CALVIN'S CATHOLIC CHRISTOLOGY

STUDIES
IN MEDIEVAL AND
REFORMATION THOUGHT

EDITED BY

HEIKO A. OBERMAN, Tübingen

IN COOPERATION WITH

E. JANE DEMPSEY DOUGLASS, Claremont, California
LEIF GRANE, Copenhagen
GUILLAUME H. M. POSTHUMUS MEYJES, Leiden
ANTON G. WEILER, Nijmegen

VOLUME II

E. DAVID WILLIS

CALVIN'S CATHOLIC CHRISTOLOGY

LEIDEN
E. J. BRILL
1966

CALVIN'S
CATHOLIC CHRISTOLOGY

THE FUNCTION OF
THE SO-CALLED EXTRA CALVINISTICUM
IN CALVIN'S THEOLOGY

BY

E. DAVID WILLIS

LEIDEN
E. J. BRILL
1966

To Irene

TABLE OF CONTENTS

                                                                    Page

Preface   xi

Abbreviations   xiii

Introduction   1

I. The Origin of the Term "Extra Calvinisticum"   8

    Conclusion   23

II. The Traditional Sources of Calvin's Doctrine of the So-
    Called Extra Calvinisticum   26

    Clues provided by Calvin for identifying the traditional sources
    (p. 26); Peter Lombard and the medieval Fathers (p. 34);
    St. Augustine and the ancient Fathers (p. 44).

    Conclusion   60

III. The So-Called Extra Calvinisticum and Calvin's Christo-
    logy   61

    The Character of Christological Knowledge and Lan-
    guage   61

    The "Extra Calvinisticum" and the *Una Persona*   63

    The "Extra Calvinisticum" and the *Vere Deus*.   67

    Calvin's uses of the term "Mediator" (p. 67); Political de-
    scriptions of the Incarnation and of God's transcendence (p. 74).

    The "Extra Calvinisticum" and the *Vere Homo*   78

    The humanity of the humbled Lord (p. 78); The "extra Calvin-
    isticum" and Christ's redemptive obedience as prophet, king,
    and priest (p. 84); The humanity of the risen and ascended
    Lord (p. 91).

    Conclusion   99

Page

IV. The So-Called Extra Calvinisticum and Calvin's Doctrine of the Knowledge of God   101

The Problem of Natural Theology in the Interpretation of Calvin.   101
The validity and limitations of the Barth-Brunner framework of investigation (p. 101); The place of the "extra Calvinisticum" in further research into Calvin's doctrine of the knowledge of God (p. 104).

The Knowledge of God only through Christ   105
Superfluous and ungrateful character of all *"theologia extra Christum"* (p. 105); The marks of saving knowledge of God through Christ alone (p. 107).

Knowledge of God *extra hanc carnem sed non extra Christum*   109
Theologia crucis et gloriae (p. 110); Concealment and revelation of God in the flesh (p. 112); Visibility and invisibility of God's revelation in the flesh (p. 114); Election and the subjective side of revelation (p. 115); Revelation and the Word joined to the Spirit (p. 117).

The *Duplex Cognitio Dei* and the Doctrine of the Trinity   120
The doctrine of the Trinity and the structure of the *Institutes* (p. 121); Revelation through the Word and Spirit in the works of God (p. 126).

Extra-Scriptural Knowledge of the Natural Order, and the Saving Knowledge of God   128

Conclusion   130

V. The So-Called Extra Calvinisticum and Calvin's Ethics . .   132

Coalescence of Knowledge and Obedience   132

Limitations and Utility of Parallels between Christological and Ethical Discourse   133
"Extra Calvinisticum": a guard against the *Analogia Unae Personae* as a method for ethical discourse (p. 134); Similarities between the "extra Calvinisticum" and descriptions of Christ's special and universal Lordship (p. 135).

Christ's Reign over the Freely Obedient Church. . . .   136
The sceptre of the Word (p. 136); Justification and sanctification of the freely obedient subject (p. 137); The Law as a guide for the freely obedient subject (p. 140).

Page

The Breakdown of the Church-World Dichotomy . . .   141

    The twofold sense of "Church" (p. 141); The twofold sense
of "world" (p. 143).

Christ's Reign *Etiam Extra Ecclesiam*   144

    Our common humanity and the order of nature (p. 145); The
order of nature and Christ's free and reluctant subjects (p. 147).

Conclusion   151

Conclusion   153

Bibliography   155

Index   161

PREFACE

Of the many challenges facing historical theology today, one of the most compelling is the ferment in theological methodology which is accompanied by a fresh discovery of the Reformers' catholicity of doctrine. Since Karl Barth shook the theological world with what was then the startling news that theology must be Christological, an intense search has taken historical theology into the writings of the Reformers for clues to the nature of the Christology which will allow theology to remain Trinitarian and anthropological.

It is this issue which whetted my interest in the "extra Calvinist-icum." Is the Word of God so fully incarnate that he has no existence also beyond the flesh he assumed? Calvin's answer brings with it a profound affirmation of God's revelation to man and man's ordered life in response to that revelation.

This study was originally undertaken as a dissertation in the Church History Department, the Divinity School, Harvard University. I am therefore indebted to those who guided my efforts in historical theology: Professor Heiko A. Oberman, for the careful and thoughtful attention he gave this research; Professor Paul L. Lehmann, for his demonstration over the years of theology's inherent sensitivity to the ethical dilemmas of contemporary men; Professor Richard R. Niebuhr, for his example in the warmth and precision of theological communication; Professor Georges Florovsky, for his instruction in the Fathers.

I am grateful for the Presbyterian Graduate Fellowship program and for the Rockefeller Doctoral Fellowship program which enabled me to pursue this work.

Finally, I want to thank Irene, without whose learned devotion to historical studies this essay would not have been completed.

E. D. W.
Princeton
Advent, 1965

ABBREVIATIONS

(full publication data given in Bibliography)

CIB   *Jean Calvin: Institution de la Religion Chrestienne, ed. Jean-Daniel Benoit*

CO   *Ioannis Calvini Opera quae supersunt omnia*

CR   *Corpus Reformatorum*

CT   *Concilium Tridentinum*

EKL   *Evangelisches Kirchenlexikon*

KCGG   *Das Konzil von Chalkedon: Geschichte und Gegenwart*

LNPF   *Select Library of the Nicene and Post-Nicene Fathers of the Christian Church*

MPG   *Patrologiae cursus completus, series Graeca*

MPL   *Patrologiae cursus completus, series Latina*

OS   *Johannis Calvini Opera Selecta*

RE   *Realencyklopädie für protestantische Theologie und Kirche*

RGG   *Die Religion in Geschichte und Gegenwart*

SC   *Sources Chrétiennes*

WA   *D. Martin Luthers Werke*, Weimar Ausgabe

INTRODUCTION

The purpose of this study is to clarify the meaning and test the legitimacy of the term "extra Calvinisticum," to trace the origins of the doctrine so designated, and to examine its function in the theology of John Calvin.

The thesis advanced is that the doctrine inadequately termed "extra Calvinisticum" operates in Calvin's thought to emphasize the fully Trinitarian character of man's knowledge of God and man's knowledge of himself.

The so-called extra Calvinisticum teaches that the Eternal Son of God, even after the Incarnation, was united to the human nature to form One Person but was not restricted to the flesh. The doctrine received its ponderous name when Lutheran theologians, upon hearing the Calvinists insist that the Son's existence also beyond the flesh of Jesus Christ (*etiam extra carnem*) was being threatened by the Lutheran version of the *communicatio idiomatum*, labelled the Reformed contention "that Calvinistic 'beyond' " (*illud extra Calvinisticum*). The Reformed theologians maintained that the Son's existence also beyond the flesh did not jeopardize the unity of the divine and the human natures in the Incarnation, while the Lutherans claimed that it did. Both sides agreed that the doctrine was part of Calvin's theology. But the Reformed evaluation was that its presence there signified that he was a faithful interpreter of Scripture and a student of the tradition, whereas the Lutherans appraised it as a mark of his being blinded on this point by philosophical considerations alien to the Christian faith.

In modern literature on the subject there is also general consensus identifying the "extra Calvinisticum" as Calvin's doctrine about the life and reality of the Eternal Son even beyond the flesh.[1] There is no

---

[1] François Wendel, *Calvin: sources et évolution de sa pensée religieuse* (Paris: Presses Universitaires de France, 1950), p. 168; Friedrich Loofs, "Kenosis," *RE*, X, p. 258; Sydney Cave, *The Doctrine of the Person of Christ* (London: Duckworth, 1925), p. 151, n. 2; Joseph Ternus, "Chalkedon und die protestantische Theologie," *KCGG*, III, p. 536; Wilhelm Niesel, *The Theology of Calvin*, trans. H. Knight (Philadelphia: Westminster Press, 1956), p. 119; Karl Barth, *Church Dogmatics*, trans. G. W. Bromiley, IV, 1 (Edinburgh: T. & T. Clark, 1956), pp. 180-81.

monograph which has gone beyond the classical passages of the *Institutes* to discover what Calvin means by it in other contexts and to pursue its ramifications for his thought as a whole. Some works concentrate on the implications of the "extra Calvinisticum" for Calvin's Christology. One view is that it reinforces a tendency in Calvin to distinguish too sharply the two natures of Christ.[1] Another view is that, when drawn out to its logical consequences, it implies two Christs, a *logos ensarkos* and a *logos asarkos*.[2] Wilhelm Niesel argues that the "extra Calvinisticum" is not central in Calvin's Christology, and that any weight it might give to a separation of the two natures is balanced by Calvin's view that the Word indwells the "temple" of Christ's humanity. Yet Niesel feels that "as a critical distinction the Extra has its value," a remark upon which he does not elaborate.[3]

A few scholars move beyond the two-natures problem to consider the effects of the "extra Calvinisticum" on Calvin's doctrine of revelation. The difficulty is this: *if* the "extra Calvinisticum" involves an implicit distinction between the *logos ensarkos* and the *logos asarkos*, is not God's full revelation of himself exclusively in Jesus Christ menaced, and is not the way opened to a natural theology alongside and complementary to revealed theology? Niesel contends that "Calvin does not teach that God is to be found in Jesus Christ but is also to be encountered fully apart from Him. No; according to Calvin, God has disclosed Himself only in Jesus Christ and we must therefore hold fast solely to this One and not attempt to seek God outside the Mediator."[4] Karl Barth feels that while it is clearly the intention of Calvin in the *extra* affirmation never to speak about God other than as we know him in Christ, it cannot be denied that Calvin, with particularly serious results in his doctrine of predestination, does

---

[1] Hermann Bauke, "Christologie II. Dogmengeschichtlich," *RGG*, I, col. 1628; Wendel, *loc. cit.*; Johannes Witte, "Die Christologie Calvins," *KCGG*, III, p. 500; Werner Elert, *Die Morphologie des Luthertums*, I (München: C. H. Beck, 1931), p. 215.

[2] Ternus, *loc. cit.*; cf. also Alexander Schweizer, *Die Glaubenslehre der evangelisch-reformierten Kirche*, II (Zürich: Orell, Füssli & Comp., 1847), pp. 296, 303. Schweizer is of special interest as a Reformed theologian saying the Reformed doctrine of the Incarnation intends always to remain within the provisions of the *finitum non capax infiniti*, and that one feature of that Christology is that it does not want to abolish the "absolute being of the Logos asarkos." These last two provisions often appear as Lutheran accusations against the Reformed position.

[3] *Op. cit.*, p. 119.

[4] *Ibid.*

travel a good way in trying to reckon with this "other" god.[1] Yet Barth finds that an asset of the "extra Calvinisticum" is its perception of the dynamic element in the ἐγένετο and its preservation of the noetic interest of Christology; he wonders at the same time, though, whether it gives adequate recognition to the static element in the ἐγένετο and therefore to the ontic relevance of Christology.[2] Paul van Buren feels that Calvin, untrue to his intention, does sometimes depart from the knowledge of God which we have in Christ.[3] Edward Dowey does not discuss the so-called extra Calvinisticum as such but deals with corresponding concerns. For relating the spheres of creation and redemption, Dowey chooses the Law as being of special use; but he also suggests that one might explore the relation between creation and redemption by inspecting the bond between the doctrine of the Trinity and Calvin's Christology.[4] The most helpful treatment of the so-called extra Calvinisticum appears in Werner Krusche's excellent study on the work of the Holy Spirit according to Calvin.[5] Krusche shows how the positive tie between creation and redemption is strengthened by the doctrine of the *Filioque*. As the Spirit of the Eternal Son as Redeemer, the Spirit is regenerator, and as the Spirit of the Eternal Son as creative Word, the Spirit is creator. Krusche says that this double character of the Spirit's work belongs systematically with the "extra Calvinisticum."[6]

Attempts have been made to draw a conclusion from the "extra Calvinisticum" about what motivates the whole of Calvin's thought. This generalized conclusion is that the "extra Calvinisticum" is the product of an effort to explain the Incarnation in terms not violating the philosophical principle *finitum non capax infiniti*, which is seen by

---

[1] *Op. cit.*, p. 181.
[2] *Op. cit.*, trans. G. T. Thomson, H. Knight, I, 2, p. 170.
[3] While it would be too much to speak of a second source of revelation in Calvin, says van Buren, yet "Calvin's understanding of the divine nature of Christ is constantly threatened ... by a concept of God as impassible Being which he inherited from the whole history of theology, from Irenaeus on, a concept that does not seem to be derived from the Cross or from the Christ who is our Lord only as He is the Crucified One." (*Christ in Our Place: The Substitutionary Character of Calvin's Doctrine of Reconciliation* [Edinburgh: Oliver & Boyd, 1957], p. 141.)
[4] Edward A. Dowey, Jr. *The Knowledge of God in Calvin's Theology* (New York: Columbia University Press, 1952), p. 222.
[5] Werner Krusche, *Das Wirken des Heiligen Geistes nach Calvin* (Göttingen: Vandenhoeck & Ruprecht, 1957).
[6] *Ibid.*, pp. 128-29.

critics as determining much of Reformed theology. Werner Elert
sees this principle operating behind the Antiochian Christology and
characteristic in Reformed Christology. From this, Elert concludes
that wherever the idea is at work, one is on a continuum with
Nestorius.[1] Friedrich Loofs and Hermann Bauke seem to take it for
granted that this precept lies behind Calvin's assertion of the distance
between God and man. They do not, however, document this with
passages in which Calvin supposedly puts the problem in the context
of a philosophical discussion of the mutual exclusiveness of the finite
and the infinite.[2] G. C. Berkouwer says that *finitum non capax infiniti*
does not occur in Calvin's works; Calvin's was not a philosophical,
cosmological theory into which he tried to fit his Christology.[3] I. A.
Dorner makes a suggestive distinction between the piety and the
metaphysics implied in Reformed Christology. The metaphysical side
refers to the predicate of infinitude which is so stressed that the essence
of the creature as such seems to consist in finitude. Zwingli's tendency
was to carry through a fixed, immovable distinction of the divine
from the human in opposition to the pagan element contained in the
theology of the Middle Ages, and Calvin develops this distinction
even more consequently. But this metaphysical view has its roots
ultimately in the peculiar shade of piety of the Swiss, that is the Reformed, theologians.[4]

---

[1] "Über die Herkunft des Satzes *Finitum infiniti non capax*," *Zeitschrift für
Systematische Theologie*, XVI (1939), pp. 500-504. Cf. also Donald G. Dawe, *The
Form of A Servant* (Philadelphia: Westminster Press, 1963), pp. 73 and 79-81.
[2] Loofs, "Christologie," *RE*, IV, p. 54; Bauke, *loc. cit.*, I, cols. 1627-28.
[3] Calvin's "... was not a philosophical, cosmological theory into which he
tried to fit his Christology; but from the gospel he learned that the riches of
Christ consisted in the fact that he redeemed us as one of us." (*The Person of
Christ*, trans. J. Vriend [Grand Rapids: Wm. B. Eerdmans, 1954], p. 282.)
[4] That piety held that reverence for God seemed to forbid the entertainment
of the idea of his actually communicating himself to the finite. According to this
piety: "It is not right either to confine the Creator, the Logos, within the limits
of finite human nature, or to expand the humanity of Christ to the dimensions
of the divine. The Logos is constantly both outside of and in the flesh: the
Almighty Deity cannot be chained with its nature to one point of the world,
not even to that with which He is personally united. Again, the humanity of
Christ would no longer have been humanity, had it had for its own the predicates
of the divine infinitude. For in that case its finite predicates would be done away
with; in other words, its creatural nature lost. Its fundamental determination,
finitude, which distinguishes it from God, being taken away, it itself would be
annihilated." (*History of the Development of the Doctrine of the Person of Christ*,
trans. D. W. Simon, II, 2 [Edinburgh: T. & T. Clark, 1866], pp. 136-37, 407.)

Despite the persistence with which the term "extra Calvinisticum" is applied to a feature of Reformed theology, surprisingly little is known about its origin,[1] and there is general obscurity about what it means. Bauke, in an influential reference work,[2] identifies the "extra Calvinisticum" as a teaching according to which "the Logos exists entirely outside of the human nature"; [3] Bauke does not note that this *extra* is only an *etiam extra*. According to Elert, the "extra Calvinisticum" holds that "the Logos, which lives in the human nature is, because of its infinity, beyond it at the same time."[4] So brief a description overlooks the Reformed affirmation of the union of the two natures in the person of Christ, a statement which claims more than just an indwelling of the Word. There is also confusion about the propriety of "Calvinisticum" in the term. It conveys the impression that the Reformed teaching constitutes an innovation, an impression which is perpetuated unless someone shows how much it belonged to a major part of the Church's tradition. In fact, the Swabian denial of the life and reality of the Eternal Son *etiam extra carnem* was the greater innovation.[5]

---

[1] See *supra*, p. 2, n. 1, and p. 3, n. 1.

[2] *Loc. cit.*, *RGG*, I, col. 1628.

[3] *Ibid.*

[4] *Morphologie . . .*, p. 215.

[5] Barth, *op. cit.*, I, 2, pp. 168-69; Wolfgang Kratz, "Christus—Gott und Mensch: Einige Fragen an Calvins Christologie," *Evangelische Theologie*, XIX (1959), p. 209. cf. Loofs, *Leitfaden zum Studium der Dogmengeschichte* (4th ed.; Halle: Max Niemeyer, 1906), pp. 95, 150, 171, 264-65; Hugh Ross Mackintosh, *The Doctrine of the Person of Christ* (New York: Charles Scribner's Sons, 1912), p. 244; Witte, *loc. cit.*, *KCGG*, III, p. 500. Witte argues that the thesis behind the "extra Calvinisticum" appears already before Calvin in "Catholic" theology; but there is a distinction between the "Catholic" and the Calvinist conceptions. The difference is, according to Witte, in part that Calvin's Christology has a certain spiritualizing tendency, which, while it emphasizes the soteriological and dynamic character of Christ's person, does not do justice to the deeper [Catholic] confession of the fact that through the Incarnation Christ enters into the unity of mankind, and in the assumption of a human nature into the divine, Christ in a certain sense assumes also manhood as a whole into the divine. Even so, Witte's judgment is far more balanced than Alexandre Ganoczy's (*Calvin: Théologien de l'Eglise et du Ministère* [Unam Sanctam, 48, Paris: du Cerf, 1964], p. 91) that "Certes, Calvin accepte Ephèse et Chalcédoine, mais en même temps sa christologie est peut-être la partie la moins patristique de toute sa théologie." On the other hand, compare the confidence of Paul Jacobs who suggests that the doctrine can be called the *Extra Evangelicum* and the *Extra Augustinum* which can never be separated from the *Infra Calvinisticum* which also is a part of Calvin's Christology. ("Pneumatische Realpräsenz bei Calvin," *Revue d'Histoire et de Philosophie Religieuse*, XLIV [1964], pp. 391-92.)

In approaching the so-called extra Calvinisticum one is faced with what is admittedly a potential weakness in Calvin's thought. A significant portion of his theology rests on his answer to the question: Are the reality and work of the Second Person of the Trinity exhausted by his life in the flesh? The so-called extra Calvinisticum, Calvin's answer to this question, has not been sufficiently scrutinized to see if it can indeed bear the weight imposed upon it by the rest of his system.

There are two problems facing contemporary theology which touch upon the issues raised by the so-called extra Calvinisticum. The first concerns the relation between the doctines of redemption and creation. Further study is needed to determine how the two are positively related and to avoid the false dichotomy inferred in a choice between redemption-oriented and creation-oriented theology. The second is the predicament concerning Christology in the present theological enterprise. We have been reminded that the distinctive characteristic of Christian theology is that it is a response to the God who reveals himself in Jesus Christ. Reaction to this reminder has set in and tends often to take two extreme forms. One uses Christology as a principle for reducing all of theology to the two-natures problem. The other consciously seeks a theological method which is non-Christological or which takes into account only marginally not only the two-natures problem (dismissed usually as a false one) but even the fact of God's revelation and redemption in Christ.

In teaching what came later to be called the "extra Calvinisticum," Calvin the Biblical theologian endeavors, with the force of his human- ist learning turned to the service of Christian theology, to safeguard an essential response to revelation which the Church before him also found it necessary to protect. It is his way for taking account of the fact that in Christ God is powerfully for us. It is not intended to evade the Christ witnessed to by the apostolic message, nor is it intended to buttress an allegedly natural theology.[1] On the contrary, the "extra Calvinisticum" emphasizes that the God at work in Jesus Christ is one and the same with the God who sustains and orders the universe. He is the Triune God, as is manifest in the prominent role assigned to the Holy Spirit in the dynamics of the Incarnate life. The humanity of Christ can develop in a special way without transgressing the bounds of genuine humanity because of the gifts which the *Logos* conveys to

---

[1] There is a natural knowledge of God in Calvin which is not a saving knowl- edge but which serves only to leave man without excuse.

it by his Spirit. In the "extra Calvinisticum," Calvin is asserting that Christ is able to be God for us because he does not cease to be God over us in the Incarnation and because the humanity of Christ never ceases to be our humanity in the movement of God towards us. In Jesus Christ the vindication of the majesty of God and the re-establishment and fulfillment of the humanity of man take place. It is this gracious relationship—Creator-created, Redeemer-redeemed, Sanctifier-sanctified—on which the right ordering of history depends: such is Calvin's affirmation in the "extra Calvinisticum," not the philosophical principle *finitum non capax infiniti*. The "extra Calvinisticum" is not a sign of the discontinuity between creation and redemption, but of the fact that by assuming our condition the Eternal Son did not relinquish part of his empire but extended that empire over lost ground. Election to the body of Christ means being united to the Head by the Holy Spirit, and conforming to the image of Christ in the world by the Holy Spirit. The "extra Calvinisticum" provides for Christ's Lordship over all the world and yet his special presence with and Lordship over the Church, through the Holy Spirit; and, it bestows a Christological content upon the role which the order of nature plays in ethics.

The following plan will guide this discussion. The first chapter will examine the origins of the term "extra Calvinisticum" to determine its meaning in the earliest context we can find and to see what issues were inherent in the very coining of it. The second chapter will consider where Calvin's doctrine, whether called the "extra Calvinisticum" or not, came from and how its widespread use by the Church before Calvin denotes that the critical factor is not its presence in a given theological system but its influence there. Chapters three, four, and five will analyze how the doctrine functions in three areas most fraught with misunderstandings about its implications: Calvin's doctrine of the person and work of Christ, his position on the revelation of God in Christ and in nature, and the relevance or irrelevance of his Christology for ethical reflection.

All translations are original with this study unless otherwise noted.

CHAPTER ONE

THE ORIGIN OF THE TERM
"EXTRA CALVINISTICUM"

A distinction must be made between "extra Calvinisticum" as a term and the so-called extra Calvinisticum as a doctrine. The former is a product of sixteenth and seventeenth century Christological debates occasioned by the divergent views of Reformed and Lutheran theologians regarding the nature of the Real Presence of Christ in the Eucharist. The latter, of which the polemical term is a misleading label, is a teaching common to a remarkably broad number of representatives of the tradition long before the sixteenth century.

This chapter will deal particularly with "extra Calvinisticum" as a term, and will disclose in what respects the term is a misnomer. The following chapters will focus upon the so-called extra Calvinisticum as a doctrine, considering first the sources in which Calvin might have encountered it and then its function in his theology at several vital points.

As to the dating of "extra Calvinisticum," modern scholarship has, for the most part, been vague. When a scholar's interest is more systematic than historical, reference to the date of the term is seldom made.[1] Sometimes an author calls attention to the doctrine in Calvin and identifies it only as that which was later to be called the "extra Calvinisticum."[2] Or again, it is said simply to have emerged in the debates between Lutheran and Reformed theologians in the sixteenth and seventeenth centuries.[3]

The attempt to date this term involves working with the elusive material of debate and polemic. Generally speaking, when a label

---

[1] Joseph C. McLelland, *The Visible Words of God: An Exposition of the Sacramental Theology of Peter Martyr Vermigli* . . . (Edinburgh: Oliver and Boyd, 1957), pp. 218-19; Loofs, *loc. cit., RE*, X, p. 258; Witte, *loc. cit., KCGG*, III, pp. 500, 506; Mackintosh, *op. cit.*, p. 244; Kratz, *loc. cit., Evangelische Theologie*, XIX (1959), pp. 209, 214; Krusche, *op. cit.*, pp. 128-29.

[2] Ternus, *loc. cit., KCGG*, III, p. 536; Wendel, *op. cit.*, p. 168; Niesel, *op. cit.*, p. 119; Bauke, *loc. cit., RGG*, I, col. 1628; Jean-Daniel Benoit, *CIB*, II, p. 250, n. 8.

[3] Walter Kreck, "Extra Calvinisticum," *EKL*, I, cols. 1245-46; Barth, *op. cit.*, I, 2, p. 168.

persists it does so because it crystallizes a prevailing sentiment about a given subject. In the case of the "extra Calvinisticum" the label crystallized the prevailing sentiment among Lutherans that it was peculiarly Calvinist to teach that after the Incarnation the Eternal Son of God had his existence also beyond the flesh. The proper dating of the term must include an examination of the growth of this sentiment, which culminated in the application of the label. In and of itself, the term is not important; it is significant only insofar as it came to be adopted as a legitimate characterization of something special in Reformed theology. Once accepted as legitimate, justifiably or not, the term "extra Calvinisticum" itself became a molding force in theology and in the history of doctrine.

The words "extra" and "Calvinisticum" appeared together as a term in the course of the crypto-kenoticist debate between the theologians of Tübingen and Giessen.[1] In order to understand the background of this Giessen-Tübingen dispute, and to appreciate the Lutheran objection to the *extra* affirmation, it will be helpful to describe at this point three main Lutheran Christologies. These are associated with the names of Johann Brenz (1499-1570), Martin Chemnitz (1522-1586), and Philip Melancthon (1497-1560). The first two types were allowed but never fully reconciled in the Formula of Concord (1580), and it was this unresolved tension which broke out in the so-called crypto-kenoticist debate. Philippist Christology became identified with Reformed theology and was not recognized by the Formula of Concord. A possible fourth kind of Christology was represented by the extreme position of Andreas Musculus who, in debates with Stancaro (in 1552) and Staphylus (in 1558), was drawn into implying that Christ suffered in his divinity as well as in his humanity.

Brenz, and the Würtemberg Christology generally, affirmed that in the hypostatic union the humanity was so united to the *Logos* in his entirety that subsequent to the Incarnation the *Logos* had no longer an existence beyond the humanity. This was possible because the *communicatio idiomatum* meant that the humanity, which in itself would have been finite, was endowed by the omnipotence of the *Logos* with infinite susceptibility. It was this infinite susceptibility, communicated to the humanity by the *Logos* in the hypostatic union, which permitted

Brenz

---

[1] Cf. G. Thomasius, *Christi Person und Werk*, II (Erlangen: Theodore Bläsing, 1857), p. 446, where the term is quoted.

the humanity to be filled with the divine fullness to constitute the Incarnation.[1] On this basis it was argued that the body of Christ united to the Word, although visibly local, filled heaven and earth even before the resurrection and the observable ascension.[2]

Chemnitz

Chemnitz claimed there was a *perichoresis* of the divine and human natures wherein the human nature manifested the attributes of the divine nature, as glowing iron manifests the attributes of fire.[3] The gifts which the human nature thus received were not restricted to finite gifts conferred by the Holy Spirit, but were infused gifts: qualities and attributes of the divine nature conferred by the Word by virtue of the hypostatic union. As a result the One Person, God-man, was able to be present with his assumed nature wherever, whenever, and however he willed.[4] Christ was ubiquitous wherever he taught and promised that he willed to be present in his assumed nature. Therefore, although the human nature possessed from the moment of the Incarnation the power of ubiquity, the divine nature refrained and withdrew the exercise of that power in and through the flesh. Chemnitz held it was wrong to teach that the person of the Word existed after the Incarnation beyond and separate from his assumed nature.[5] In expressing this Christology, Chemnitz stood between Brenz and the Philippist theologians, especially on the meaning to be given the *communicatio idiomatum*. He rejected a concept of a physical or natural communication or a transfusion of properties; he likewise rejected a mere *communicatio dialectica*. Chemnitz distinguished among three kinds or stages of the *communicatio idiomatum*, an arrangement generally used in subsequent Lutheran orthodoxy.[6] This differentiation was

---

[1] Dorner, *op. cit.*, pp. 178-90.

[2] Johann Brenz, *De majestate Domini Nostri Jesu Christi* . . . (Frankfurt: Peter Brubach, 1562), p. 150; Otto Fricke, *Die Christologie des Johannes Brenz in Zusammenhang mit der Lehre vom Abendmahl und der Rechtfertigung* (München: Kaiser Verlag, 1927), pp. 195-206.

[3] *De Duabus Naturis in Christo* (Frankfurt and Wittenberg: Tobias Meuius and E. Schumacher, 1653 [first published in 1571]), chap. vi, pp. 28-29.

[4] *Ibid.*, chap. xxx, p. 184.

[5] *Ibid.*, chap. v, p. 24.

[6] (1) *genus idiomaticum*, whereby the attributes of each nature are ascribed to the entire Person; (*ibid.*, chap. xiii); (2) *genus apotelesmaticum*, whereby the redemptive acts and functions proper to the entire Person are attributed to only one or the other of the two natures; (*ibid.*, chap. xvii); (3) *genus majestaticum*, whereby the human nature is clothed with and magnified by the attributes of the divine nature; (*ibid.*, chap. xxiii). cf. Johann Heinrich Schmid, *Die Dogmatik der evangelisch-lutherischen Kirche* (3rd ed., Frankfurt a.M. and Erlangen: Heyder & Zimmer, 1853), p. 246ff. The Reformed orthodox theologians accepted the

helpful only because it served temporarily to limit the area of dispute to the third one, *genus majestaticum*. Chemnitz claimed that although the humanity could never have infinitude "according to itself, subjectively, formally, or inherently," the divine majesty was communicated to it above and against its nature by the union of the Word with it. Only in this sense was Chemnitz willing to speak of the divine majesty of the man Christ.[1]

Melancthon, in elucidating the Christology implied in his doctrine *Melanchthon* of the Eucharist which was congenial to that of the Reformed Churches, interpreted the *communicatio idiomatum* in the sense of a dialectical communication. He rejected any physical and real communication,[2] but of course he insisted on the indissoluble unity of the two natures in the One Person. The Wittenbergers, of which Melancthon was the chief spokesman, differed from Chemnitz by teaching that the special gifts communicated to the humanity were finite gifts, and by emphasizing the work of the Holy Spirit in the communication of the gifts, whereas Chemnitz emphasized the activity of the Word in the *communicatio idiomatum*.[3]

In the emergence of the term "extra Calvinisticum," the Colloquy of Maulbronn (1564) had decisive significance because it marked the convergence of two growing trends in the doctrinal and polemical development of this period. One was the increasingly widespread practice among Lutherans of calling their sacramentalist adversaries the "Calviniani," instead of just "Zwingliani." The other was the increasingly explicit teaching by Reformed theologians of the importance of the *extra* affirmation. Both of these were aggravated in no small measure by the changing political climate. Elector Frederick III's support of Reformed theology in the Palatinate and especially the appearance of the Heidelberg Catechism (1563) were widely interpreted as an infringement of the Peace of Augsburg. Frederick's neighboring Lutheran princes urged him to call a conference of the rival theologians. The result was the Colloquy of Maulbronn which

---

genus idiomaticum and the *genus apotelesmaticum* but rejected the *genus majestaticum* in favor of a *communicatio gratiarum*. cf. Heinrich Heppe, *Die Dogmatik der evangelisch-reformierten Kirche*, ed. Ernst Bizer (Neukirchen: Neukirchener Verlag, 1958), p. 345ff.

[1] Dorner, *op. cit.*, pp. 199-205.

[2] Fricke, *op. cit.*, pp. 233-34.

[3] Dorner, *op. cit.*, pp. 173-74, 195; Otto Ritschl, *Dogmengeschichte des Protestantismus*, IV (Göttingen: Vandenhoeck & Ruprecht, 1927), pp. 35-46.

brought together in April of 1564 a distinguished body of theologians in the presence of Frederick and Duke Christopher of Würtemberg. Pierre Bouquin, Zacharias Ursinus, Kaspar Oliveanus, and Emanuel Tremellius, among others, represented the Reformed position; Jakob Andreas, Johann Brenz and Theodore Schnepff, among others, represented the Lutherans.[1] The first six days were spent disputing only about the person of Christ and whether his majesty was shared with his humanity; so much controversial matter was brought to light in those six days that the Colloquy was dismissed by the princes and the two parties departed without having come at all closer to one another.[2]

Literature contemporary with the Colloquy indicates the shift that was occurring in Lutheran terminology for the Calvinists. "Calvinist" had become a special term of opprobrium among Lutherans with the appearance in 1552 of Joachim Westphal's *Farrago confusanearum et inter se dissidentium Opinionum de coena Domini ex Sacramentariorum libris congesta* (Magdeburg), in which he charged the Melancthonians with departing from Luther's doctrine of the Real Presence and agreeing with the Sacramentarians including, among others, Zwingli, Oecolampadius, Bucer, Bullinger, Schwenkfeld, Martyr, and especially Calvin. In 1553 he wrote another tract, *Recta fides de Coena Domini*, in which the Zwinglian position was called the Calvinist heresy.[3] At the conclusion of the Conference of Worms, 1557, a letter was written

---

[1] *Pierre Bouquin*, d. 1582, Carmalite who embraced the Reformation, teacher successively in Strasbourg (appointed to lecture in Calvin's place, 1542), Bourges (where he had taken his doctorate in theology in 1539), Strasbourg again, Heidelberg (1557-1577), and Lausanne. *Kaspar Oliveanus*, 1536-1587, best-known for cooperation in composition of the Heidelberg Catechism, student of law at Orléans and Bourges, under the influence of Farel and Calvin turned preacher in Trier (1559), teacher and preacher successively at Heidelberg (1560-1576), Berleberg, and Herborn (1584-1587). *Emanuel Tremellius*, 1510-1580, hebraist born in Italy of Jewish parents, baptized c. 1540, teacher successively in Strasbourg (1542), Cambridge (1549-1553), Hornbach, Heidelberg (1561-1567), and Sedan. *Johann Brenz*, 1499-1570, learned Swabian Reformer, participant in Marburg Colloquy (1529), writer of widely-used Catechism (1551), preparer of the *Confessio Wirtembergica* presented to the Council of Trent in 1552. *Theodore Schnepff*, 1525-1586, professor of theology at Tübingen (from 1557), son of better-known Erhard Schnepff, 1495-1558, who joined with Brenz in the *Syngramma Suevicum* (1525) but later, on accepting a chair at Jena, broke not only with Melancthon but with Brenz and Andreas as well.

[2] Gottlieb Jakob Planck, *Geschichte der protestantischen Theologie*, Buch VI (Leipzig: S. L. Crusius, 1799), pp. 485-491.

[3] Philip Schaff, *History of the Christian Church*, VII (New York: Charles Scribner's Sons, 1892), pp. 661-62.

in which Zwinglianism and Calvinism were equated.[1] And on July 23, 1563, in the dedicatory epistle to the Commentary on Jeremiah, Calvin remarked that quarrelsome men were trying to discredit Prince Frederick of the Palatinate by applying to the religion he was guarding the name "Calvinism."[2]

One explanation for this shift is certainly that the Consensus Tigurinus of 1549 had made the title "Zwinglian" less usable. According to some Lutherans, it was more than just the Zwinglians who were sacramentarian in a "Zwinglian" way. Another explanation is more political. Zwingli could not subscribe to the Augsburg Confession's article on the Lord's Supper, and those who opposed the Confession for the same reasons were Zwinglian sacramentarians. The Peace of Augsburg (1555) provided that only those who subscribed to that Confession were to be tolerated alongside the Roman Catholics in Germany. The Reformed theologians claimed that their views of the Real Presence as enunciated in a general way in the Consensus Tigurinus were not finally inconsistent with the Augsburg Confession. In his *Final Admonition to Westphal*, 1557, Calvin said: "In regard to the Confession of Augsburg, my answer is that as it was

---

[1] Erhard Schnepff, Victor Strigel, and other Lutherans wrote a "Protestatio" in which they explained the meaning of "Zwinglianism."

"Zum Andern [the first danger mentioned was "Osiandrismus"] bedarf es nicht langer u. weitläufiger Erklärung, was wir mit dem Namen Zwinglianismi wollen verstanden haben. Denn wir hiermit begreifen allerlei Sekten u. Rotten, die sich unter die einfältigen Worte des h. Nachtmals innerhalb dreissig Jahren gesetzt haben, sie kommen gleich her von Carlstadt, Zwingli, Oecolampadio, Calvino oder Andern. Denn wiewol die Sacramentschwärmer bekennen, dass unser lieber Herr u. Heiland Jesus Christus im Nachtmal sei, gleich wie die ganze Dreifaltigkeit in der heiligen Taufe gegenwärtig u. kräftig ist, so leugnen sie doch, dass denjenigen, so das Brod empfangen, wahrhaftig u. wesentlich gegeben werde der Leib Christi, welcher von der Jungfrau Maria geboren, gekreuzigt, von den Todten auserstanden ist, u. nun zu der rechten Hand Gottes sitzt." (Heinrich Heppe, *Geschichte des deutschen Protestantismus in den Jahren 1555-1581*, I [Marburg: Elwert, 1852], Appendix, p. 19.)

[2] "Dum ergo Calvinismum obiciendo aliqua infamiae nota tuam Celsitudinem aspergere conantur, nihil aliud quam suam privitatem cum stultitia frustra et magno suo cum dedecore produnt." (*CO* 20: 73.) In September of the same year, Princes Wolfgang of Palatinate, Karl of Baden and Christoph of Würtemberg wrote a joint letter to Prince Frederick in which they placed side by side as almost synonymous the terms "Zwinglianism" and "Calvinism." In speaking of the "Zwinglische und Calvinische" books written and printed at Heidelberg, they said: "Nun erkennen wir aus gnediger verliehung gottes, das der *Zwinglianismus* und *Calvinismus* im Articull vom Abenthmall Christi ein verfurischer und verdamblicher Irthumb sey . . ." (Heppe, *op. cit.*, II [Marburg, 1853], Appendix, p. 7. cf. also pp. 8-9.)

published at Ratisbon there are not things which emerge contrary to our doctrine. If there is any ambiguity in its meaning, there cannot be a more competent interpreter than its author to whom, as his due, all pious and learned men will rapidly pay this honor."[1] As far as the non-Philippist Lutherans were concerned, the Reformed doctrine that Christ is present in the Eucharist *realiter et spiritualiter*, was just a more subtle, dangerous, sacramentarian threat to the reality of Christ's Presence in the Eucharist.[2] It was only another watering down of Christ's explicit words: *Hoc est corpus meum*. This new threat was related directly or indirectly to Calvin, through Calvin's own views and those of men who studied with him including especially those responsible for the Heidelberg Catechism.

In the Consensus Tigurinus a new form had been found enabling the Reformed churchmen of Geneva and Zürich to affirm their basic solidarity on the doctrine of the Eucharist. The emphasis was placed on the Real Presence of Christ, an emphasis heretofore made overtly by the Genevan theologians, but never entirely lacking in their Zürich brethren. This Consensus, however, did not have the effect of mediating between the Zwinglians and the Lutherans. Instead, the gap between Reformed and Philippist theologians on the one hand and non-Philippist Lutherans on the other, grew ever wider. The controversy which partially caused and also filled this widening hiatus concentrated in the 1550's largely on the sacramental implications of the respective views. The Christological implications were not ignored, but attention was generally centered on the question: "Given the respective views of the character of Christ's session at the right hand of God, how can he be truly and really present in his Supper?" In the 1560's, however, the controversy concentrated on the formal Christological implications of the respective convictions regarding Christ's Presence in the Eucharist. The sacramental implications were not ignored, but attention was generally focused on the question: "Given the character of Christ's Real Presence in the Eucharist, how can the reality of the two natures and their hypostatic union into the One Person be most faithfully and accurately confessed?"

It was as a part of the Reformed attempt to answer this last question that the *extra* affirmation, which had already been present in less explicit forms and had functioned in different contexts, came into unmistakable prominence.

---

[1] *CO* 9:148.
[2] Dorner, *op. cit.*, II, 2, pp. 173-76.

Question 47 of the Heidelberg Catechism confessed that the ascension of Christ means that according to his human nature he is no longer on earth but according to his divinity, majesty, grace, and Spirit he is never absent from us. Question 48 went as follows:

> But in this way are not Christ's two natures separated, if the human nature is not wherever the divine nature is? By no means! For since the divinity cannot be enclosed and is present in every place, it necessarily follows that the divinity is indeed beyond that human nature which the divine nature assumed, but it is no less within the human nature and it remains personally united to it. [1]

At the Colloquy of Maulbronn, discussion converged on the differences arising over the doctrine of the person of Christ, a major source of disagreement being the ramifications of the view expressed by Question 48 of the Catechism. In these discussions, as in others, the Reformed similitudes spurred bitter contention. It was apparently at this Colloquy that the figure of Antwerp and the ocean was introduced by Olivean as an analogy for testing logical statements about the nature of Christ's ubiquity. Andreas argued: (1) the right hand of God is everywhere, (2) the man Christ is at the right hand of God, (3) therefore the man Christ is everywhere. Olivean said this conclusion did not follow unless a fourth term were introduced: that Christ is the right hand of God. He claimed Andreas' syllogism resembled: (1) the ocean goes around the whole earth, (2) Antwerp is on the ocean, (3) therefore Antwerp goes around the whole earth; or, (1) the power of Caesar extends to every place of his empire, (2) Caesar possesses this power, (3) therefore Caesar is in every place of his empire. To draw the proper conclusions in the sample syllogisms it would be necessary to imply: Antwerp is the ocean and Caesar is his

---

[1] "Werden aber auf diese Weise die zwei Naturen in Christo nicht von einander getrennt, so die Menschheit nicht überall ist, da die Gottheit ist? Antwort. Mit nichten: denn weil die Gottheit unbegreiflich und allenthalben gegenwärtig ist, so muss folgen, dass sie wohl ausserhalb ihrer angenommenen Menschheit, und dennoch nichts desto weniger auch in derselben ist, und persönlich mit ihr vereiniget bleibt."

"An vero isto pacto duae naturae in Christo, non divelluntur, si non sit natura humana, ubicunque est divina? Minime: Nam cum divinitas comprehendi non queat, et omni loco praesens sit, necessario consequitur, esse eam quidem extra naturam humanam, quam assumsit, sed nihilo minus tamen esse in eadem, eique personaliter unitam permanere."

(Philip Schaff, *The Creeds of Christendom*, III [4th ed.; New York: Harper & Bros., 1931,] p. 322; Hermann Agathon Niemeyer, *Collectio Confessionum in Ecclesiis Reformatis Publicatarum* [Leipzig: J. Klinkhardt, 1840], p. 440.)

power. Just as there is a difference between being on the ocean and being the ocean, and between possessing the imperial power and being the imperial power, so there is a difference between sitting at the right hand of God and being the right hand of God. Andreas countered that Olivean, with this argument, was making something earthly of the reign of Christ because to limit Christ bodily to one place is to make Christ like Caesar.[1]

In a tract of 1588, Jakob Andreas [2] wrote against the Calvinist views which de Bèze expressed at the Colloquy of Montbéliard (1586). Andreas complained that Calvinist thoughts about the ubiquity of Christ were too crass, as demonstrated by their homely figures of speech. They thought of ubiquity only in terms of extension, and thereby rejected a ubiquity which Lutherans themselves were not even proposing.[3] The Colloquy of Montbéliard (also Mümpelgart, Mömpelgard) was called by Count Frederick of Würtemberg, who wished to see a settlement of the disputes between the Reformed and Lutheran populations of Montbéliard when that city, by inheritance, was brought into the Duchy of Würtemberg. Among those representing the Reformed Churches were Théodore de Bèze and Antoine de la Faye of Geneva, Claude Aubery of Lausanne, and Abraham Musculus and Peter Hubner of Bern.[4] Among those representing the Lutheran

---

[1] *Protocollum, hoc est, Acta Colloquii inter Palatinos et Wirtebergicos Theologos . . .* (Heidelberg, 1566), pp. 32-33.

[2] *Jakob Andreas,* 1528-1590, student at Tübingen (doctorate 1553), professor of theology there starting in 1561, well-known as chief architect, along with Martin Chemnitz and Nikolaus Selnekker, 1530-1592, of the Formula of Concord (1580).

[3] *Epitome Colloquii Montis Belgartensis . . .* (Tübingen: G. Gruppenbach, 1588), pp. 34-35.

[4] *Antoine de la Faye* (Fayus, Fagus), d. Geneva c. 1615, pastor, doctor in theology and medicine, rector of the academy of Geneva and professor of theology and philosophy, close friend of de Bèze, and his biographer. *Claude Aubery* (Auberius, Alberius, Albertinus, surnamed Triuncuranus), d. Dijon 1596, physician who became Reformed and fled from Paris to Lausanne where he was made professor of philosophy. Later, disillusioned by the doctrinal controversies he was involved in (including controversies with de Bèze, who thought views expressed in Aubery's *Apodictae orationes,* a sort of commentary on the Letter to the Romans, were not orthodox), went to Dijon where he renounced Calvinism before his death. *Abraham Musculus* (Meuslin, Meusel), pastor and dean in Bern, son of noted hebraist and theologian Wolfgang Musculus, 1497-1563, professor of theology in Bern from 1549. Not to be confused with the ardent anti-Calvinist and anti-Philippist Lutheran theologian Andreas Musculus, 1514-1581, preacher and teacher in Frankfurt-a.d.-Oder from 1542. Little is known of *Peter Hubner,* professor of Greek in Bern.

position were Andreas, and Lucas Osiander the Elder (1534-1604), son of Andreas Osiander (1498-1552). It is worth noting that the alignment at the Colloquy was national as well as theological: the titles given the Reformed representatives in the Lutheran report of the proceedings were "Galli" and "Gallici Doctores."

The main portion of the discussion was borne by de Bèze and Andreas. According to the Lutheran report of the debate, de Bèze at one point stated:

> The Word is so in the assumed humanity that even beyond that humanity it is in the other creatures, not scattered about in pieces so that here is one part of the Word and there another part, but the same whole Word who is entire within the assumed humanity is also beyond that humanity. Therefore, because of that union, it is not necessary nor does it follow to say that wherever the Word is, there also is his humanity. For the reality and property of the true body which the Son of God assumed in this way does not allow or permit such a thing. [1]

Andreas had pointed out how objectionable were the images used by Reformed theologians in illustrating what they meant by the Word's being *etiam extra carnem*. De Bèze defended their use by saying:

> Our theologians used these memory-serving illustrations in order to make this clear: because the humanity has boundaries it does not extend as far as the divinity, since in the union itself the humanity remains finite, bounded and organic. From this it does not follow that the divinity does nothing beyond the humanity, just as the divinity is not so contained by the humanity that it cannot act beyond that humanity. My position is that the man Christ, but not the humanity, fills all things and is everywhere present. [2]

In retrospect, it must be conceded that these Reformed similes, which de Bèze was defending, were indeed incongruous. They lent

---

[1] "Λόγος ita in humanitate assumpta est, ut etiam extra eam sit in reliquis creaturis, neque in partes distributus, ut hic sit pars λόγου, illic altera pars: sed totus λόγος, qui totus est in humanitate assumpta, idem totus quoque est extra illam. Ideoque propter illam unionem, non necesse est, neque sequitur: ubicunque est λόγος, ibi quoque est eius humanitas. Nam veritas et proprietas veri corporis, cuiusmodi Filius Dei assumpsit, non patitur neque admittit istud." (*Acta Colloquii Montis Belligartensis . . . 1586* [Tübingen: G. Gruppenbach, 1587], p. 321.)

[2] "Nostri usi sunt commemoratis similitudinibus, quod his significare voluerint: Humanitatem, cum sit circumscripta, non tam late patere quam divinitatem, ut quae in ipsa unione maneat finita, circumscripta, et organica. Unde non sequitur, quod divinitas extra eam nihil agat, sicut non ita ab humanitate continetur, ut non possit extra illam agere. Ego dico, hominem Christum implere omnia, et ubique praesentem esse: sed non humanitatem." (*ibid.*, p. 319.)

themselves easily, by extension, to being considered as statements regarding the relation between the two natures, and they were singularly ill-fitted for this. Antwerp is merely tangential to the ocean; a setting holds a gem in place by attachment and not by union. The planet-orbit analogy, although unfortunate also, was not quite as bad as the others: a heavenly body and an orbit are generally conceived in conjunction with one another, especially if the orbit is taken as a description of the power structure which is presupposed by a planet's presence in one "place" at one "time." These illustrations, according to de Bèze's testimony at Montbéliard, were supposed to protect and they functioned only to restrain exaggerated conclusions about the hypostatic union. They intended to say that however the union is described it must maintain the finitude of the humanity of Christ without which the humanity is not human, and the unlimited character of the divine power without which the humanity cannot be sustained.

The crucial anthropological assertion made by this Reformed Christology was that humanity by definition is finite. Christ was human in all respects like us: sin and not finitude was excepted. Here is one of the ironies continually emerging in the history of doctrines. Reformed Christology has been pilloried for refusing to recognize the capacity of the finite for the infinite. Here Reformed Christology asserts that this is but one fact; the other is the capacity of the infinite for the finite. In other words, can the infinite be related to the finite in a way not destructive to the finite? Or, can the Word of God be united to the humanity of Jesus Christ so as not to nullify that finitude without which his humanity is only illusory? Amid the perplexities of the issues and the tempting alternatives, the Reformed theologians, even at their most awkward moments, were rightfully stubborn about the finitude of the humanity which the Word assumed. Although none of the disputants put it this way, the logic of the Reformed position was that the majesty of the humanity of Christ consisted in the very fact that it remained finite and creaturely even when hypostatically joined to the infinite Creator.

Although it is possible that the term "extra Calvinisticum" appeared already during these discussions, all that can be indicated with certitude is that in literature from the 1580's the emphasis on the *extra* is identified as being particularly Calvinist. But one can gather from a work of A. Hunn (1550-1603) of 1592 that already by that date the *extra* had become a subject of special discussion between Lutheran and Reformed theologians. Hunn did not label his adversaries as

Calvinists but instead called them "Pezeliani" who teach a Zwinglian and Nestorian doctrine. Hunn identified the emphasis on the *extra* as characteristic of this group: "illud Extra (Pezelianae videlicet scriptionis Helena)."[1]

Hunn understood the *extra* to be used by Pezel in an exclusive sense; that is, in a sense which would preclude the Word's being also entire within the flesh. Therefore he was willing to substitute the preposition *praeter* for *extra*. "The orthodox formula is, as I say, that the Word is not elsewhere *outside* the flesh. The false and inconsistent statement is the one which says the Word is not elsewhere *beyond* the flesh."[2] This is our opinion, said Hunn: "Although *beyond* the flesh the Word is in the Father and dwells in the saints and is with all creatures by one or another kind of presence, nevertheless *outside* the flesh the Word is and subsists nowhere."[3] If Pezel really did use the *extra* in an exclusive sense, Hunn was quite justified in his protest. If however, as is more probable, Pezel was saying that after the Incarnation the Word was so *intra carnem* as to be *etiam extra carnem*, then he indeed approached the necessary qualification which Hunn sought with his suggested use of *praeter*. At stake was undoubtedly a genuine theological issue, but nonetheless the impression is inescapable that on this particular portion of Christological reflection Hunn and Pezel were separated by a difference that was largely semantic in nature (provided, of course, that Pezel did not use the *extra* in an exclusive sense). In any event, Hunn was quite right in adhering to the general Lutheran objection to the awkward and even inadmissible similitudes which had come to be associated with the Christology of those who taught "illud Extra." The analogies mentioned specifically by Hunn were Antwerp and the ocean, a gem and its setting, a body and its orbit, and a root and the branches joined to it.[4]

---

[1] *Assertio Sanae et Orthodoxae Doctrinae de Persona et Maiestate Domini* . . . (Frankfurt a.M., 1592), p. 191. The classical reference is intended, perhaps, to mean that the *Extra* is the doctrine for the sake of which the Pezeliani are willing to sacrifice all else as Paris was willing to sacrifice a kingdom for Helen.

[2] "Orthodoxa phrasis est, cum dico, λόγος non est alibi EXTRA carnem. Falsa est et absona, qua dicitur: λόγος PRAETER suam carnem non est alibi." (*ibid.*, p. 152.)

[3] ". . . etsi PRAETER carnem ὁ λόγος etiam sit in Patre, habitet in sanctis, et adsit omnibus creaturis, alio atque alio praesentiae modo, tamen EXTRA carnem sit aut subsistat nuspiam." (*ibid.*, pp. 152-53.)

[4] *Ibid.*, p. 146.

In the first quarter of the seventeenth century, attention was given by Johann Gerhard of Jena (1582-1637) to the doctrine set forth by men like Zanchius, de Bèze, and Ursinus. Gerhard argued:

> Thus one ought to teach that after the Incarnation took place the person of the Word was neither beyond the flesh nor was the flesh beyond the person of the Word; nor were the two natures joined by a certain bare side-by-side existence but by a profound interpenetration which the Fathers teach with the example of the glowing iron and the animated body. [1]

This passage is to be dated at about 1610, judging from the fact that it appeared in the first volume of Gerhard's nine-volume *Loci*, first published 1610-1622.[2] Also in Gerhard there is a rejection of similes used by the Calvinists (Antwerp and the ocean, a gem and its setting, head and feet, planet and orbit) [3] which, as will be seen, continued to plague Reformed and Lutheran discussions from the time they were first introduced.

Turning now to the Giessen-Tübingen dispute of the 1620's, we find that one group represented the Brenz and one the Chemnitz emphasis.[4] The theologians of both schools agreed that by the *communicatio idiomatum* the human nature of Christ had communicated to it the divine property of ubiquity from the moment of the Incarnation. But both parties to the debate had to account for the fact that during the period of Christ's earthly ministry his body evidently was not everywhere. The Tübingers said Christ's body was evidently not everywhere because there was a hiding (κρύψις) of the power of Christ's humanity to be everywhere: there was an abstention only of the visible use of the humanity to be everywhere. The Giesseners said Christ's body was evidently not everywhere because there was an abstention (κένωσις) of the use, and not just of the *visible* use, of the humanity's power to be ubiquitous. The Tübingen theologians said the man Jesus abstained only from the visible use of his power to govern the world while actually exercising it in a concealed way. The

---

[1] "Post factam igitur incarnationem, nec persona λόγου extra carnem, nec caro extra personam λόγου statui debet: nec per nudam quandam παράστασιν duae illae Naturae conjunctae sunt, sed per intimam περιχώρισιν, [sic] quod veteres declarant exemplo ferri igniti et corporis animati." (*Locorum Theologicorum* ... *Tom. I* [3rd ed.; Jena: Steinmann, 1628], "De Persona et Officio Christi," I, 3, 30, p. 649.)

[2] Cf. *EKL*, I, col. 1508.

[3] *Op. cit.*, pp. 649, 656.

[4] *Supra*, pp. 9-11.

Giessen theologians provided for the world's governance during the time of the *exinanitio* by saying that Christ reigned over the world but not through his flesh.[1]

To teach as the Giessen theologians did, said Thumm, was to reintroduce "illud ipsum *extra* Calvinisticum."[2] The context of the Thumm statement as quoted by Thomasius indicates that the *extra* part of the term was well known in Lutheran circles as an undesirable charge against any given theology. It is impossible from the passage, however, to decide whether what was notorious was the full term "extra Calvinisticum" or just the *extra*, which was granted as being Calvinist. It is possible, therefore, that the term itself was first used by Thumm in 1623; but a small variation of the term appeared slightly earlier in the works of Balthazar Mentzer (1565-1627), one of the major theologians of Giessen with whom Thumm was in debate on the doctrine of the person of Christ.

Mentzer dealt at great length with the teaching of the Calvinists that after the Incarnation the Word was also *extra carnem*. In his *Exegesis Augustanae Confessionis*, 1615,[3] Mentzer had a paragraph (Art. III, 6) on the "Sententia Zwinglii, Calvini et sociorum de Christo." Despite its title, this section in effect concentrated on the associates rather than on Zwingli or Calvin; Calvin was cited only three or four times and was never quoted. Mentzer listed the views of de Bèze, Zanchi, Pezel, and Sohn [4] who did not hesitate to affirm that ". . . the

---

[1] "Regnavit quidem Christus et regnat semper ut Deus cum patre et spiritu sancto, verum humanitatem suam in statu exinanitionis non adhibuit gubernando universo, sed potius eam in servili forma continuit, retraxit; regnavit mundum non mediante carne." (Justus Feurborn, 1587-1656, [cited by] Thomasius, *op. cit.*, pp. 439-40.

[2] Thomasius, *op. cit.*, p. 446; cf. Bauke, *loc. cit.*, *RGG*, I, cols. 1628-29; Loofs, *loc. cit.*, *RE*, X, pp. 261-62; Barth, *op. cit.*, IV, 1, pp. 181-82.

[3] Judging from the date of the dedicatory epistle.

[4] *Théodore de Bèze*, 1519-1605, well-known co-worker with Calvin in Geneva and Calvin's successor as leader of the Genevan Reformed Church. *Girolamo Zanchi*, 1516-1590, Italian and Reformed theologian, teacher successively at Strasbourg (for a time alongside his compatriot Peter Martyr Vermigli), at Heidelberg, and at Neustadt-an-den-Hardt. *Christoph Pezel*, 1539-1604, a Philippist turned Calvinist, chief author of several catechisms (Wittenberg Catechism, 1571; Bremen Catechism) and the *Consensus ministerii Bremensis ecclesiae*, 1595; teacher and preacher successively in Wittenberg, Siegen, Dillenburg, Herborn, and Bremen. *Georg Sohn*, 1551-1589, student of jurisprudence and theology at Wittenberg, theology at Marburg where he was professor of Hebrew (1574) until, because of disputes, he accepted a call to Heidelberg (1584).

whole Word was in the flesh and the whole Word was beyond the flesh or his human nature."[1]

> Pezel, Sohn and others concede that after the Incarnation the divine person of the Word (which Holy Scripture and pious antiquity maintain is communicated to that assumed humanity subsisting personally in the divine nature) is not beyond the assumed nature. But then they affirm that with respect to his infinite essence the Word is beyond the flesh in boundless places. There you have it—the infinite divinity of the Word but the finite person of the same Word! How will God's perfectly simple unity be demonstrated? [2]

And in a work from 1621, *Anti-Crocius*,[3] he referred to what he called "Extra Calvinianum" in this context:

> One ought not, therefore, to say that something of the Word dwells in the flesh, or that the Word according to some part dwells there, for indeed the whole humanity is united to the whole divinity in the person of the Word. Whence there is in Christ that mutual and personal *perichoresis* of the natures, which the 'Extra Calvinianum' is completely unable to provide for. [4]

Mentzer called attention to two different interpretations, given by Calvinists, of the manner in which the *Logos* is not confined to the flesh. One said it was the divine essence which remained also beyond the flesh; the other said it was the *hypostasis* which was also beyond the flesh. What is important is that Mentzer, as a Lutheran, rejected both assertions of the life of the Eternal Son beyond the flesh.[5]

---

[1] ". . . totum λόγον esse in carne, et totum λόγον esse extra carnem, sive naturam suam humanam." (Balthazar Mentzer, *Opera Latina*, ed. B. Mentzer, Jr., I [Frankfurt, 1669], p. 48.)

[2] "Personam divinam τοῦ λόγου (quam communicatam esse assumptae Humanitati, quae in ipsa personaliter subsistit, ex divinis Literis et pia Antiquitate constat) post factam incarnationem, non esse extra carnem assumptam, concedunt Pezelius et Sohnius, et alii: Sed tamen, quia essentia τοῦ λόγου sit infinita, proinde hujus respectu affirmant, τὸν λόγον infinitis locis esse extra carnem. Vides infinitam τοῦ λόγου Deitatem, sed finitam ejusdem personam! Ubi demonstratibur simplicissima in Deo unitas?" ("Collatio Augustinae Confessionis cum Doctrina Zwinglii, Calvini, Bezae et Sociorum," *op. cit.*, I, p. 311.)

[3] The reference is to *Ludwig Crocius*, 1585-1655, who took his doctorate at Basel (1609) and was pastor and professor at Bremen. He is not to be confused with Johannes Crocius, 1590-1659, also a Reformed theologian, who took his doctorate at Marburg, was preacher in Königsberg and professor of theology at Marburg.

[4] *Op. cit.*, I, p. 584.

[5] Johann Andreas Quenstedt, 1617-1688, writing some sixty-five years later (his *Theologiae Didactico-Polemicae Pars Tertia* was first published in 1685), indicated this same two-fold possibility of interpreting the *extra* affirmation. He had a

CONCLUSION

"Extra Calvinisticum" as a term may have been first introduced by Theodore Thumm in 1623. The synonymous term "Extra Calvinianum" appeared still earlier in a 1621 work of Balthazar Mentzer. The appearance of both terms, however, crystallized an idea long held among Lutheran theologians that it was characteristically Calvinist to teach that after the Incarnation the Eternal Son had an existence *etiam extra carnem*. This Lutheran sentiment appeared as early as the Colloquy of Maulbronn, in 1564. Already by that date "Calvinist" was becoming synonymous with, or was even replacing, "Zwinglian" as the most comprehensive term to describe the "sacramentarians," and the Reformed theologians were giving increased attention to the *etiam extra* affirmation.

Closely associated with this affirmation was the use, by Reformed theologians, of similitudes such as "Antwerp and the ocean." These images were originally intended to illustrate the relation between Christ's bodily presence in heaven (Antwerp) and his ubiquity according to the power of his divinity (the ocean). But they, unfortunately, came to describe, and were accepted by the Reformed theologians themselves as describing, the relation between the two natures of the One Person. Although the *etiam extra* was not an innovation on the

---

Question entitled, "An post factam Unionem personalem totus λόγος ita existat intra carnem assumptam, ut etiam totus sit extra eam?" (*Theologiae Didactico-Polemicae Pars Tertia* [4th ed.; Wittenberg, 1701], "De Christi," cap. III, memb. I, sect. II, quest. V, p. 138.) There he said Calvinists teach:

"λόγον, qui humanam assumpsit naturam, non minus totum extra naturam humanam esse, quam in natura humana, totamque naturam divinam λόγου esse et intra et extra corpus suum, post factam unionem. Abeunt vero Calviniani circa hanc assertionem in duas classes; Quidam et naturam et hypostasin λόγου ita dicunt esse in carne, ut tamen sit etiam extra carnem . . . [e.g., de Bèze, Zanchi, Crocius, Ursinus (*Zacharias Ursinus*, 1534-1583, Reformed theologian most prominent for his part in the composition of the Heidelberg Catechism (1563), and his project for Church discipline in the Palatinate), and others]. Quidam concedunt hypostasin λόγου non esse extra suam carnem, interim naturam divinam τοῦ λόγου dicunt esse extra humanam naturam propter infinitatem . . . [e.g., Sohn and Wendelin (*Markus Friedrich Wendelin*, 1584-1652, student at Heidelberg, teacher in Geneva [as tutor, 1609] Dessau and rector of the Gymnasium Illustre in Zerbst from 1612 until his death)]." (*ibid.*, p. 139)

Over against both forms of the Calvinists' extra, Quenstedt's thesis was:

"Uti post factam unionem hypostaticam τοῦ λόγου et carnis, assumpta caro nunquam et nuspiam est extra et citra λόγον, ita et λόγος nunquam et nuspiam est extra vel citra suam carnem, ita tamen, ut nec caro immensa sit, nec λόγος includatur, finiatur vel circumscribatur, sed et illa finita, et hic infinitus permaneat." (*ibid.*, p. 138)

part of the Reformed theologians, the special use of the similitudes as explications of this affirmation did constitute an innovation which was naturally met by Lutheran objections.

The Lutheran aversion for the *etiam extra*, apart from the peculiar form given it by the similitudes, was itself an innovation, however, but one understandable in the light of the special Lutheran use of the *communicatio idiomatum*. For, as the Lutherans saw it, the *extra* was superfluous since it provided nothing not already contained in Lutheran Christology. Christ's activity after the Incarnation was not restricted to the places where Jesus of Nazareth appeared. By virtue of the *communicatio idiomatum* the One Person continued to govern the universe, with the humanity abstaining from or concealing the use of its power to be ubiquitous while appearing to be limited to a place on earth. An even more fundamental cause for the objection was a form of the theology of glory which the Lutherans felt was implied in the *extra* confession. On this point Luther's dictum remained decisive for his followers: "...Neither in heaven nor on earth do I have or know God outside this flesh, cared for in the womb of the Virgin Mary."[1]

The Reformed theologians, for their part, maintained that a denial of the *extra* affirmation threatened the integrity of both natures which were united in the One Person. While for the Lutherans it was crass to limit Christ bodily, the Reformed scholars could not visualize Christ bodily as being anything other than limited since in taking on our flesh Christ took on that which by definition was limited. In an effort to restrict themselves to the flesh of Christ the Lutherans could only engage in a new kind of theology of glory, fatally speculating away the reality of precisely that flesh.

Both Lutheran and Reformed theologians were intent, in different ways and with differing degrees of success, on maintaining the unity of the Person and the reality of the natures there hypostatically united. Both were intent on confessing that in this One Person, in this fashion, and in this Incarnate Lord, God himself was dealing with the world. And both were intent on affirming that the Incarnation did not require that the Eternal Word cease to govern the universe. But on this last point the Lutherans generally insisted that the majesty of Christ's

---

[1] "...Ego nullum nec in coelo neque in terra Deum habeo aut scio extra hanc carnem, quae fovetur in gremio Mariae Virginis." (*Scholia in Esaiam*, Cap. 4:6; *WA* 25:107.)

humanity exalted it, by virtue of the *communicatio idiomatum*, to governing the universe in union with the divine nature. The Reformed theologians never agreed with the Lutherans that Christ's humanity shared the majesty of the divine nature. They resorted instead to a more traditional provision for the Word's governance of the universe after the Incarnation: the doctrine that the Incarnate Lord never ceased to have his existence *etiam extra carnem*.

CHAPTER TWO

THE TRADITIONAL SOURCES OF
CALVIN'S DOCTRINE OF THE SO-CALLED
EXTRA CALVINISTICUM

This study now turns from "extra Calvinisticum" as a term to the
larger question of the so-called extra Calvinisticum as a doctrine. The
purpose of this chapter is not to give a complete history of the doctrine
before Calvin, nor to reiterate the scattered acknowledgment others
have already made of the so-called extra Calvinisticum before Calvin.[1]
It will become clear that these previous findings have been sketchy,
at best, and that the doctrine was far more widespread than anyone
has indicated. Furthermore, it is one thing to show that the "extra
Calvinisticum" was present in the tradition before Calvin; it is another to show that Calvin was aware of its presence there and consciously availed himself of the tradition in his own use of the doctrine.
This chapter will seek, therefore, from Calvin's own writings, clues
as to the parts of the tradition on which he drew. Another area
neglected in modern literature is the unique position of the doctrine
as a subject of consensus among medieval and ancient Fathers whose
theologies in other respects differed radically. A second goal of this
chapter, then, will be to account for the use of this doctrine in dis-
parate Church Fathers, including the heterodox and the orthodox.
It will become apparent that the significance of the doctrine in any
theological system was not its presence but its function.

Clues provided by Calvin for identifying the traditional sources

There are two passages in the *Institutes* which are commonly
accepted as Calvin's classical statements of the "extra Calvinisticum."
These are II, 13, 4 and IV, 17, 30 of the 1559 edition.[2] While the II,
13, 4 statement appears only in the 1559 edition, the IV, 17, 30 for-

    [1] Wendel, *op. cit.*, p. 168; Benoit, *loc. cit.*, *CIB*, II, p. 250, n. 8; Loofs, *Leit-
faden* . . ., *op. cit.*, pp. 95, 150, 171, 264-65; Kreck, *loc. cit.*, *EKL*, I, cols. 1245-46;
Barth, *op. cit.*, I, 2, pp. 168-69, IV, 1, pp. 180-81; Mackintosh, *op. cit.*, p. 244.
    [2] Benoit, *op. cit.*, II, pp. 250-51; Wendel, *op. cit.*, p. 168; Niesel, *op. cit.*, p. 118;
Loofs, *loc. cit.*, *RE*, X, p. 258; and *Leitfaden* . . ., *op. cit.*, pp. 880, 891; Witte,
loc. cit., *KCGG*, III, p. 499; Krusche, *op. cit.*, p. 129.

mulation is a significantly expanded version of a section already present in the first edition of the Institutes, 1536. It is noteworthy that the doctrine first appeared in Calvin in a discussion of the Eucharist and that its appearance within the context of the two-natures problem did not come, as far as the *Institutes* is concerned, until the final edition. This fact more than coincidentally reflects the way in which Calvin progressively formulated and refined his Christology in response to what he feared were threats to the Church's confession of the person of the Savior. From 1536 onwards the so-called extra Calvinisticum was used to thwart menacing eucharistic speculation. By the 1559 edition the doctrine was also used to forestall menacing Trinitarian and anti-Trinitarian speculation.

Institutes II, 13, 4. Although the II, 13, 4 passage is later than the IV, 17, 30, it is worth considering first if only to note that it offers no clues about the traditional sources from which Calvin drew his knowledge of the doctrine. In addition, however it indicates the affirmations Calvin sought to preserve in his use of the doctrine.

In 1536 Calvin referred briefly to the Manichaeans who did not recognize the full humanity of the flesh of Christ.[1] In the 1543 edition, VII, 11-12 were directed against the Manichaeans and the Marcionites, both of whom threatened the reality of Christ's humanity. The Manichaeans did so in their doctrine of the heavenly body of Christ, the Marcionites in their teaching that his body was only an appearance.[2] In the 1559 edition this section appeared in II, 13, a paragraph devoted to the true substance of Christ's flesh. There Calvin dealt with those who argued that humanity would make Christ's human body impure and that such an Incarnation would restrict God within the limits of a small place. This last was false, according to Calvin,

> ... because although the immeasurable essence of the Word joined with the human nature into One Person, still we do not imagine that was an enclosure. For the Son of God descended marvelously from heaven in such a way that he did not leave heaven; and marvelously he was borne in the womb of the Virgin and walked about the earth and willed to be crucified, but in such a way that he always filled the world as from the beginning. [3]

---

[1] OS I, pp. 80-81.

[2] "Humanitatis veritas partim a Manichaeis, partim a Marcionitis impugnata est. Quorum hi quidem spectrum Christo pro corpore affingebant, illi autem coelesti carne praeditum somniabant." (*Institutes* (1543), VII, 11; *CO* 1:519.)

[3] "... quia etsi in unam personam coaluit immensa Verbi essentia cum natura hominis, nullam tamen inclusionem fingimus. Mirabiliter enim e caelo descendit

Institutes IV, 17, 30. The IV, 17, 30 passage discloses Calvin's reliance on Lombard and St. Augustine for his particular interpretation of the so-called extra Calvinisticum. Examination of this passage reveals three stages in the development of the doctrine within the context of the eucharistic discussion, all leading to its final form in the 1559 and 1560 editions.

1. In 1536 Calvin was maintaining the reality of the humanity of Christ against those who attributed to him only a spiritual body. The truth in summary form, said Calvin, is that

> Christ, since he put on our true flesh when he was born of the Virgin, suffered in our true flesh when he made satisfaction for us; so by rising again he received and bore into heaven this self-same flesh. For this is where our hope in our resurrection and ascension rests, that Christ rose again and ascended. And how weak and fragile would this hope be unless our flesh truly were aroused and entered the Kingdom of heaven? But the abiding reality of the body is that it be contained in a place, that it retain its dimensions, that it have its outward appearance. [1]

There are those, Calvin went on, who teach that Christ's body never had any other dimensions but those which by length and breadth extend to heaven and earth; that by a certain dispensation he performed a human role in being born, growing, being stretched on the cross, and being shut in the tomb; that the resurrection appearances and the ascension were by the same dispensation in order for him to declare himself in the sight of men the established King in heaven.

> What is this but to raise Marcion from hell? For who will doubt that the body of Christ was an apparition if it were in this condition? They contend that it was said by Christ himself 'No one ascends into heaven except he who descends from heaven, the Son of Man who is in heaven.' (John 3) But are they not of obtuse sense that they

---

Filius Dei, ut caelum tamen non relinqueret: mirabiliter in utero Virginis gestari, in terris versari, et in cruce pendere voluit, ut semper mundum impleret, sicut ab initio." (*Institutes*, II, 13, 4 fin.; OS III, p. 458.)

[1] "Christus, ut veram nostram carnem induit, cum e virgine natus est, in vera carne nostra passus est, cum pro nobis satisfecit; ita eandem veram carnem et resurgendo recepit et in coelum sustulit. Haec enim nobis nostrae resurrectionis et in coelum ascensionis spes est, quod Christus resurrexit et ascendit. Porro, quam infirma et fragilis spes foret ista, nisi haec ipsa nostra caro in Christo vere suscitata et in regnum coelorum ingressa esset? Atqui haec est perpetua corporis veritas, ut loco contineatur, ut suis dimensionibus constet, ut suam faciem habeat." (OS I, p. 140.)

do not see this was said through the communication of properties? For as the Lord of glory is said by Paul (I Cor. 2) to be crucified, not because he suffered according to the divinity, but because Christ when he was abject and held in contempt suffered in the flesh, so the same was God and the Lord of glory. In this way he was also the Son of Man in heaven because the very same Christ who, as Son of Man, dwelt on earth according to the flesh, was God in heaven. Wherefore by this same passage he is said to have descended according to the divinity, not because the divinity left heaven in order to remove himself into the workhouse of the body but because although he filled all things, nevertheless in Christ's very humanity he dwelt bodily, that is, naturally, and in some indescribable way (Col. 2). [1]

2. This 1536 passage became XVIII, 23 and 25 of the 1543 edition. Paragraph 24, a new insertion, consisted largely of a testimony drawn from St. Augustine. Since the new Marcionites appealed to the Fathers, Calvin called them to hear Augustine who was commonly held as a most faithful interpreter among the ancients in dogmatic affairs of the Church.

He says, 'Do not doubt, Christ the man is now there whence he is to come; contemplate by memory and hold faithfully the Christian confession, that since he arose from the dead and ascended into heaven he sits at the right hand of the Father. Nor otherwise is he to come to judge the living and the dead. And he is to come, according to the testimony of the angelic voice, as he was seen to go into heaven, in that same visible form and substance to which, because he carried it, he gave immortality and whose nature he did not remove. Accordingly it is not to be believed that this form is everywhere diffused. For we have to be careful lest we so construct the divinity of the man that we give up the truth of the body. For it does not follow that what is in God is everywhere as God is everywhere.' [2]

---

[1] "Qualiter a Paulo (I Cor. 2) Dominus gloriae crucifixus dicitur, non quia secundum divinitatem sit passus, sed quia Christus, qui abiectus et contemptus in carne patiebatur, idem Deus erat et Dominus gloriae. Ad hunc modum et filius hominis in coelo erat, quia ipse idem Christus, qui secundum carnem hominis filius habitabat in terris, Deus erat in coelo. Qua ratione, eo ipso loco, descendisse dicitur secundum divinitatem; non quod divinitas coelum reliquerit, ut in ergastulum corporis se abderet, sed quia, tametsi omnia impleret, in ipsa tamen Christi humanitate corporaliter, id est, naturaliter habitabat et ineffabili quodam modo (Col. 2)." (ibid., pp. 140-141.)

[2] "Noli, inquit, dubitare, ibi nunc esse hominem Christum unde venturus est; memoriterque recole et fideliter tene christianam confessionem, quoniam resurrexit a mortuis, ascendit in coelum, sedet ad dexteram patris. Nec aliunde venturus est ad vivos mortuosque iudicandos. Et sic venturus est, angelica illa voce testante, ut ire visus est in coelum, et eadem visibili forma atque substantia, cui profecto immortalitatem dedit, naturam non abstulit. Secundum hanc formam non est putandus ubique diffusus. Cavendum est enim ne ita divinitatem astruamus

Calvin felt this passage demonstrated the extent to which Augustine differed from the Marcionites. As Calvin saw it, whatever doctrine the Marcionites offered tended to assert the local presence of Christ in the Supper, and this is because the only participation they could conceive of was one consisting either of spatial contact or crude enclosure.

3. A third revision brought this passage into its final form in the 1559 and 1560 editions. What had been introduced in 1543 as XVIII, 24 became in 1559 IV, 17, 28, a section on the interpretation of Augustine's doctrine concerning the nature of Christ's Real Presence in the Supper. The portion which had been carried over from the 1536 edition into the 1543 edition as XVIII, 25 was broken into two parts in the final edition of the *Institutes*. The first part, which said Christ's body was not an apparition, served as the basis of IV, 17, 17. The second part, which dealt with John 3: 13, became the framework for the final IV, 17, 30.

Concentrating now on that part of the 1536 passage which remained in 1559 as IV, 17, 30, one finds Calvin added John 1: 18 ("The only Son, who is in the bosom of the Father, he has made him known.") to John 3: 13 as a saying of Jesus spoken *per communicationem idiomatum*. This supplemented his refutation of those seeking a doctrine of Christ's bodily ubiquity based on these verses.

A much more important addition, however, was Calvin's use of the scholastic distinction between *Christus totus* and *Christus totum*. The end of IV, 17, 30 stated that Christ

> ... is said to have descended according to the divinity, not because the divinity left heaven in order to remove himself into the workhouse of the body but because although he filled all things, nevertheless in Christ's very humanity he dwelt bodily, that is, naturally, and in some indescribable way (Col. 2). There is a trite distinction in the schools to which I am not ashamed to refer. Although the whole Christ is ubiquitous, yet everything which is in him is not ubiquitous. And would that the scholastics themselves had wisely explored the force of this opinion, because thus would the absurd comment about the carnal presence of Christ have been avoided. Therefore our Mediator, since as *totus* he is ubiquitous, always is with his own

---

hominis, ut veritatem corporis auferamus. Non est autem consequens, ut quod in Deo est ita sit ubique ut Deus." (*CO* I: 1006; the quote is from St. Augustine's letter to Dardanus, Ep. 187, chap. iii (10); *MPL* 33: 835-36.)

people, and shows himself present in a special way in the Supper, yet he is there *totus* not *totum*. Because, as was said, in his flesh he is contained in heaven until he appears in judgment. [1]

The *totus-totum* distinction and the "*extra Calvinisticum*"

Calvin used the *totus-totum* distinction as an explication of the "extra Calvinisticum," identifying this distinction as a commonplace of the "Scholastici" or the "Théologiens Sorboniques." Unfortunately, Calvin did not name here the men to whom he was referring. It is necessary now to determine their identity, and compare Calvin's interpretation of the distinction with theirs. In the process, consideration will be given to explicit statements of the "extra Calvinisticum" in certain scholastic theologians who used the *totus-totum* distinction and in others who did not.

The *totus-totum* distinction was most clearly described by Peter Lombard in his *Sententiarum Liber III*, d. 22, 3. Although Calvin did not in the *Institutes* identify Lombard as his source in this matter, he did so elsewhere in his writings.

In the *Final Admonition to Westphal*, 1557, Calvin replied to those who objected that the person of Christ is dissolved if one denies that he can be present in his human nature wherever he wishes.

> If this is a dissolution of the Person, then it will be necessary for that which above all is his to be ripped from his human nature, lest he cease to be Mediator. What then can be imagined to be more absurd than that the flesh of Christ was in heaven while it hung on the cross? Nevertheless undoubtedly the whole Christ, God and man, then indeed was in heaven. But these proud critics ought to hold to the common distinction which was not unknown either to Peter Lombard nor to the sophists who followed afterwards: indeed that the Mediator Christ, God and man, is everywhere *totus* but not everywhere *totum*: because with respect to his flesh he walked about on

---

[1] ". . . Trita est in scholis distinctio, quam me referre non pudet, Quanvis totus Christus ubique sit, non tamen totum quod in eo est, ubique esse. Atque utinam Scholastici ipsi vim huius sententiae probe expendissent: quia ita occursum fuisset insulso commento de carnali Christi praesentia. Mediator ergo noster quum totus ubique sit, suis semper adest: et in Coena speciali modo praesentem se exhibet, sic tamen ut totus adsit, non totum: quia, ut dictum est, in carne sua caelo comprehenditur donec in iudicium appareat." (*Institutes* IV, 17, 30; *OS* V, p. 389.) The 1560 edition illumined this distinction (which Calvin there attributed to "les Théologiens Sorboniques") as Calvin interpreted it: "C'est que Iesus Christ est par tout en son entier, mais que tout ce qu'il a en soy n'est point par tout." (Benoit, *op. cit.*, IV, p. 419.)

the earth for a while, and now dwells in heaven. And it is strange the way those men so impudently rush against the consensus of the ancient Church. [1]

Calvin used the distinction again in 1561, this time against Heshusius. There he reiterated that in insisting on Christ's place at the right hand of the Father he was not narrowly confining him. It was not a matter of philosophical or physical details but rather of the testimony of Scripture; Scripture, not geometry, makes it plain that the body of Christ is finite and has its own dimensions.

> We do not deny that the whole and entire Christ in the person of the Mediator fills heaven and earth. I say 'totus, non totum' because it would be absurd to say this of the flesh. The hypostatic union of the two natures is not equivalent to a communication of the immensity of the Godhead to the flesh, since the peculiar properties of both natures are perfectly in accord with the unity of the Person. [2]

Then Calvin insisted that he was teaching, and for more than twelve years had taught, that Christ's sitting at the right hand of the Father does not mean that Christ is confined to heaven, but rather that while the humanity of Christ is in heaven his power is everywhere diffused as reigning power.[3]

In a dedicatory letter of 1563 to Frederick of Palatinate, Calvin again discussed what the session at the right hand of God means for the eucharistic presence and for the relation of the divine to the human in the person of Christ. Calvin contended that Christ, while he sits at the right hand of the Father, is in a way everywhere.

> ... because he who watches over and tends all parts of heaven and earth and who by his mastery regulates and controls all things above and below cannot be enclosed in a place. Yet by the name Christ I embrace the whole Person of the only begotten Son, as he was manifested in the flesh. I say that that one, God and man, is everywhere by mastery and incomprehensible power and infinite glory—just as

---

[1] "Si haec est personae solutio, humanae Christi naturae eripi necesse erit quod eius maxime proprium est, ne desinat esse mediator. Quid autem absurdius fingi potest, quam in coelo fuisse Christi carnem dum in cruce pendebat? Neque tamen dubium est quin totus Christus deus et homo tunc quoque in coelo fuerit. Sed istis superbis censoribus tenenda erat vulgaris distinctio, quae nec Petro Lombardo, nec sophistis qui postea sequuti sunt, fuit incognita: nempe quod Christus mediator deus et homo totus ubique sit, sed non totum: quia carnis suae respectu in terra aliquamdiu versatus est, et nunc in coelis habitat. Ac mirum est homines istos tam proterve contra veteris ecclesiae consensum ferri." (CO 9:194-95.)

[2] De Vera Participatione Christi in Coena, 1561: CO 9:507.

[3] Ibid.

the faithful experience his presence by evident effects. And Paul is not beside the point when he proclaims that Christ dwells in us (Eph. 3, 17). But there is no sense in twisting what is said about the immensity of power, which appears in spiritual gifts and in all the invincible aid for our salvation, to make it apply to the essence of the flesh. I wish at least that many who with little reason are angry with us would remember that trite saying which is famous in the Papal schools: 'Christus ubique totus est sed non totum.' [1]

Granted, said Calvin, that this is expressed in the unpleasant and barbarous language of Lombard: "It is yet wisely expressed from whomsoever it may have come and I willingly adopt it." [2] Calvin poked fun at the daintiness of those who rejected Lombard's language and who yet delighted in Berengarius' words of recantation which spoke of Christ's body being broken by the teeth and digested by the stomach. The sober teaching should not be loathed that:

> ... Christ the Mediator is everywhere in his entirety, but not with respect to his flesh which is contained by its limits, since his power is infinite and his operation is felt no less on earth than in heaven. There are two customary words, 'union' and 'unity.' The first refers to the two natures; the second is proper to the Person alone. Those who nevertheless impudently throw themselves into this absurdity would also be ashamed, unless I am mistaken, to assert the unity of flesh and deity. For unless the flesh differ and be distinguished in its properties from the divine essence, they are coalesced by a confused mixture into one. [3]

---

[1] "... quia loco includi non potest qui omnes coeli et terrae partes fovet ac tuetur, omniaque sursum et deorsum suo imperio moderatur ac temperat. Dum nunc Christum nomino totam unigeniti filii personam complector, ut est in carne manifestatus. Ipse, inquam, Deus et homo ubique est imperio virtuteque incomprehensibili et infinita gloria: sicuti claris effectis eius praesentiam experiuntur fideles. Neque vero abs re praedicat Paulus (Eph. 3,17) eum in nobis habitare. Verum quod de immensitate virtutis dicitur, quae in donis spiritualibus, invicto auxilio totaque nostra salute apparet, ad essentiam carnis torquere minime consentaneum est. Utinam saltem multus, qui parum considerate nobis succensent, in mentem veniret dictum in scholis papalibus tritum ac celebre: Christus ubique totus est, sed non totum! (Lib. 3 Sentent. dist. 22)" (*CO* 20:75.)

[2] *Ibid.*

[3] "... Christum mediatorem esse ubique integrum, sed non carnis respectu quae finibus suis continetur, quum infinita sit eius potentia et operatio in terra non minus quam in coelo sentiatur. Duae sunt usitatae voces, unio et unitas: quarum prior ad naturas duas refertur, altera soli personae convenit. Unitatem carnis et deitatis asserere eos quoque, nisi fallor, puderet qui tamen in hanc absurditatem imprudenter se coniiciunt: quia nisi differat suaque proprietate distinguatur caro ab essentia divina, confusa permixtione in unum coalescent." (*CO* 20:75.)

Peter Lombard and the medieval Fathers

Peter Lombard (c. 1100-1160). Lombard used the *totus-totum* distinction to account for the nature of Christ's presence during the period between his death and resurrection, not to reconcile Christ's bodily ascension and his presence in the Eucharist. During those three days, Christ was, according to Lombard, *totus* in hell, *totus* in heaven, *totus* everywhere. For as Person he was never diminished or enlarged by union with the flesh or lack of union therewith. Christ, entire and perfect, was everywhere. But while he was everywhere *totus*, he was not everywhere *totum*. "Totus" refers to *hypostasis* or person, while "totum" refers to nature, just as "alius" refers to someone and "aliud" refers to something.[1]

---

[1] "Et utique totus eodem tempore erat in inferno, in coelo totus, ubique totus; persona enim illa aeterna non major erat, ubi carnem et animum simul unitam sibi habebat, quam ubi alterum tantum; nec major erat ubi utrumque simul vel alterum tantum unitum habebat, quam ubi erat neutrum habens unitum. Totus ergo Christus et perfectus ubique erat ... Ex his [Augustine's words] apparet quod Christus eodem tempore totus erat in sepulcro, totus in inferno, totus ubique; sicut et modo totus est ubicumque est, sed non totum. Nec in sepulcro, nec in inferno totum erat, etsi totus, sicut Christus totus est Deus, totus homo, sed non totum; quia non solum est Deus vel homo, sed et Deus et homo. Totum enim ad naturam refertur, totus autem ad hypostasim; sicut aliud et aliquid ad naturam, alius vero et aliquis ad personam referuntur." (*Sententiarum Liber III*, d. 22, 3; *MPL* 192: 804.) Lombard cited the *totus-totum* distinction as made by John of Damascus (c. 675-c. 749) in a passage containing not only the *totus-totum* distinction but a statement of the so-called *extra Calvinisticum* itself. The Damascene said:

"We indeed confess one incarnate nature of the Word of God meaning by this 'incarnate' which we say, the substance of the flesh, following the blessed Cyril. And therefore the Word was incarnate and did not give up his own immateriality, and he was incarnate in his entirety (ὅλος) and he was unbounded (ἀπερίγραπτος) in his entirety (ὅλος). As regards his body, he is diminished and contracted, and as concerns his deity he is unbounded, for his body is not co-extensive with his unbounded divinity. (οὐ συμπαρεκτεινομένης τῆς σαρκὸς αὐτοῦ τῇ ἀπεριγράπτῳ αὐτοῦ θεότητι) Indeed on the one hand he is perfect God in his entirety (ὅλος), yet on the other hand the whole thing (ὅλον) is not God; for he is not only God but also man. Also he is perfect man in his entirety, but the whole thing is not man; for he is not only man but also God. For while the ὅλον stands for nature, so even the ὅλος stands for person, just as ἄλλο stands for nature while ἄλλος stands for person." (*De Fide Orthodoxa*, III, 7; *MPG* 94: 1011-12.) John of Damascus himself referred to a passage in Gregory Nazianzus (329-389), from whom he drew the grammatical analogy which supported the ὅλος-ὅλον distinction. Gregory's main concern in that passage was to affirm that although the two natures are God and man who is in fact soul and body, yet there are not two Sons, much less two Gods. There are two natures but not two Persons, for both are One in the σύγκρασις. Then Nazianzus applied ἄλλο καὶ ἄλλο to the two natures of the Incarnation, whereas in speaking of the Trinity

The distinction thus was between Christ as the second *hypostasis* of the Trinity, the Eternal Son of God, and Christ the second *hypostasis* with what he united to himself in the Incarnation. Making this distinction provided another way of accounting for the fact that the Eternal Son of God was united to the flesh but also had his existence and reality beyond that flesh.[1] In contrast with Lombard, Calvin assigned to the distinction the special eucharistic role already noted, but he did not use it to support the more traditional view of the descent into hell. This he described instead as the anguish of Christ's soul on the cross.[2]

---

he used ἄλλος καὶ ἄλλος. For in speaking of the Trinity ἄλλος καὶ ἄλλος was appropriate lest there be confusion about the *hypostases*; but ἄλλο καὶ ἄλλο was inappropriate because the three *hypostases* are one and the same as divinity. (Gregory of Nazianzus, Ep. 101 [listed in the Damascus text under the old ordering as Orat. 51], "Ad Cledonium Presbyterum contra Apollinarium, Ep. 1"; *MPG* 37: 179-80.)

[1] Cf. J. Lebon:

"La théologie actuelle réserve le neutre (*totum, aliud*) à la prédication de la nature et emploie le masculin pour la prédication de la personne. Mais, comme l'observe déjà dom Coustant [*sic*], en note à cet endroit, cette règle de terminologie n'existait pas encore au temps d'Hilaire, au moins dans sa rigeur présente. La pensée de notre Docteur [Hilary] reste claire; elle est nettement opposée, non pas à la distinction réelle des natures dans le Christ, mais à la distinction de deux sujets ou personnes, ce qui serait la *divisio* rejetée." ("Une ancienne opinion sur la condition du corps du Christ dans la mort," *Revue d'Histoire Ecclésiastique*, XXIII (1927), p. 223, n. 3; cf. also pp. 5-43 esp. on Athanasius, and pp. 209-41 esp. on Hilary of Poitiers.)

The reference is to P. Constant whose general preface to the edition of the works of St. Hilary, published in 1693, has been preserved in *MPL* 9: 11-126. Constant points out this distinction in Fulgentius Ferrandus' (fl. 530, deacon of Church in Carthage) *Ep. ad Severum*, 8:

" 'Totus Christus apud inferos fuit secundum animam rationalem, sed non totum; quia caro ibi non fuit, cum qua est totum; totus Christus in sepulcro fuit secundum carnem, sed non totum; quia anima ibi non fuit, cum qua est totum. Verbum tamen Dei et cum anima sua apud inferos, et cum carne sua in sepulcro fuit.' [cf. *MPL* 67: 918] Et [Constant goes on] quia Verbum cum anima apud inferos, et cum carne in sepulcro fuit, subinde declarat consequens esse, ut totus Christus apud inferos et totus in sepulcro recte dicatur, ob unitatem scilicet personae Verbi, animae rationalis, et carnis." (*MPL* 9: 86.)

[2] It should be noted that *totus Christus* has another and larger meaning in theological works than the one given it in this context by John of Damascus, Peter Lombard, Calvin, and (as will be seen) St. Thomas. *Totus Christus* is also used to designate Christ, Head and Body, or Jesus Christ and his Church. Depending on how broadly one interprets Christ's effective and not just potential redemption, *totus Christus* may mean Jesus Christ together with all humanity. For example, A. Piolanti means by *totus Christus* Christ united to the faithful in his Church. ("Il mistero del 'Christo totale' in S. Agostino," *Augustinus Magister*, III [Paris:

St. Thomas Aquinas (c. 1225-1274). Such a distinction between *totus,* the Son as he is eternally, and *totum,* the Son as he is eternally but including also what he united to himself, offered no little difficulty. For one thing, if *totus* pertained to the person, and the person were composed of divinity and humanity, it could be argued that the humanity of Christ was everywhere and so also Christ the man was

---

Congrès International Augustinien, 1954], p. 467.) Barth uses the term to mean Christ and Christians, or Christ and the earthly form of his body:

"To His heavenly form of existence as Son of God and Son of Man He has assumed this earthly-historical—the community as His one body which also has this form. He carries and maintains it in this unity with Himself as the people which not merely belongs to Him but is part of Himself. In God's eternal counsel, in His epiphany, and finally in His revelation at the end of the age, He was and is and will be this *totus Christus*—Christ and Christians." (*op. cit.,* trans. G. W. Bromiley, IV, 2 [Edinburgh: T. & T. Clark, 1958], p. 60.) Emile Mersch is even more explicit:

"Le Christ total, c'est le Christ considéré avec tout ce dont il est inséparable dans la réalité des choses: avec toute la Trinité, dans laquelle il ne fait qu'un seul Dieu, avec toute l'humanité dont il fait un seul corps, le sien, c'est le *totus et integer Christus,* dont parlent les documents de la foi, qui a en lui la plénitude de la divinité et qui est la plénitude de l'humanité, ce Christ tout en tous, dans lequel tous les hommes ne font qu'un, εἷς, et qui est un de la Trinité *unus de Trinitate.*" (*La Théologie du Corps Mystique,* I [Paris: Museum Lessianum, Sect. Théol. no. 38, 1944], p. 60.) This same concept lies behind the thought of J. A. T. Robinson when he says:

". . . to say that the Church is the body of Christ is no more of a metaphor than to say that the flesh of the incarnate Jesus [sic] or the bread of the Eucharist is the body of Christ. None of them is 'like' His body (Paul never says this): each of them *is* the body of Christ, in that each is the physical complement and extension of the one and the same Person and Life. They are all expressions of a single Christology." (*The Body: A Study in Pauline Theology,* Studies in Biblical Theology no. 5 [Naperville, Illinois: A. R. Allenson, 1957], p. 51.) According to Robinson, when Paul speaks of the Church as the Body of Christ,

". . . it is in fact no other than the glorified body of the risen and ascended Christ. 'We are members of that body which was nailed to the Cross, laid in the tomb and raised to life on the third day. There is only one organism of the new creation; and we are members of that one organism which is Christ' (L. S. Thornton, *The Common Life in the Body of Christ,* 298)." (*ibid.,* pp. 51-52)

The Church that Paul was trying to stamp out was none other than Jesus Christ Himself:

"The appearance on which Paul's whole faith and apostleship was founded was the revelation of the resurrection body of Christ, not as an individual, but as the Christian community." (*ibid.,* p. 58.)

This language reflects a view of the Church as an extension of the Incarnation, or of ecclesiology as an extension of Christology. It is crucial to note that this widely-used meaning of *totus Christus* is not the same the meaning it has in the *totus-totum* distinction under discussion.

everywhere. St. Thomas listed this as a possible line of reason,[1] but replied that the person is not correctly said to be composed of the natures.

> . . . 'totus' does not apply to the person as a thing is called whole because it has parts, but 'totus' applies to the person in the same way a thing is called whole because it is perfect and nothing is missing from it. Thus he is said to be everywhere in his entirety because there is nothing missing from his existence as person which enables him to be everywhere. For since the 'totus' is of the masculine gender, it applies to the person. Insofar as he is everywhere, he is missing something of what pertains to the human nature, because according to the human nature he is not everywhere. And therefore it is said that he is not everywhere 'totum,' because since 'totum' is of the neuter gender it applies to the nature. [2]

So according to Thomas the Person in and of himself and by reason of the divine nature is everywhere; but the man, or the human nature, cannot be said to be everywhere. For Thomas, three different statements might be made but not all of them would be correct. If "man" signifies the subject of the human nature and also the human nature itself, then it is false to say "the man Christ is everywhere." On the other hand, because being everywhere is an attribute of the Person, it is true to say "*this* man is everywhere." The statement, "Christ as man is everywhere," may be true or false. Insofar as it

---

[1] *Commentum in Quatuor Libros Sententiarum*, III, 22, Quest. I, Art. 2, *Opera Omnia*, VII (Parma, 1857), p. 227.

[2] ". . . *totus* non fertur ad personam, secundum quod totum dicitur quod habet partes, sed secundum quod totum dicitur perfectum, cui nihil deest: et secundum hoc dicitur totus ubique, quia nihil deest sibi de sua personalitate, secundum quod est ubique: *totus* enim cum sit masculini generis, ad personam pertinent. Deest ei autem aliquid de his quae ad humanam naturam pertinent secundum quod est ubique: quia secundum humanam naturam non est ubique; et ideo dicitur quod non est totum ubique: quia *totum* cum sit neutrius generis, ad naturam pertinet." (*ibid.*, p. 228.)
This same distinction is reflected in the remarks of Maurice Gilbert:
"Munis de méthodes plus scientifiques, ils [les scholastiques] reprirent l'explication des Grecs pour l'approfondir et la développer. S'arrêtant aux formules de la foi: deux natures dans une personne, ils s'attachèrent à montrer la différence profonde et réelle qu'il y a entre être une nature et être une personne. Cette distinction établie, on comprend qu'il leur était facile de défendre la possibilité d'une union *in persona* qui ne fût pas une union *in natura*. Pareillement, cette précision les mit en mesure de déterminer d'une façon plus claire en quoi consiste au juste cette union, le mystère même de l'Homme-Dieu." ("La structure ontologique du Christ selon saint Thomas," *Revue de l'Université d'Ottawa*, Section Spéciale, XI (1941), p. 40.)

says something about the condition of the nature, it is false; but insofar as it says something about the reality of the subject it is true.[1]

It is probable, though not demonstrable beyond a doubt, that St. Thomas is included among those Calvin knew had maintained this distinction. Of special interest with St. Thomas is the way in which this *totus-totum* distinction was present in his teaching along with remarkably clear presentations of the "extra Calvinisticum."

In the *Summa Theologiae*, St. Thomas said Christ descended from heaven in two ways, by reason of his divine nature and by reason of his body. The descent by reason of the body means that his body was formed by heavenly power, that is, by the Holy Spirit, not that the very body of Christ came down from heaven in its substance. The descent of Christ by reason of the divine nature means that here below he existed in a new way, that is, according to his assumed nature (and here Thomas quoted John 3:13), not that the divine nature ceased to be in heaven.[2]

> . . . Nor is it to be said that even in the hypostatic union is the Word of God or the divine nature comprehended by the human nature. Although that divine nature was wholly united to the human nature in the One Person of the Son, nevertheless the whole power of the divinity was not as it were circumscribed.[3]

In the *De Unione Verbi Incarnati*, St. Thomas reiterated that the Incarnation is a unique union, unlike any other known to us: God *is* essentially his unity, as he is his existence and goodness. Just as his existence and goodness surpass what is discoverable among creatures, so by his infinite power he can make a union in which the human nature is taken into the person of the Word.[4] This union, involving

---

[1] "Et ideo, quia homo signat suppositum humanae naturae, et ipsam naturam humanam, inde est quod haec est falsa: *Christus est homo ubique*; quia non convenit sibi ubique habere humanitatem . . . Sed haec est vera: *Iste homo est ubique*: quia esse ubique convenit personae. Haec autem, *Christus secundum quod homo, est ubique*, potest esse vera et falsa: secundum quod enim potest importare conditionem naturae, sic est falsa; sed veritatem suppositi, et sic est vera." (*op. cit.*, p. 228.)

[2] *Summa Theologiae*, III, 5, 2, ad. 1 (Ottawa: Institute of Medieval Studies, 1944), p. 2455.

[3] " . . . Nec etiam in unione quae est secundum esse personale, natura humana comprehendit Dei Verbum, sive naturam divinam; quae quamvis tota unita fuerit humanae naturae in una persona Filii, non tamen fuit tota virtus divinitatis ab humana natura quasi circumscripta." (*ibid.*, III, 10, 1, ad. 2, p. 2492.)

[4] I. Backes adopts the habitus-assumptus-subsistence scheme of the Middle Ages interpretation concerning the union of the two natures. Seen in this pattern, Thomas is of Christological significance as one who put an end to the dominance

the relation of the one *hypostasis* or subject to the two natures,[1] differs
from the relation of form to matter. Matter is not brought into being
except by form, and therefore form requires determinate matter
which it brings into actuality. But a subject is constituted not only out
of the nature of a species but may also have certain other properties
as well. Therefore nothing need prevent a particular nature from being
attributed to the subject of another nature.[2] Further on, Thomas
pointed out that the person of the Word is contained in the nature of
the Word so that the person cannot extend beyond the nature of the
Word. But the nature of the Word, because of its infinity, compre-
hends all finite natures. Therefore when the person of the Word assumed human nature he did not extend beyond the divine nature but took
up that which was within (*infra*) the divine nature. Paul's meaning in
Philippians 2 is indeed not that the Son of God put aside the grandeur
of the form of God but that he took on the smallness of human
nature.[3] As the nature of the Word is infinite, so is the person of the
Word infinite. Therefore the divine nature of the Word corresponds
exactly to the person of the Word himself as he is in himself; but the
human nature corresponds to the Word insofar as he became man.
Whence it is not necessary for the nature in the man who is the in-

of the assumptus theory and made instead the subsistence theory the most viable
one for regarding the union of the two natures. ("Die christologische Problematik
der Hochscholastik und ihre Beziehung zu Chalkedon," *KCGG*, II, pp. 923-39.)
See also Backes, *Die Christologie des hl. Thomas v. Aquin und die griechischen Kirchenväter* (Paderborn: Schöningh Verlag, 1931), esp. p. 136 on Thomas' use of
Damascus in discussing the three days, and pp. 218-33 on the assuming and the
assumed in the hypostatic union. cf. also Maurice Gilbert, *loc. cit.*, p. 109.

[1] On the relation of "persona" to "suppositum" in St. Thomas, see Thomas
Bonhoeffer, *Die Gotteslehre des Thomas von Aquin als Sprachproblem*, Beiträge zur
historischen Theologie, no. 32 (Tübingen: Mohr-Siebeck, 1961), pp. 126-29.

[2] ". . . Quod non eodem modo se habet natura ad suppositum, sicut se habet
forma ad materiam. Materia enim non constituitur in esse nisi per formam;
et ideo forma requirit determinatam materiam, quam faciat esse in actu; sed
suppositum non solum constituitur per naturam speciei, sed etiam alia quaedam
potest habere. Et ideo nihil prohibet naturam aliquam attribui supposito alterius
naturae." (*De Unione Verbi Incarnati*, Quaest. I, a. 1, 11, *Opera Omnia*, VIII [Parma
ed.; New York: Musurgia Publishers, 1949], p. 536.)

[3] ". . . Quod persona Verbi comprehenditur sub natura Verbi, nec potest se
ad aliquid ultra extendere; sed natura Verbi ratione suae infinitatis comprehendit
omnem naturam finitam; et ideo cum persona Verbi assumit naturam humanam,
non se extendit ultra naturam divinam, sed magis accipit quod est infra; unde
dicitur ad Philip. 12: 6 [sic] quod *cum in forma Dei esset* Dei Filius, *semetipsum
exinanivit*; non quidem deponens magnitudinem formae Dei, sed assumens
parvitatem humanae naturae." (*op. cit.*, ad. 14, p. 536.)

carnate Word, constituting him insofar as he is man, to be any simpler or more formal than the nature of other men.[1]

Duns Scotus (c. 1264-1308). Duns Scotus, although familiar with the _totus-totum_ distinction, did not use it, as did Thomas and Lombard, to account for Christ's existence between his death and resurrection. The influence of Scotus on Calvin is found more in Calvin's doctrine of the merit of Christ and his stress on predestination than in his treatment of the two-natures problem.[2] Duns argued that the body is a part of man and therefore forms a part of the "quiddity" of the man, since the "quiddity" of a thing must include, for Scotus, the matter as well as the form.[3] On this basis Scotus concluded that _in triduo_ Christ was not man. It should be noted that Scotus still maintained that the soul of Christ descended into hell and that both soul and body were united to the divine _hypostasis;_ but since soul and body were not joined together _in triduo,_ Christ was not man then.[4]

While Scotus did not have an explicit statement of the doctrine of the "extra Calvinisticum" in his discussion of the Incarnation, he did set forth a series of distinctions which parallel that doctrine. Regarding the way Christ will come as judge, Scotus said Christ will be judge and now has his governance in human form but not according to his humanity.[5] In discussing the Incarnation, Scotus taught that in the hypostatic union the two natures are not confused. Christ has two essential beings, although he has only one being of personal subsistence: one essential being is created and one is uncreated.[6] The

---

[1] ". . . Quod sicut natura Verbi est infinita, ita et persona Verbi infinita est; et ideo natura divina Verbi correspondet ex aequo ipsi personae Verbi secundum se; natura autem humana correspondet Verbo secundum quod factum est homo. Unde non oportet quod natura sit simplicior et formalior illo homine qui est Verbum caro factum, et constituens ipsum inquantum est homo." (_ibid.,_ ad. 15.)

[2] On Duns Scotus' Christology in general, see Karl Werner, _Die Scholastik der Späteren Mittelalters,_ I (pub. 1881; reprinted New York: Burt Franklin, n.d.), pp. 427-40; A. Goudel, "La Théologie de l' 'Assumptus Homo'," _Revue des Sciences Religieuses,_ XVII (1937), pp. 219-33 (a comparison of Thomas' and Scotus' Christologies); Reinhold Seeberg, _Die Theologie des Johannes Duns Scotus_ (Leipzig: Dieterich, 1900), pp. 234-75.

[3] _Joannis Duns Scoti . . . Opera Omnia_ (Paris: L. Vives, 1891ff.) _Quaestiones in Tertium Librum Sententiarum,_ d. 22, q. 1, n. 4, n. 18, n. 19. cf. also In Lib. III, d. 2, q. 2.

[4] "Cum igitur hoc nomen _Christus_ significet suppositum existens in duabus naturis, et in triduo non existebat in natura humana tota, quamvis partes naturae essent sibi unitae, ideo haec propositio: _Christus fuit homo in triduo,_ est falsa . . ." (In Lib. III, d. 22, q. 1, n. 19.)

[5] In Lib. IV, d. 48, q. 1, n. 4.

[6] In Lib. III, d. 6, q. 1, n. 2, n. 5, n. 6.

divine and uncreated being as con-substantial with the Father is infinite and immutable and ubiquitous by his immensity. Only God, not the creature, is immutable and Christ *secundum quod homo* is a creature.[1] It is quite clear for Scotus that both propositions, *Verbum est homo* and *Deus factus est homo* may be admitted in describing the Incarnation, but with the qualifications that they are not statements of identity.[2]

Concerning the Eucharist, Scotus declared that Christ's body is locally in heaven: it has always been believed that Christ's bodily presence in heaven did not change.[3] In the Sacrament, Christ's body exists under the elements possessing internal quantity but not local extension.[4] Scotus was careful, however, to point out that this manner of sacramental Presence does not limit the freedom of God. By the divine power, one and the same body could be in several places, locally or by dimension, even independently of the miracle of transubstantiation.[5] Although God alone is everywhere because of his immensity, this does not mean that God, by his power, cannot make something not himself to be everywhere also.[6] Especially interesting was Scotus' insistence that the eucharistic Presence does not mean a diminution of Christ's powers and functions belonging to his presence in heaven.[7] Here is a direct transposition of the "extra Calvinisticum" into the doctrine of the Eucharist. What the "extra Calvinisticum" says about the Incarnation, this teaching of Scotus says about the eucharistic presence of Christ. The one says that the Word's presence in the flesh does not mean the Eternal Son of God forsook his governance of the world. The other says Christ's presence under the sacramental elements does not mean he forsook those operations which belong to his heavenly presence.

---

[1] In Lib. III, d. 11, q. 2, n. 4.
[2] In Lib. III, d. 7, q. 1, q. 2.
[3] In Lib. IV, d. 10, q. 1, n. 9.
[4] In Lib. IV, d. 10, q. 1, n. 14-17.
[5] In Lib. IV, d. 10, q. 2.
[6] In Lib. IV, d. 10, q. 2, n. 15.
[7] "Ex hoc sequitur corollarium, quod Christus propter suum *esse* in Eucharistia, non tantum non privatur aliqua operatione quam habet, ut in coelo: sed ut in Eucharistia est, habet aliquam operationem primo, quam per consequens concomitanter habet, ut in coelo, utpote intellectionem et volitionem cuiuscumque objecti, cujus Angelus hic praesens haberet, et per consequens non est ad imperfectionem suam, quod sit in Eucharistia, sed ad ampliorem perfectionem." (In Lib. IV, d. 10, q. 5, n. 5.)

William Occam (*c.* 1300-*c.* 1349) *and Gabriel Biel* (*c.* 1420-1495).

Following Scotus, William Occam did not use the *totus-totum* distinction to account for Christ's existence *in triduo*. Occam left no commentary on Lombard's *Lib. III*, d. 22; but where Occam did discuss the problem, in the *Centiloquium Theologicum*, he was satisfied with the use of the *communicatio idiomatum* to account for the truth of the propositions that Christ was in the grave and that he descended into hell.[1]

In his Exposition on the Canon of the Mass, Gabriel Biel discussed Christ's existence *in triduo*.[2] In this particular passage, Biel, like Occam, did not rely on the *totus-totum* distinction, but rather on the *communicatio idiomatum*. Such statements as "Christ descended into hell" and "Christ lay in the tomb" are not figuratively true but are true by virtue of the *communicatio idiomatum*.

Biel made explicit statements of the "extra Calvinisticum."[3] In Sermo II, on the Ascension, he said:

> We know then there are two natures in Christ, namely the divine and the human. According to the divine nature, by which he is eternally one with the Father and the Holy Spirit, he is everywhere, unbounded, without place, incomprehensible; he holds all things, fills all things, embraces all things, transcends all things, as Gregory says in the eighth homily on Ezekiel. But the human nature which he assumed from the body, from the Virgin, because it is creaturely, is bounded, precisely located, movable from one place to another, although hypostatically united to the immovable nature. Wherefore even the man is resplendent. Although Christ is everywhere and eternal,

---

[1] *Centiloguium Theologicum* (Lyon, 1495), Conclusio 13, Responsio ad objectionem secundam; cf. Ernst Borchert, *Der Einfluss des Nominalismus auf die Christologie der Spätscholastik*, Beiträge zur Geschichte der Philosophie und Theologie des Mittelalters, Bd. 35, Heft 4/5 (Münster, 1940), pp. 78-79.

[2] *Sacri canonis missae expositio* (Tübingen: 1499), Lectio 42, D.

[3] Heiko A. Oberman, in *The Harvest of Medieval Theology: Gabriel Biel and Late Medieval Nominalism* (Cambridge: Harvard University Press, 1963), cites the following passages:

"Si autem extrema huius unionis consideramus quid mirabilius cogitari potest: deus immutabilis eternus sine sua mutatione fit homo novus in tempore. Deus infinitus, incomprehensibilis, ubique existens sine contradictione sui nihil perdens eorum que ipse est, unitur personaliter nature finite et loco circumscripte —ita ut nec minus in assumpta natura esset quia in se infinita, nec minor in se existeret quia in ista fuerat totum."

"Ita de celo descendisse dicitur non quia suam amitteret plenitudinem, sed quia in unitatem persone naturam terrenam suscepit."

(p. 265, n. 59.)

yet the human nature in Christ is temporal and does not fill every place, according to Ambrose in the book on the Holy Spirit. To be in all things and everywhere is peculiar to divinity and dominion. [1]

Biel went on to explain that the divine nature and dignity did not ascend: the ascent was proper to the human nature. John 3: 13 is not to be interpreted as meaning that the human nature descended from heaven. Because Christ is eternal and yet truly man, born of the virgin mother, he is eternal and temporal, suffering and unable to suffer, the same Christ everywhere but not everywhere in the same way, because according to the divinity he is God and according to the humanity he is man. Thus it is the same person who ascended and descended.[2]

Jacques LeFèvre d'Estaples (c. 1455-1536). It may be that Calvin had immediate access to these passages of Biel. At least their existence demonstrates that the doctrine was present in the tradition just before Calvin. Another appearance directly accessible to Calvin was in LeFèvre d'Estaples' commentaries on the Gospels. On John 3: 13, LeFèvre commented that because Christ exposed the secret thoughts of his hearers, he hinted that he was God, which indeed he was.

For the same Son of Man is he who, without being moved, ascended into heaven from the foundation of the world, the same one who descended from heaven without change when the Word was made flesh, and the same one who is in heaven because he never left the right hand of the Father. And this saying of the Son of Man is to be understood according to the *hypostasis* which is the divine Word,

---

[1] "Novimus autem in Christus duas fore naturas, Divinam et humanam. Divinam secundum quam eternaliter una est cum patre et spiritu sancto, ubique est, incircumscriptus, illocalis, incomprehensibilis, omnia tenet, omnia implet, omnia complectit, omnia supercedit, ut dicit Greg. homel. viii in Ezech. Humanam vero quam ex corpore sumpsit ex virgine, quia creatura, est circumscripta, in certo loco existens, ad aliud locum localiter mobilis: licet naturae immobili hypostatice sit unita. Ex quo etiam homo relucet. Quod licet Christus sit ubique et eternus, tamen natura humana in Christo temporalis est et non replet omnem locum: quam secundum Amb. lib. de Spiritu Sancto. In omnibus et ubique esse, divinitatis et dominationis est proprium. ("In die ascensionis domini," *Sermo II, in ordine XXX*, Fol. CCXLV, *Sermones de festivitatibus Christi* [Hagenau, 1510].)

[2] ". . . eternus et temporalis, passibilis et impassibilis, idem ubique Christus sed non secundum idem, quia secundum divinitatem deus, secundum humanitatem homo. Ita eadem persona est quae ascendit et descendit." (*ibid.*)
In this same passage Biel referred to Augustine's teaching of the doctrine in his *Book on the Symbol* (probably *De Fide et Symbolo* [393], 3 and 4; *MPL* 40: 183-87). cf. also Biel's use of Augustine (in *Sermo IX*, F, *op. cit.*, Fol. CXC) and Fulgentius (in *Sermo XI*, A, *ibid.*, Fol. CXCIII) in support of this doctrine.

according to which understanding he was both in heaven and on earth and in every people and nation. And he was no less in Africa, in Europe, in Pannonia, Germany, France, Italy, and Spain when he preached to the Jews, and the very same who preached to the Jews, than he was in Asia and Judea—although he appeared bodily only to the Jews. Therefore let the inhabitants of Pannonia, the Germans, the Italians, the French, the Spanish rejoice because the Son of Man even while he was mortal was equally among them and among the Jews—among them only in an impassible way but among the Jews in a passible way. [1]

This statement of LeFèvre's is of interest not only for its universal emphasis, but for the way in which it differs from Calvin's doctrine. In his desire to stress Christ's universal presence, LeFèvre depreciates here the scandalous, particular presence of Christ in his body among the Jews, a tendency which does not appear equally in Calvin's use of the doctrine.

St. Augustine and the ancient Fathers

St. Augustine (354-430). Although Calvin was in contact with the "extra Calvinisticum" in Lombard and his followers in the *totus-totum* distinction, and although he was probably aware of the explicit statements of it in the thought of St. Thomas, Biel, and LeFèvre, he utilized Augustinian expressions of the doctrine with a frequency which leads one to identify Augustine as Calvin's major traditional source of the "extra Calvinisticum." [2] This comes as little surprise, given Calvin's favoritism for Augustine, whom he referred to and

---

[1] "Quod secretas cogitationes eis pandit, se ipsis deum insinuat, ut revera est: ipse enim est filius hominis, qui immobiliter ascendit in coelum a constitutione mundi: et qui immutabiliter descendit de coelo, cum verbum caro factum est: et qui est in coelo, quia nunquam dexteram patris deserens. Et hic sermo de filio hominis, secundum hypostasin, quae divinum verbum est, intelligitur: secundum quam intelligentiam et in coelo, et in terra erat, et in omni gente et natione. Nec minus in Africa, in Europa, in Pannonia, Germania, Italia Gallia, Iberia, quando praedicabat Iudaeis, et ille idem qui praedicabat Iudaeis, quam in Asia et Iudaea: licet solis Iudaeis corporaliter appareret. Exultent ergo Pannonii, Germani, Itali, Galli, Hispani, quod filius hominis etiam dum mortalis esset, aeque inter ipsos fuerit atque inter Iudaeos: sed inter illos modo solum impassibili, inter Iudaeos etiam passibili." (*Commentarii initiatorii in quatuor evangelia* [Basel, 1523], Fol. 297 [25].)

[2] In speaking of Augustine's concept of the integrity of the divine nature of Christ, T. J. van Bavel says rightly in his excellent study:
"Son [Augustine's] idée maîtresse est que la venue de Dieu en ce monde n'empêche pas le Verbe de rester intégralement au ciel et d'être en même temps intégralement parmi nous. Il n'est pas question d'une diminution de la nature

quoted more than any other Father, acknowledging his priority among the ancients as a Biblical interpreter for matters of dogma.[1]

Calvin was well acquainted with the Epistle to Dardanus, written in 417, in which Augustine expressed what was later to be called the "extra Calvinisticum." According to Smits' reckoning, Calvin quoted from this letter some forty-three times between 1536 (the Lausanne Disputation) and 1561 (his work against Heshusius). Twenty-two of these citations appeared in Calvin's *Final Admonition to Westphal*. Dardanas' question had had to do primarily with the nature of the ascended Christ's presence. Even while on the cross, Christ had said to the robber: "This day you shall be with me in paradise." From this, one might have gathered that paradise is some place in heaven, or that since God is everywhere, the God-man is also everywhere and

---

divine. La kénose signifie seulement que le Verbe a voilé sa dignité et sa puissance divine à cause de notre infirmité. Toutefois, la communication des idiomes permet de dire que la Sagesse est devenue faible par la susception d'une nature humaine." (*Recherches sur la Christologie de Saint Augustin*, Paradosis, X [Fribourg, Suisse, 1954], p. 48.)

[1] Even so, of course, Augustine's position was a qualified one for Calvin: he had authority because he confirmed Scripture. J. Cadier says Calvin considered Augustine as his master, despite clear differences on problems such as evil and illumination:

"Or nous remarquons que ces deux doctrines sont liées, et surtout qu'elles se ratachent toutes deux à l'influence néo-platonicienne, à celle de Plotin en particulier, sur le grand docteur africain. Calvin suit Saint Augustin quand il le trouve en accord avec la Bible, il le quitte quand il sent qu'il se laisserait entraîner sur les chemins de traverse de la philosophie platonicienne." (*Augustinus Magister*, II [Paris: Congrès International Augustinien, 1954], p. 1055.) Luchesius Smits comes to the same conclusion:

"L'authorité dont jouit saint Augustin auprès de Calvin dépend logiquement du critère qu'il applique toujours aux docteurs anciens comme aux premiers conciles, à savoir: la conformité de leur doctrine avec la Parole de Dieu. L'évêque d'Hippone, aux yeux de Calvin, est demeuré plus que tout autre fidèle à cette norme." (*S. Augustin dans l'oeuvre de Jean Calvin*, I [Assen, 1957], pp. 270-71.)

Smits has comprehensively traced Calvin's use of Augustine. He shows that Calvin progressively drew on Augustine's sacramentarian doctrine (first edition of the *Institutes*), his doctrine of free will and predestination (second edition of the *Institutes*), his doctrine of the Church (third edition of the *Institutes*), and again his doctrine of predestination and the Lord's Supper in the final edition (there is no general characterization for the fourth edition). (*ibid.*, pp. 30ff, 42ff, 59ff, 82ff, 104ff.) Smits also points out, correctly, that from 1550 onward, Calvin turned more to Irenaeus and Tertullian than to Augustine for the development of his Trinitarian doctrine. True as this is, however, it is also true that Calvin did rely on Augustine to confirm certain parts of his doctrine concerning the person of Christ, especially insofar as they bore on the eucharistic controversy. Such was the case with the "extra Calvinisticum," taken as a general teaching.

so, by his will, he was at that time capable of being in heaven also.[1] Augustine replied that as God, Christ was indeed everywhere, but as man he was in the tomb in his body and in hell in his soul during the three days between his death and resurrection.[2]

In Ep. 137, written in 412 to Volusianus, Augustine again expressed the doctrine. Volusianus had posed a number of questions to Augustine, all relating to whether the Lord and director of the world was limited to the body born of the Virgin. Augustine remarked it is not a Christian doctrine which teaches

> . . . that God was so poured into the flesh in which he was born of the Virgin that he either abandoned or lost the care of the government of the universe or that he transferred this care into that small body as into a gathered and contracted material. [3]

Men err in trying to judge the divine presence after earthly and corporeal standards; our minds cannot penetrate the mystery of God. But if the soul is able by the sense of sight to experience the heavenly bodies far removed from the body, or if a human word when spoken is entire in the several persons who hear it, how can we consider it incredible that the Eternal Word of God took the flesh of the Virgin without leaving the bosom of the Father? Bodies with which we are humanly familiar have parts which have to fill different places; but it is not so with the soul, and much less so with the creator of body and soul. The Word of God, by whom all things were made, is not subject to change.

> He remains as he is, and he is everywhere whole. [4] But he comes when he is manifested, and he goes away when he is hidden. Yet he is present

---

[1] Ep. 187, II (3); *MPL* 33: 833.

[2] "Homo quippe Christus illo die secundum carnem in sepulchro secundum animam in inferno futurus erat: Deus vero idem ipse Christus ubique semper est. Est enim lux quae lucet etiam in tenebris, quamvis eam tenebrae non comprehendant." (*ibid.*, III [7]; *MPL* 33: 834.) cf. *ibid.*, III [10]; *MPL* 33: 836. "Una enim persona Deus et homo est, et utrumque est unus Christus Jesus; ubique per id quod Deus est, in coelo autem per id quod homo." It is from this context that Calvin drew his citation of Augustine in the Institutes: "Noli . . . corporis auferamus." (*supra*, p. 29, n. 2.)

[3] ". . . quod ita sit Deus infusus carni, qua ex virgine nasceretur, ut curam gubernandae universitatis vel deseruerit vel amiserit, vel ad illud corpusculum quasi contractam materiam collectamque transtulerit." (Ep. 137, 2 *ad Volusianum*; *MPL* 33: 517.)

[4] Note here *totum*, not *totus* refers to what is ubiquitous; yet it is not as man that Christ is everywhere, according to Augustine. The *totus-totum* distinction as used by Lombard rested on the grammatical analogy which Augustine did not use.

> whether hidden or manifested, as light is present to the eyes of the seeing and the blind, but is present to the seeing as present and present to the blind as absent. [1]

God is great not in mass or size but in power.

The same teaching was pronounced in *De Civitate Dei*, IX, 15, 2 (a section which was cited for Calvin in a letter of 1561).[2] There Augustine said:

> And while as Mediator he was in the form of a servant and wished to be among the angels, he remained in the form of God above the angels. The same was the way of life in the lower beings who was the life in the superior beings. [3]

Elsewhere, in *De Peccatorum Meritis et Remissione*, I, 60 (31), written in 412,[4] there is a passage intriguing for its statement of the corporate nature of the Christian's saving relationship to Christ. Augustine said John 3:13 describes the regeneration Nicodemus asked about; it also describes the only way to reach heaven, namely, by participation in the unity of Christ so that in his body we may ascend to heaven.

> For although he became Son of man on earth, nevertheless he did not consider his divinity—by which he remained in heaven while he descended to earth—unworthy of the name 'Son of man', just as his flesh is worthy of the name 'Son of God', lest these be taken as two Christs, the one God and the other man, instead of the one and same God and man. *God* because, 'In the beginning was the Word, and the Word was with God, and the Word was God,' *man* because 'the Word became flesh and dwelt among us.' (John 1:1,14) Thus according to the distinction of divinity and infirmity, the Son of

---

[1] "Manet sicuti est, et ubique totum est. Venit autem cum manifestatur, et cum occultatur abscedit. Adest tamen sive occultum sive manifestum, sicut lux adest oculis et videntis, et caeci: sed videnti adest praesens, caeco vero absens." (*ibid.*, II [7]; *MPL* 33: 518.) cf. also:
"Non sic Deus dicitur implere mundum, velut aqua, velut aer, velut ipsa lux, ut minore sui parte minorem mundi impleat partem, et majore majorem. Novit ubique totus esse, et nullo contineri loco: novit venire non recedendo ubi erat: novit abire non deserendo quo venerat." (*ibid.*, II [4]; *MPL* 33: 517.)
[2] From Leopolitanus, Feb. 25; *CO* 18: 375.
[3] "Ideo quando in forma servi (Philipp. II, 7), ut mediator esset, infra Angelos esse voluit, in forma Dei supra Angelos mansit: idem in inferioribus via vitae, qui in superioribus vita." (*MPL* 41: 269.)
[4] A work quoted by Calvin over one hundred times, but never at the precise spot mentioned here. cf. Smits, *op. cit.*, II, pp. 216-19.

God remained in heaven, the Son of man walked on earth. But according to the unity of the Person which binds both substances into one,
Christ the Son of God both walked on earth and the selfsame one
remained Son of Man in heaven. [1]

In *De Libero Arbitrio* III, 10, 30, Augustine made use of a familiar
image in saying the Word of God became bread to us without ceasing
to be the eternal bread for the angels.

> He descended towards us without, however, abandoning the angels;
> but he is at the same time whole with them, whole with us; nourishing
> them inwardly through that by which he is God, teaching us out-
> wardly by that which we are, he enables us to partake of by faith
> what they eat by vision. [2]

---

[1] "Quamvis enim in terra factus sit filius hominis, divinitatem tamen suam
qua in coelo manens descendit ad terram, non indignam censuit nomine filii
hominis, sicut carnem suam dignatus est nomine filii Dei, ne quasi duo Christi
ista accipiantur, unus Deus, et alter homo: sed unus atque idem Deus et homo;
Deus, quia *in principio erat Verbum, et Verbum erat apud Deum, et Deus erat Verbum*;
homo, quia *Verbum caro factum est, et habitavit in nobis.* (Joan. 1: 1, 14) Ac per
hoc per distantiam divinitatis et infirmitatis filius Dei manebat in coelo, filius
hominis ambulabat in terra: per unitatem vero personae, qua utraque substantia
unus Christus est, et filius Dei ambulabat in terra, et idem ipse filius hominis
manebat in coelo." (*MPL* 44: 144.)

[2] "Nec sic descendit ad nos, ut illos desereret; sed simul integer illis, integer
nobis, illos intrinsecus pascens per id quod Deus est, nos forinsecus admonens
per id quod nos sumus, idoneos facit per fidem, quos per speciem pascat aequaliter."
(*MPL* 32: 1286.)

Dorner recognized the doctrine in Augustine, citing especially Augustine's
words, "Accessit ad nos, sed a se non multum recessit, immo a se quod Deus
est, nunquam recessit, sed addidit quod erat, naturae nostrae. Accessit enim ad
id quod non erat, non amisit quod erat." (Sermo 122, De Verbis Evang. Joh. 1.;
Dorner, *op. cit.*, II, 1, p. 399.) But Dorner argued that if the Word were everywhere
in its entirety, as Augustine maintained, it would appear to have no distinctive
manner of being, and the only difference between Christ and others would seem
to be that he possessed a degree of susceptibility to God no one else had. (*ibid.*)
Augustine

"did scarcely anything in the way of showing that the incarnation was more
than a close . . . . 'relatio,' σχέσις, of the 'Verbum quod ubique totum est,' to that
particular point of humanity which became Jesus in consequence of its special
and unquestionably God-created susceptibility to God." (*ibid.*, p. 400.)

Augustine's Christology contained traces of Ebionitic and Docetic views. For
what reality, Dorner asked, can be attached to the expression *factus est, quod
non erat,* or to *accessit quod non erat* if attention be directed merely to the unchangeableness and omnipresence of the Verbum who was *ubique totum* despite his union
with Christ? "How can Christ be seriously regarded as an incarnation of the
Son, if He did not actually come into the possession, not even by love, of something He had not possessed before?" (*ibid.*, p. 401.) Thus Dorner in this criticism
was describing more a danger or a tendency in Augustine's work than what

Et alii. Besides appearing in the writings of the foregoing men, the "extra Calvinisticum" is to be found in a sufficiently great number of other works as to be regarded as having commanded a consensus of the ancient Fathers.[1] Without launching into a full survey of the doctrine in the ancient Fathers, which would be as prohibitively long as it would be interesting, this discussion will restrict itself to certain Fathers, chosen as representing main Christological currents.[2]

Orthodox and heterodox precursors of Chalcedon. The "extra Calvinisti-cum" was prominent in the works of theologians who occupied varying Christological positions. The positions differed not so much because some theologians taught the doctrine and so emphasized the

---

was in fact Augustine's position. Augustine was emphatic in his confession that the Son who is unchangeable in his eternity began to be in a new way in the Incarnation; the conditions of this beginning to be in a new way remained for Augustine a mystery and remained undescribed by much Christological speculation. Augustine's Christology might indeed have been strengthened had it given more attention to the manner of the Incarnation. But it is not correct to imply Augustine felt he was confessing anything less than the Incarnation of the Eternal Son. Augustine was quite certain that in taking on our flesh the Eternal Son assumed to himself what was not united to him before the Incarnation.

Charles N. Cochrane has called attention to Augustine's significance for stating a view of history which assures man a respondible place in a meaningfully ordered world. In Cochrane's analysis, it is the Christian doctrine of the Word which provides the clue to a history not subject to the caprice of fate and fortune. (*Christianity and Classical Culture*, Galaxy Books [New York: Oxford University Press, 1957], pp. 479-80.) One function of the "extra Calvinisticum" as a doctrine in Augustine was to identify the Incarnate Lord with him who never ceases to govern in a beneficially ordered, universal, historical coherence.

[1] See Calvin's reference to a consensus of the ancient Church: "Ac mirum est homines istos tam proterve contra veteris ecclesiae consensum ferri." (*Ultima Admon. ad Westph.*; *CO* 9: 195; *supra*, p. 32, n. 1.)

[2] In addition to the representative Fathers mentioned in this chapter, the following men, at least, included the doctrine in their writings:
Eustathius of Caesarea (d.c. 337), *ex oratione in Eccles.* 24: 14, quoted by Theodoret; *MPG* 83: 288d-289a.
Eusebius of Caesarea (d.c. 339), *Demonstratio Evangelica*, IV, 6 and 13; *MPG* 22: 263-268, 283-288.
Ephraem Syrus (d. 373), *Ephraem Syri Hymni et Sermones*, II, 6-8 (Mechliniae, 1886), pp. 432-34.
Apollinaris of Laodicea (d.c. 390), ἡ κατὰ μέρος πίστις 11; H. Lietzmann, *Apollinaris von Laodicea und seine Schule* (Tübingen, 1904), p. 171.
Gregory of Nyssa (d.c. 395), *Oratio Catechetica*, 10; *MPG* 45: 41-44.
Peter Chrysologus (d.c. 450), *Sermo 63*; *MPL* 52: 375-79, and *Sermo 83*; *MPL* 52: 432-36.
Theodoret of Cyr (d. 466), *Expositio rectae confessionis* [*fidei*], 13-17; MPG 6: 1232-40 (Pars I, S. Justini Opera Spuria).
Fulgentius of Ruspe (d. 533), *ad Trasimundum*, II, "De Immensitate Divinitatis Filii Dei"; MPL 65: 245-68.
Pelagius I (d. 561), *Fides Papae Pelagii*; MPL 69: 407-10.

distinction of the two natures (e.g., the Antiochians), while others did not teach the doctrine and so emphasized the unity of the Person (e.g., the Alexandrians). The doctrine was in fact commonly held, and the diversity lay rather in its function than in its form.

The "extra Calvinisticum" was generally accepted because all Fathers were compelled to keep together (1) the impassible and immutable character of God and its correlate, the reality of Jesus Christ's atoning suffering [1] and (2) the constancy of God's ordering of the

---

[1] See article of T. E. Pollard on "The Impassibility of God," *Scottish Journal of Theology*, VIII (1955), pp. 353-64. Pollard blames the Greeks for introducing this concept in competition to the Biblical picture of the personality of God who acts in history:

"Among the many Greek philosophical ideas imported into Christian theology, and into Alexandrian Jewish theology before it, is the idea of the *impassible* God (ἀπαθὴς θεός), and this idea furnishes us with a particularly striking illustration of the damage done by the assumption of alien philosophical presuppositions when they are applied to Christian theology. So alien is this idea, so foreign is it to Hebraic-Christian thought, that it makes nonsense of the revelation of God in the Old Testament, it makes the Incarnation no real Incarnation, and it reduces the sufferings and death of Christ to a purely human work." (p. 356.) Pollard's article is useful as a reminder of the difficulties posed by the concept of the ἀπαθὴς θεός for Christian theology. However, Pollard's article offers several complications of its own. It indulges in particularly spirited historical judgments:

". . . It took Christian theology nearly four hundred years to work this one Greek philosophical idea out of its system. It was not to remain outside Christian theology, however, for it was brought back by the Scholastic theology, which, in place of the Platonist presuppositions of the Early Fathers, brought in Aristotelian presuppositions." (p. 359.)

Pollard says only that:

"Some of the Early Fathers [footnote: Tertullian, Athanasius, *inter alios*; the same attempted solution is found in Anselm, *Cur Deus Homo*, 1. 8] tried to overcome this dilemma by saying that the divine in Christ is impassible, but that the human is passible; it was His human nature that suffered, not His divine nature." (p. 362.)

Although Pollard cites Anselm as one who attempted in this way to overcome the dilemma, he also says,

"Even if we disagree with St. Anselm's theory of the Atonement, we must agree with him that the death on the Cross achieves nothing for man, unless it be at one and the same time a *human* and *divine* act." (p. 363.)

Pollard uncritically takes for granted that Greek philosophy (which in this article apparently means Platonic philosophy) and Biblical thought (which in this article is equated with Semitic thought) are mutually exclusive. More important, however, is his seeming presupposition that all would be well if the idea of the impassibility of God should be dropped. He seems perfectly willing to affirm a position which is difficult to distinguish from a form of Patripassianism he himself mentions on page 362. He says only that the transcendence of God, his perfect moral freedom, and his perfect blessedness and pure joy can be maintained surely in "some other way" than by holding to the impassibility of God. Unfortunately, Pollard makes no suggestion as to what this other way might be.

universe and the identity of this ordering God with the Savior.[1] Two solutions, judged by the Church as heretical, were offered to meet the problem these realities posed for theological reflection: (1) to rest content with a loose relation between the divine and the human in Christ, or (2) to mix the divine and the human. The first jeopardized the identification of this atoning, revealing Person with the impassible, ordering God; and the second threatened the Christian affirmation of the constancy of the divine order and the reality of Christ's human experience. While the "extra Calvinisticum" went manifestly ill with the second solution, it did not lend support to the first one either. Indeed, the doctrine was taught in some of its most beautiful and eloquent formulations by the Fathers who best avoided both false routes.

If it appears at first puzzling that the "extra Calvinisticum" should have functioned among both the orthodox and the heterodox, a partial explanation can be cited in referring to the *Deus in se-Deus ad nos* distinction and how it was variously regarded or disregarded. Where no such distinction was made, or where it did not work significantly, the "extra Calvinisticum" tended to bolster a Christology separating the two natures and to imply that the *Logos'* existence also beyond the flesh means his existence immanently in creation. Where such a distinction functioned in a properly guarded fashion, the "extra Calvinisticum" tended to bolster a Christology emphasizing the hypostatic union and to imply that the *Logos'* existence also beyond the flesh is his transcendence.

Origen (185-254). The doctrine is to be found in a certain form in Origen. It is ambiguous, however, existing as it does alongside seemingly contradictory statements, and being supported by Scriptural references which make it difficult to determine just what Origen meant by that which exists beyond the flesh after the Incarnation. In *De Principiis*, IV, 1, 30-31, commenting on the nature of Christ's presence in the world and with his disciples, Origen spoke about the bodily advent of the Word and his presence everywhere even during his bodily advent. The main point of the passage was that since the Word

---

[1] It will be noted that "God" here did not refer to God the Creator one time and God the Redeemer the other. Rather, the two realities involved were the identity and distinction of the one God who is Creator and Redeemer inasmuch as we are reconciled and governed by him. It is only with reference to the work of the Holy Spirit that these two were properly held together by the theologians who best succeeded in this task.

is incorporeal, he can be everywhere without being less in one place than another, because as regards his divinity the spatial categories are misleading.

> When it comes to the Incarnation and bodily advent of the only begotten Son of God, we should not think that the majesty of all his divinity was shut within the confines of a very small body so that the whole Word of God and his wisdom and his life and substantial truth were either separated from the Father or forced and drawn into the smallness of his body nor be considered operative nowhere else. But a cautious confession of piety ought to be between both [alternatives] so that it not be believed that something of divinity was lacking in Christ, and there should be confessed that there was no division made inwardly in the substance of the Father, which substance is everywhere. [1]

John the Baptist indicated such a thing when he said while Christ was bodily absent from the crowd, "There stands in the midst of you one whom ye know not, he the latchet of whose shoes I am not worthy to loose."

> However, let no one think that by this we affirm that some part of the deity of the Son of God was in Christ, but that the remaining part was elsewhere or everywhere. This is the way those are able to feel about the matter who do not know the nature of incorporal and invisible substance. For it is impossible to talk about a 'part' of something incorporal or to teach some sort of division of an incorporal thing; but [he] is in all things, through all things, over all things, in the same way we said above, that is, in the way he is understood to be Wisdom or Word or Life or Truth. By this thought all local confinement is without a doubt excluded. [2]

---

[1] "Post haec vero competenter admonebimus de adventu corporali et incarnatione unigeniti Filii Dei: in quo non ita sentiendum est, quod omnis divinitatis ejus majestas intra brevissimi corporis claustra conclusa est, ita ut omne Verbum Dei et sapientia ejus ac substantialis veritas ac vita, vel a Patre divulsa sit, vel intra corporis ejus coercita et conscripta brevitatem, nec usquam praeterea putetur operata; sed inter utrumque cauta pietatis debet esse confessio, ut neque aliquid divinitatis in Christo defuisse credatur, et nulla penitus a paterna substantia, quae ubique est, facta putetur esse divisio." (*MPG* 11: 404.)

[2] "Ne quis tamen nos existimet per haec illud affirmare, quod pars aliqua deitatis Filii Dei fuerit in Christo, reliqua vero pars alibi vel ubique: quod illi sentire possunt qui naturam substantiae incorporeae atque invisibilis ignorant. Impossibile namque est de incorporeo partem dici, aut divisionem aliquam fieri, sed in omnibus, et per omnia, et super omnia est, eo modo quo superius diximus, id est quo vel sapientia, vel Verbum, vel vita, vel veritas intelligitur; per quem intellectum omnis sine dubio conclusio localis excluditur." (MPG 11: 405.)

It is by a certain dispensation that the Word who, by his incorporeal nature is everywhere, was present in a special way in the flesh. He was present in the midst of those who were unaware of his presence, "the only-begotten of God, the God Word, even Wisdom, Justice and Truth who is not bounded by bodily space. According to the nature of divinity he did not walk about but he walked about according to the dispensation of the body which he took on."[1]

In *Contra Celsum*, II, 9, Origen dealt directly with Christ's sufferings. Origen was arguing against the position of the Jews who asked how Jesus could be God since he submitted to death and was deserted even by his disciples. Origen replied that Christians do not suppose that the body of Jesus, then an object of sight and perception, was God. Rather, he who spoke was the Lord of all flesh and was using the body and soul of the prophet. It was, therefore, the Jews who did not acknowledge him to be God, to whom witness was borne in many passages of the prophets, "to the effect that he was a mighty power and a God alongside the God and Father of all things."[2]

> And that the Gospels do not consider him who in Jesus said the words 'I am the Way, the Truth, and the Life' to have been of so circumscribed a nature as to have an existence nowhere outside the soul and body of Jesus is evident . . . [3]

Origen asked: if John the Baptist had thought the Son of God were only there where the visible body of Jesus was, how could he have said, "There stands in the midst of you one whom ye know not"? [4]

The doctrine functioned for Origen to account for the special presence of the Word in the flesh in Jesus Christ. At the same time, it also emphasized the real significance of the invisible behind the visible as that giving importance to the visible.[5] Origen had several

---

[1] *Series veteris interpretationis Commentarium Origenis in Matthaeum*, 65; *MPG* 13: 1703.

[2] καὶ Θεὸν κατὰ τὸν τῶν ὅλων Θεὸν καὶ Πατέρα. (*MPG* 11 : 809.)

[3] (*MPG* 11: 809.)

[4] *Ibid.*

[5] Jean Daniélou remarks that:
"The theology of the Incarnation here merges with exegesis of the New Testament and the theology of the sacraments. All three spheres are dominated by Origin's idea of the relationship between the visible and the invisible. He by no means belittles the visible. He is no more a Docetist in his theology of the Incarnation than he reduces everything to the spiritual in his theory of the sacraments. He believed that Christ really did become incarnate. But just as in his theory of the Eucharist he lays little stress on the visible eating and makes much of the invisible feeding on Christ, so here he does not dwell for long on the

explanations for how the Word cannot be enclosed or limited to one place: because of his invisible and incorporeal substance, his divinity, what he shares with the Father, and his assigned role as Wisdom and Truth and the Way of Life. But while this incorporeal nature of the Word means he is not circumscribed, it also means that it is false to think of a "part" of him in the body and a "part" of him elsewhere and everywhere. His special presence in the flesh and Jesus' suffering take place by dispensation (καθ' οἰκονομίαν). It is unclear from these passages what Origen meant by the Word's presence everywhere; however, there is a strong suggestion that he meant an immanent presence of the *Logos* as life principle within creation.[1] Origen's use of Scriptural texts was especially suggestive of this, with no reference being made, at least in the passages examined for this study, to the Holy Spirit as the instrument for effecting the presence Christ promised in Matthew 18: 20 and Matthew 28: 20. Lacking the technical terminology at the disposal of later Fathers, Origen conveyed an ambiguity which was to provide much of the material for subsequent Christological disagreement and constructive formulation.

Theodore of Mopsuestia (d. 428). Theodore of Mopsuestia taught that the Son continued to have his existence even beyond the flesh after the Incarnation. According to him, Christ is everywhere accord-

---

historical aspect of Christ, because he is in a hurry to examine its spiritual significance." (*Origen*, trans. Walter Mitchell [New York: Sheed and Ward, 1955], p. 264.)

This perspective on Origen's Christology is an important corrective to one which overplays Origen's logical difficulties with the doctrine of the Incarnation, e.g., the judgment of J. N. D. Kelly:

"It must be recognized that the incarnation as such really stood outside the logic of Origen's system. While assigning it a place, out of loyalty to God's revealed word and the Church's tradition, he did not regard the Son's participation in human nature as either permanent or essential." (*Early Christian Doctrines* [New York: Harper and Bros., 1958], p. 157.)

[1] The Word and the Spirit for Origen are clearly transcendent in the sense that they are superior to the *logikoi* and the *psychikoi*, while they are inferior to the Father. "If the Son and the Spirit transcend all λόγικοι, they are themselves transcended to a still greater extent by the Father." (Daniélou, *op. cit.*, p. 254.) With this suggestion of subordinationism in Origen (which should never be isolated from the emphasis, also in Origen, on the full divinity of the Word) went a view of the *Logos*' immanent presence in creation. The rational beings share in the Son in a way analogous to the sharing of the Son in the Father.

"Origen has no hesitation in representing the Son as the Father's image in little. Contrariwise, he does not allow difference enough between the Logos and the *logikoi*. On that point he was influenced by the Stoic idea that the Logos is imminent [*sic*] in all individual *logikoi*." (*ibid.*, p. 261.)

ing to his essence and energy, which for Theodore cannot finally be distinguished one from the other. But Christ's special indwelling in the Incarnation is by good pleasure. In his seventh book on the Incarnation, Theodore considered the way the inhabitation in the Incarnation took place. He rejected the teachings of those who said it took place by essence and those who said it took place by efficacy. According to Theodore, Christ is always everywhere in essence and efficaciousness.

> Therefore it is manifest that it is necessary to say that the indwelling occurs by good pleasure ... For since he is infinite and by nature unbounded, he is present to all things. But by good pleasure he is far distant from some and near to others ... [1]

Therefore as nearness and distance are effected by good pleasure, when Christ indwells it is by good pleasure, not because the essence and efficaciousness are circumscribed.[2] The indwelling of Christ in the Incarnation differs from his inhabitation of just persons. The special character of the Incarnation is that "when he indwelt, he united to himself everything he assumed and he made him to share every honor with him who, Son by nature, did the indwelling, since he wished to have him common with him."[3]

In this passage, there is an attempt to clarify how in the Incarnation the Son is united to the flesh of the man Jesus, but not restricted to it or circumscribed by it. The concept of the εὐδοκία, or the good pleasure, is an emphasis which Theodore kept before the eyes of the Church in its reflection about the Incarnation: the Incarnation came about not because God was under any constraint or necessity, for his Being, to be Incarnate, but because it so pleased him. However, Theodore's language did mislead when it implied more separation between the two natures than even he wished to maintain when he stressed that the One who did the assuming *united* what was assumed to himself in that special inhabitation.[4] Moreover, Theodore's use

---

[1] ... Ἄπειρος μὲν γὰρ ὢν καὶ ἀπερίγραφος τὴν φύσιν, πάρεστι τοῖς πᾶσι· τῇ δὲ εὐδοκίᾳ, τῶν μὲν ἔστι μακρὰν, τῶν δὲ ἐγγύς. (*Ex Libris de Incarnatione Filii Dei*, VII; *MPG* 66: 973.)

[2] *Ibid.*

[3] *Ibid.*

[4] See Paul Galtier, "Théodore de Mopsueste: sa vrai pensée sur l'Incarnation," *Recherches de Science Religieuse*, XLV (1957), pp. 161-86, 338-60. On general and particular inhabitation by the Word according to Theodore, *ibid.*, pp. 353-54. Galtier points out that Theodore and Cyril were agreed in attributing the sufferings of Jesus Christ to the body; *ibid.*, pp. 338-39.

of οὐσία, ἐνέργεια and εὐδοκία was crucial. He did not admit that the distinction between God in his hiddenness and God in his revelation to us was the distinction between God's being and God's action. He was wise in recognizing that a sharp separation between these might foster knowledge of an idol instead of knowledge of God. Yet in rejecting this distinction altogether, along with anything like it, he could not finally differentiate between the special ontological character of the indwelling of the Word in Jesus Christ and the Word's general presence everywhere. Theodore's Christology, especially in the light of research which has fairly conclusively reversed the judgment of long standing (from the Fifth General Council, 553) that he was a Nestorian before Nestorius,[1] has the strength of being an early formulation of a "Logos-Mensch" Christology. That is, the Word assumed not just flesh but all which belongs to man, including a soul. Within this Logos-Mensch framework, however, it is not always plain that Theodore avoided the thought of the Word's adopting a human nature already in existence.[2] Theodore's formulations have a particular attractiveness for us because of the sober exegesis which restrained philosophical speculation and because of his awe before the mystery of the Incarnation. Yet more would have had to be said to make certain the mystery which was being guarded was precisely the mystery of the Incarnation.

Athanasius (c. 299-373). The "extra Calvinisticum" was not a teaching unique to the school of Antioch, bound up with a Christology separating the two natures. Indeed, one of its most eloquent exponents was Athanasius, whose language exhibited the keen soteriological intent he considered to be preserved by the doctrine. This appeared in *De Incarnatione*, 17. Athanasius had been arguing that the Word, by becoming man, accomplished two works of love as Savior. (1) He put death away from us and renewed us, and (2) being invisible, he made himself known by his works to be the Word of the Father and the ruler and king of the universe.

> For he was not bounded within the body, nor was he so in the body that he was not elsewhere, nor did he so move that body that the government of the universe was left empty of his efficacy and provi-

---

[1] See Robert Devreesse, *Essai sur Théodore de Mopsueste*, Studi e Testi, **141** (Vatican City, 1948), pp. 103-20.

[2] Kelly, *op. cit.*, pp. 304-05; Aloys Grillmeier, "Die theologische und sprachliche Vorbereitung der christologischen Formel von Chalcedon." *KCGG*, I, p. 145ff.

dence. But the thing most marvelous is that the Word was not at all contained by anything, but himself rather contained all things. And just as while present in the whole of creation he is at once distinct in being from the universe and present in all things by his power—giving order to all things and revealing his own providence over all and in all, and giving life to each thing and to all things, including the whole, without being included but being in his own Father alone wholly and in every respect—so existing in the human body and being the life-giver to it, he was also quickening the universe and still was in everything and was also beyond all things. And while he was known from the things he did by the ministry of the body, yet also he was not hidden in the operations of nature. [1]

The soul in man functions to behold even what is outside its own body. A man by observing the heavenly bodies does not move them.

But the Word of God was not in man in a similar way, for he was not bound by the body but rather contained it, so that he was in it and in all things and beyond all things and rested only in the Father. And this was the wonderful thing, that he was at once walking as man and as the Word was quickening all things and as the Son was dwelling with his Father. So that when the Virgin bore him he himself did not suffer, nor by the body in which he was was he dulled, but rather he sanctified the body. [2]

One reason why the doctrine appeared with such clarity and effectiveness in Athanasius was that in his own linguistic milieu he successfully made the effort to distinguish between the Word's immanence and his transcendence. This in turn rested on his recognition of the distinction between statements which are appropriate to God according to nature and those appropriate to God according to dispensation.

---

[1] *MPG* 25: 125. cf. *Library of Christian Classics*, III (Philadelphia: Westminster Press, 1954), pp. 70-71.

[2] ... Οὐ γὰρ συνεδέδετο τῷ σώματι, ἀλλὰ μᾶλλον αὐτὸς ἐκράτει τοῦτο, ὥστε καὶ ἐν τούτῳ ἦν καὶ ἐν τοῖς πᾶσιν ἐτύγχανε, καὶ ἔξω τῶν ὄντων ἦν, καὶ ἐν μόνῳ τῷ Πατρὶ ἀνεπαύετο. Καὶ τὸ θαυμαστὸν τοῦτο ἦν, ὅτι καὶ ὡς ἄνθρωπος ἐπολιτεύετο, καὶ ὡς Λόγος τὰ πάντα ἐξωογόνει, καὶ ὡς Υἱὸς τῷ Πατρὶ συνῆν ... (*Ibid.*)

Père Th. Camelot, commenting on this passage, remarks that the *Logos* of the stoic philosophers also contained all of creation and constituted the order and unity of that creation:

"... mais il se distingue difficilement du monde lui-même auquel il est immanent. Le Verbe de la révélation chrétienne est à la fois immanent et transcendant, 'en tous et en dehors de tous.' Présent au monde qui trouve 'en lui l'être, la vie, le mouvement,' il en est cependant infiniment séparé. Cette transcendance fait que, même incarné, son action n'est pas restreinte par les limites de son corps." (*Contre les Païens et sur l'Incarnation du Verbe, par Athanase d'Alexandrie*, ed. P. Th. Camelot, *Sources Chrétiennes* (18) [Paris: du Cerf, 1946], p. 237, n. 1.)

All statements about Jesus Christ are not statements about God according to dispensation; the dispensation is the vehicle of God's revelation of himself. But since he reveals *himself* and not just his dispensation, there is a possibility of saying something, if not much, about God's being, even apart from the beatific vision. One such statement is that he is the one who governs all creation; when this is said, it becomes a statement about God's being in a relation of action toward the creation which is not God.

> But the expressions used about His Godhead, and His becoming man, are to be interpreted with discrimination and suitably to the particular context. And he that writes of the human attributes of the Word knows also what concerns His Godhead: and he who expounds concerning His Godhead is not ignorant of what belongs to His coming in the flesh: but discerning each as a skilled and 'approved money-changer,' he will walk in the straight way of piety; when therefore he speaks of His weeping, he knows that the Lord, having become man, while He exhibits His human character in weeping, as God raises up Lazarus; and he knows that He used to hunger and thirst physically, while divinely He fed five thousand persons from five loaves; and he knows that while a human body lay in the tomb, it was raised as God's body by the Word Himself. [1]

Using this distinction as a tool, Athanasius said the Word after the Incarnation was not restricted to the flesh, and he meant by the existence beyond the flesh the Word's transcendence. It meant the Word's never ceasing to be at the right hand of God, to be in the bosom of the Father, to have all creation under his feet or bowing down before him. This, however, is a special kind of transcendence, resembling the relation of a ruler to subjects. It is not a transcendence of abstract and negative otherness with the resultant lack of contact. [2]

Cyril of Alexandria (376-444). It was Cyril of Alexandria who taught the matured Alexandrian Christology. His Christology was mature in the sense that he was able to build on Athanasius and to surpass him in affirming the soul of Christ as being also part of that which was assumed; he profited positively from Didymus the Blind and negatively from Apollinaris.

In the autumn of 430, Cyril wrote to Nestorius the letter containing

---

[1] *De Sententia Dionysii*, 9; *MPG* 25: 493-94. Trans. is from *LNPF*, IV (New York, 1896), p. 179.

[2] ... οὕτως ὁ αὐτὸς ὤν καὶ ἄνθρωπος γενόμενος, κληθείς τε 'Ιησοῦς, οὐδὲν ἧττον ἔχει πᾶσαν ὑπὸ πόδα τὴν κτίσιν ... (*Oratio I Contra Arianos*, 42; *MPG* 26: 99-100; *LNPF*, p. 330.) cf. *Oratio II Contra Arianos*, 47; *MPG* 26: 245-48.

the famous twelve anathemas. A part of the letter before the anathemas contained the following:

> ... When seen as a babe and wrapped in swaddling clothes, even when still in the bosom of the Virgin who bore him, he [the only-begotten Word of God] filled all creation as God, and was enthroned with him who begot him. For the divine cannot be numbered or measured and does not admit of circumscription. So confessing the Word [to be] hypostatically united, we worship one Son and Lord Jesus Christ, neither putting apart and dividing man and God, as joined with each other by a union of dignity and authority -for this would be an empty phrase and no more- nor speaking of the Word of God separately as Christ, and then separately of him who was of a woman as another Christ, but knowing only one Christ, the Word of God the Father with his own flesh. [1]

This passage from Cyril presents a typically balanced statement confessing the unity of the Person in no uncertain terms and affirming the unchangeableness of the Word in his unity with the Father.[2] Here is also an expression of the Son's existence even beyond the flesh, in the creation which he governs and orders and at the same

---

[1] ... Ὁρώμενος δὲ καὶ βρέφος ἐν σπαργάνοις μένων ἔτι, καὶ ἐν κόλποις τῆς τεκούσης Παρθένου, πᾶσαν ἐπλήρου τὴν κτίσιν, ὡς θεὸς, καὶ σύνεδρος ἦν τῷ γεγεννηκότι. Τὸ γὰρ θεῖον, ἀποσόν τέ ἐστι καὶ ἀμέγεθες, καὶ περιορισμὸν οὐκ ἀνέχεται ... ἕνα μόνον εἰδότες Χριστὸν, τὸν ἐκ Θεοῦ Πατρὸς Λόγον μετὰ τῆς ἰδίας σαρκός ... (Epistola XVII; *MPG* 77: 109-12; trans. LCC 3: 350.)
cf. also "Homilia Paschalis," XVII (429), 9:
"Natus est enim continuo infans ille divinus et omni mundo excellentior. Et erat quidem in cunabulo gremioque genetricis, propter morem conditionis humanae; sed quoniam ad haec erat etiam Deus, arma Satanae virtutibus detrahebat arcanis ... Ergo divina quidem illa generatio, etsi propter conditionem hominum, more agebatur humano. Deus vero vere et naturaliter Emmanuel, qui videbatur more hominum quidem contineri, attamen divino modo coelum et terras inferiora etiam, sua majestate utpote Deus implebat, et continebat omnia quae per ipsum bene fuerant constituta." (*MPG* 77: 796.)
[2] Cf. G. Joussard, "'Impassibilité' du Logos et 'impassibilité' de l'âme humaine chez saint Cyrille d'Alexandrie," *Recherches de Science Religieuse*, XLV (1957), pp. 209-24. The debate in recent scholarship is not over whether the Word is impassible, according to Cyril, but over whether the soul of Christ is also impassible. Cf. also Dom H. M. Diepen, *Aux Origines de l'Anthropologie de Saint Cyrille d'Alexandrie* (Bruges: Desclée de Brouwer, 1957). Over against Joussard, Diepen finds Cyril's phrase ἀπαθὲς ὅτι ἀσώματων does not mean either the impassibility which was the ideal of the Stoics or the impassibility which was the reality of the platonizing philosophers. According to Diepen, Cyril "sait que l'impassibilité de l'âme est toute relative et très différente de l'impassibilité absolue de la nature divine. Notamment, il envisage expressément une 'compassion' de l'âme à l'égard de son propre corps qu'il exclut dans le cas du Verbe s'appropriant la Passion de son humanité." (p. 55.)

time above that creation: here is the immanence and yet the transcendence of the Son.[1]

CONCLUSION

The label "extra Calvinisticum," applied to the affirmation that in the Incarnation the Eternal Son of God was united to but not restricted to his humanity, is misleading, to say the least. There is nothing uniquely Calvinist about the doctrine, for as a means of interpreting the Biblical witness to Christ it had a widespread and ancient usage.

There is a direct liaison from Calvin to Lombard and especially to St. Augustine. That he learned the doctrine from other portions of the tradition cannot be proved from his writings, but it was in fact almost universally confessed—from Origen and Theodore of Mopsuestia, to Athanasius and Cyril, to St. Thomas and Gabriel Biel. The "extra Calvinisticum" was taught by some whose tendency was to separate the two natures of Christ, and by some who resolutely maintained above all the unity of the Person; for some it affirmed God's transcendence, and for others it ministered to a view of his immanence in nature. It could show the uniqueness of God's revelation in Christ or it could provide a rationale for general saving knowledge of God even beyond the Biblical witness.

If one wished to add to the terminological explosion which threatens and delights the theological world, one might coin "extra Catholicum" or "extra Patristicum" as being more appropriate than "extra Calvinisticum."

---

[1] Cf. Epistola IV; *MPG* 77: 45c-48a, and *Adversus Anthropomorphitas*, 18-20; *MPG* 76: 1107-16.

CHAPTER THREE

THE SO-CALLED EXTRA CALVINISTICUM
AND CALVIN'S CHRISTOLOGY

THE CHARACTER OF CHRISTOLOGICAL
KNOWLEDGE AND LANGUAGE

The theme which dominates Calvin's Christology is that Christ is to be known fruitfully not in his essence but in his power to save, not as he is invisibly in himself, but as the Father willed him to be towards us in his office.

> Indeed, faith ought not to fix upon the essence of Christ alone, so to speak, but should be intent upon his power and office. For there was little profit in knowing who Christ was unless this second thing happened, that Christ be known as he willed to be towards us and for what purpose he was sent by the Father. Hence it is that the Papists have nothing but a little shadow of Christ because while they were concerned to grasp the bare essence they neglected his kingdom, which consists in the power of serving. [1]

Right Christological knowledge and language do not deny that Christ's essence is divine; but they concentrate on the way Christ is revealed to us in his benefits. Thus, in the "I am" of John 14: 10, because he was talking not simply about who he was in himself but about how he ought to be recognized by us, Christ spoke about power

---

[1] "Et certe fides non in sola Christi essentia (ut ita loquar) haerere debet, sed eius virtutem et officium attendere. Parum enim prodesset scire quisnam sit Christus, nisi hoc secundum accederet, qualis erga nos esse velit, et in quem finem missus fuerit a patre. Hinc factum est ut papistae nonnisi umbratilem Christum habeant, quia nudam essentiam apprehendere illis curae fuit: regnum vero eius, quod servandi virtute constat, neglexerunt." (Commentary John 1 : 49; *CO* 47 : 36.) cf. "Argementum," Commentary Hebrews; *CO* 55 : 6, and Commentary Colossians 1 : 12; *CO* 52 : 83. Calvin makes use of Augustine on this intimate connection between a fruitful knowledge of Christ and the identity of the Church: the proper foundation of the Church is Jesus Christ, not as name but as reality. cf. *Institutes* II, 15, 1; *OS* III, pp. 471-72; Augustine *ad Laurentium Enchiridion*, 5; *MPL* 40: 233. cf. also Commentary I Corinthians 3: 11; *CO* 49: 354.

rather than essence.[1] Calvin is not impugning that which is presupposed in Christ's being for us, namely, who he is in himself; Calvin is only insisting that the object of our Christological knowledge is the mode of revelation.[2] We know Jesus Christ only as he is towards us according to his office and power. But we can so know him only because of the way he *is* towards us, only because of the unity of the Person which is the consequence of the divine initiative.

That unity of Person which underlies and is presupposed by our knowledge is described by Calvin in shorthand fashion as *Deus manifestatus in carne* (I Timothy 3: 16). "There is no better way to speak of the person of Christ than with these words: *Deus manifestatus in carne.*"[3]

Calvin's partiality for I Timothy 3: 16 is a natural result of his doctrine of the "extra Calvinisticum."[4] The *Deus manifestatus in carne* formulation points to the fact that Jesus Christ, the empirically observable person ministering in Palestine, was the Eternal Son of God among us in a bodily existence; but as the Eternal Son of God, he was not limited to his bodily existence.

One might well conclude that Calvin's penchant for this formula is proof of his alleged inability to confess consistently the union of the two natures in One Person. Does not this formula concentrate on a divine appearance among men at the expense of a gracious identification with men and assumption of their predicament? Does it not suggest the divine nature is *in* the flesh instead of being *united* to it? And does it not intimate, by making "manifestation" the determining

---

[1] "Sed quia non simpliciter disputat Christus, quis sit in se, sed qualis debeat agnosci a nobis, virtutis potius quam essentiae elogium, est." (Commentary John 14: 10; *CO* 47: 326.)

[2] "Haec verba non ad divinam Christi essentiam refero, sed ad modum revelationis." (*ibid.*) In commenting on Hebrews 1: 3, the passage employed by the Fathers to defend the use of *hypostasis* in the Christological formulae, Calvin says that: "Caeterum etsi hic non est propositum apostolo, disserere qualis in se sit Christus, sed qualem se nobis re ipsa declaret: tamen Arianos et Sabellianos satis confutat . . ." (*CO* 55: 12-13.) "Haec igitur vera est Christi cognitio, si eum qualis offertur a Patre suscipimus, nempe Evangelio suo vestitum." (*Institutes* III, 2, 6; *OS* IV, p. 13.)

[3] "Non potuit magis proprie de Christi persona loqui, quam his verbis: Deus manifestatus in carne." (*CO* 52: 289-90.)

[4] Niesel, *op. cit.*, p. 119, and Witte, *loc. cit.*, *KCGG*, III, p. 506, have called attention to the importance of the phrase *Deus manifestatus in carne* for Calvin's Christology and have indicated the intimate relationship between that phrase and the "extra Calvinisticum."

manner of the Mediator's presence, that redemption is nothing more than revelation?

Not really—as Calvin uses *Deus manifestatus in carne*, it does indeed function to protect the fact that Jesus was Mediator as God manifested in the flesh, and that in the flesh he was never less God than he was before this fleshly manifestation.[1] *Deus manifestatus in carne* serves also, however, to indicate the reality of both natures, their distinction, and their unity in the person of the Mediator Jesus Christ.[2] As a corollary to the "extra Calvinisticum," *Deus manifestatus in carne* is for Calvin precisely one way of affirming the unity of the Person. That the Eternal Son of God was not restricted to the flesh does not mean he was not united to it. To confess the unity of the two natures in One Person is to confess that mysterious way in which he who was boundless in majesty and power joined himself to that which was weak and limited.

THE "EXTRA CALVINISTICUM" AND THE UNA PERSONA

It is Calvin's clear intention, in his use of the term *Deus manifestatus in carne*, to state the unity of the Person so unambiguously that all the Christological heresies threatening the Church might be avoided. Calvin is indeed "unoriginal" in his Christology in the sense that he rejects with the ancient Church the positions jeopardizing a correct view of the person of Christ. Calvin does this not because his love

---

[1] *Institutes* II, 14, 7; *OS* III, pp. 468-69.

[2] "Verum enim Deum et verum hominem simul pronuntiat. Secundo, notatur inter duas naturas distinctio: quum hinc vocat Deum, inde manifestationem in carne ponit. Tertio, unitas personae significatur, quum unum eundemque esse tradit: qui quum Deus esset, manifestatus fuit in carne. Ita hoc uno testimonio vera et orthodoxa fides adversus Arium, Marcionem, Nestorium et Eutychem egregie munitur. Caeterum magnum emphasin continent ista antitheta, *Deus in carne*. Quantum enim interest inter Deum et hominem? Et tamen immensam Dei gloriam sic videmus in Christo coniunctam cum hac nostra carnis putredine, ut unum efficiant." (Commentary I Timothy 3: 16; *CO* 52: 290.) cf. Sermon on same text, in which Calvin says the word *manifesté* shows us that there are two natures to be distinguished (*CO* 53: 321), and that we must know Christ to be One Person and not double (*CO* 53: 325). Further, *manifesté* assures us that our God so became one of us that we are freed from the burden of sin and are given perfect riches in him (*CO* 53: 327). cf. also Commentary John 17: 1; *CO* 47:376, and Commentary Genesis 28: 12; *CO* 23: 391. "Proprie autem convenit hoc nomen filio Dei in carne manifestato cui data est a Patre omnis potestas, et qui ordinatus est summus coeli et terrae princeps, per cuius manum Deus omnia gubernet." (Commentary Luke 1: 43; *CO* 45: 35.) cf. also Sermon on Luke 1: 39-43; *CO* 46: 110.

for the Church includes an inability to disagree with the Church Fathers. Rather, it is because the ancient heresies are not simply ancient but in fact constitute perpetual threats to the right understanding of our salvation.[1]

Even when Calvin says the Son "indwelt" the flesh or "clothed" himself with the flesh, he explicitly wishes to avoid Nestorianism. He obviously considers that what makes one Nestorian is not the use of such language in itself, but the misuse of this terminology to suggest something less than the unity of the two natures into One Person.[2]

---

[1] It was because of our need for the Mediator (*Institutes* II ,1-11) that he came to us (*Institutes* II, 12-17). Because of our iniquities, no man could reach to God, and even the angels had need of a Head.

" Deplorata certe res erat nisi maiestas ipsa Dei ad nos descenderet: quando ascendere nostrum non erat. Ita Filium Dei fieri nobis Immanuel oportuit, id est nobiscum Deum: et hac quidem lege, ut mutua coniunctione eius divinitas et hominum natura inter se coalescerent; alioqui nec satis propinqua vicinitas, nec affinitas satis firma, unde nobis spes fieret Deum nobiscum habitare." (*Institutes* II, 12, 1: *OS* III, p. 437.) "Christum ergo, ut Deus est et homo, unitis, licet non confusis, naturis constans, Dominum nostrum verumque Dei Filium esse constituimus, etiam secundum humanitatem: etsi non ratione humanitatis." (*Institutes* II, 14, 4; *OS* III, p. 463.) St. John's words that the Word became flesh are apt for driving back the sacrileges of both Nestorius and Eutyches.

"Quum sermonem dicit carnem esse factum, clare hinc personae unitas colligitur. Neque enim convenit alium nunc esse hominem quam qui verus semper fuit Deus, quum dicatur Deus ille factus esse homo. Rursum, quum distincte Christo homini sermonis nomen tribuat, sequitur Christum, quum homo factus est, non desiisse tamen esse quod prius erat, et nihil in aeterna illa Dei essentia, quae carnem induit, esse mutatum. Denique sic filius Dei homo esse coepit, ut tamen adhuc sit ille aeternus sermo qui nullum habet temporis initium." (Commentary John 1: 14; *CO* 47: 14.) cf. *Institutes* II, 12, 3; *OS* III, pp. 439-40.

[2] In the *Institutes* II, 14, 1, Calvin says that John 1: 14 does not mean the Word was turned into flesh or was confusedly mingled with it. Instead, it means that the Word

". . . e Virginis utero templum sibi delegit in quo habitaret, et qui Filius erat Dei, filius hominis factus est: non confusione substantiae, sed unitate personae. Siquidem ita coniunctam unitamque humanitati divinitatem asserimus, ut sua utrique naturae solida proprietas maneat, et tamen ex duabus illis unus Christus constituatur." (*OS* III, p. 458.) Calvin carries over the *templum* figure from the 1539 to the 1559 edition, so it must be considered as being his mature form of expression. But he is aware of the misunderstanding this might engender and elsewhere guards against it more adequately than in 1559. In 1553, Calvin says that Christ's body is rightly called a temple (in John 2: 19), yet that Nestorius made a wrong use of it. For there is a difference between the way our soul inhabits our body as in a tabernacle and the way the eternal majesty of God inhabited Christ's body as in a sanctuary. In Christ, the fulness of the Godhead dwelt bodily so that he was truly God manifested in one flesh. (Commentary John 2: 19; *CO* 47: 47.) In 1558, in his reply to the question of George Blandrata, Calvin says,

To put on, or to clothe oneself in, human nature is uniquely descriptive of the Incarnation, for Calvin. The angels indeed appeared in human form, but it was the form they took on, not the very human nature. To say that the Eternal Son clothed himself with human nature is to confess the unity of the Person; it is not to maintain a separation of the natures which could permit them to be known somehow abstractly and apart from their being united in the person of Jesus Christ.

Calvin's use of the *communicatio idiomatum* strengthens rather than weakens his affirmation of the unity of the person of Jesus Christ. If it is in II, 14 that the kernel of Calvin's Christological discussion in the *Institutes* is to be found,[1] and if Chapter 14 is really an elaborated statement of the meaning and implications of the *communicatio idiomatum*, then that doctrine plays not a minor but a major role in Calvin's Christology.

Already in the 1536 *Institutes* Calvin's use of the *communicatio idiomatum* comes to light.[2] What he means by it and how he uses it remain basically the same throughout the editions of the *Institutes*. In II, 14, however, Calvin expands his use of it, especially to counteract the Christological implications of Servetus' thought and of the Lutheran doctrine of the ubiquity of Christ's body. In that passage, Calvin begins by stating the outlines of the mystery of the Incarnation. He then significantly introduces the simile of the relation between body and soul in the human constitution. The point of this simile is that though man is composed of two substances, body and soul, he is only one person: things can be said of man as soul, others of man as body, others of man as both. Yet he who consists of these parts is one man, not many. There is one person in man composed of two things joined together, and the two diverse underlying elements constitute one person. The Scriptures speak even of Christ in this way when they attribute to him what must refer sometimes peculiarly to his humanity, sometimes to his divinity, and sometimes to what embraces both natures together but is not sufficient to either alone. "And indeed

---

"Sermo enim caro factus dicitur, quia carnem induit, ut qui aeternus erat Deus, idem homo quoque mortalis esset: nec solum ut humanitas templum esset deitatis, sed ut naturis duabus in unam personam unitis, ille per quem eramus creati, idem esset et redemptor noster." (*Responsum ad G. Blandratae Quaestiones*; *CO* 9: 332.)

[1] Witte, *loc. cit.*, *KCGG*, III, p. 500.
[2] *OS* I, p. 80.

the Scriptures so earnestly express this conjunction of both natures which is in Christ that they sometimes interchange them, a figure of speech called by the ancients ἰδιωμάτων κοινωνία."[1] Subparagraph 2 applies the *communicatio idiomatum* to the divinity and the humanity of Christ, respectively. Calvin cites Scriptural passages which, by interchanging the two natures, speak of the divinity of Christ and of the humanity of Christ. Subparagraph 3 concentrates on those passages which comprehend both natures at once and set forth Christ's true substance most clearly. Thus, in "God laid down his life for us," a property of humanity is shared with the other nature. On the other hand when Christ, still living on earth, said, "No one has ascended into heaven, but the Son of man who was in heaven," then surely as man and in the flesh he put on he was not in heaven, but since he, the same, was God and man because of the union of two natures he attributed to the one what belonged to the other.[2]

Witte insists that Calvin remains faithful to the Chalcedonian formulation in the sense that he emphasizes certain worthwhile Antiochian elements, especially the adverb "without confusion" and the expression, *salva proprietate utriusque naturae*.[3] However, he warns that Calvin would have more fully reflected other elements in the Chalcedonian formula if he had taught that kind of *communicatio idiomatum* which provides for the ontological foundation of the unity of the Person.

Witte is correct in his judgment that the *dabat* in *alteri dabat quod erat alterius*[4] does not mean for Calvin that by which the ontological foundation of the personal union is established. He is also probably correct in his judgment that Calvin has no clear concept of the ontological foundation of the Incarnation. Calvin's awe before the mystery and his distaste for speculation set limits to his inquiry into what, in retrospect, may be called the ontological foundation of the Incarnation. Witte is wrong, however, when he goes on to say, "Für Calvin ist die *communicatio idiomatum* nicht in einer ontologischen Vereinigung zwischen den beiden Naturen grundgelegt, sondern ausschliesslich im Amte Christi als Mittler, was eine persönliche

---

[1] *OS* III, pp. 458-59.

[2] "... certe tunc secundum hominem et in carne quam induerat non erat in caelo, sed quia ipse idem erat Deus et homo, propter duplicis naturae unionem [1536-43: *unitatem*] alteri dabat quod erat alterius." (*OS* III, p. 460.)

[3] Witte, *loc. cit.*, *KCGG*, III, p. 529.

[4] *Supra*, n. 2.

Vereinigung ('persönlich' im Sinne Calvins) erforderte."[1] That is, Witte accurately says the *communicatio idiomatum* does not provide this ontological foundation of the person of Christ, but he is mistaken in saying the *communicatio idiomatum* is not grounded in an ontological unity between both the natures. For Calvin, the *communicatio idiomatum* is primarily a hermeneutical tool to keep in balance the varied Scriptural witness to the One Person; but it rests upon and presupposes the hypostatic union.

THE "EXTRA CALVINISTICUM" AND THE VERE DEUS

Whatever else the union of the two natures may mean, this Redeemer in the flesh is one with the Eternal Son of God who, even before his manifestation in the flesh, was the Mediator between God and man. The *Deus manifestatus in carne* was possible because the Eternal Son of God freely chose to stoop to our condition and by this very descending initiative constituted the One Person of the Redeemer. These two belong together: the identity of the Redeemer with the Mediator of revelation in all ages, and the Eternal Son's freedom for humility which enabled the Incarnation.

Calvin's uses of the term "Mediator"

Calvin inherits from the tradition an ambiguity in the use of the term Mediator as applied to Christ. In I Timothy 2: 5, Paul refers to "the one Mediator between God and man, the man Jesus Christ". This text occasioned the discussion about whether Christ is Mediator only as man or also as God. If one concludes that he is Mediator as God, how does one avoid the erroneous Arian conception of the Son as superior to the created order but inferior in nature to the Father? If one concludes that he is Mediator only by virtue of his humanity, one is faced with the question: why was it necessary for *God* to become man?

Augustine did not resolve these difficulties; but neither did he get caught denying the role of the divinity in mediation. On the one hand he said that insofar as Christ was man he was Mediator.[2] On the other hand he said that if Christ were either God alone or man alone he

---

[1] *Loc. cit.*, p. 503.

[2] "In quantum enim homo, in tantum mediator; in quantum autem Verbum, non medius, quia aequalis Deo, et Deus apud Deum et simul cum Spiritu Sancto unus Deus." (*Confess.* 10, 43, 68; *MPL* 32: 808.)

would not be Mediator.[1] In any event, "the Mediator" meant for Augustine the incarnate Word, and the only ambiguity left was how and in what measure the mediation belongs to the human and to the divine nature of the incarnate Word.

The primary sense of "Mediator" for Calvin is *Deus manifestatus in carne*. When he speaks of the Mediator, without any explicit or contextual qualifications, Calvin means the One Person formed by the *assumptio carnis*.[2] Even in restricting "Mediator" to this, however, Calvin is especially cautious to see that the divinity's part in the mediation is not denied. Interpreting I Timothy 2: 5, he says Paul could have said "God"; that is, the Pauline phraseology could have been: "the one Mediator between God and men, the God Jesus Christ." Or, he could at least have omitted the word "man"; that is, the verse could have been: "the one Mediator between God and men, Jesus Christ." But the Spirit speaking through Paul's mouth and knowing our weakness willed, by specifying the "man," to emphasize the Mediator's nearness to us.[3]

---

[1] "... mediator Dei et hominum; quia Deus cum Patre, quia homo cum hominibus. Non mediator homo praeter deitatem; non mediator Deus praeter humanitatem. Ecce mediator: Divinitas sine humanitate non est mediatrix, humanitas sine divinitate non est mediatrix; sed inter divinitatem solam et humanitatem solam, mediatrix est humana divinitas et divina humanitas Christi." (Sermo 47, 12, 21; *MPL* 38: 310.) And, "Sed si homo solum esset, hoc sequendo quod es, nunquam pervenires; si Deus solum esset, non comprehendendo quod non es, nunquam pervenires." (*Enarratio in Psalmum* 134, 5; *MPL* 37: 1741-42.)

[2] Thus in the *Institutes* I, 13, 11, he says that the Apostles spoke of Jesus Christ as Mediator; yet every text he subsequently cites applies also to Christ as eternal God. When he treats the deity of Christ as recorded in the Old Testament, Calvin says, "I do not yet touch upon the person of the Mediator but postpone it until we reach the treatment of redemption." (*Institutes* I, 13, 9; *OS* III, p. 119.) In the *Institutes* I, 13, 24, Calvin says the Eternal Son of God took upon himself the person and office of the Mediator that he might join us to God. Then in the *Institutes* II, 13, 1, Calvin announces that with the divinity of Christ already proved, it remains for us to see "how, clothed with our flesh he fulfilled the office of Mediator (quomodo carne nostra indutus Mediatoris partes impleverit)." (*OS* III, p. 447.)

"Or notons qu'en Jesus Christ il y a deux choses à considerer, l'une c'est qu'il est la sagesse de Dieu devant la creation du monde. Voyla donc comme tousiours il a esté exalté par dessus tout: mais d'autant qu'il est constitué Mediateur afin de nous approcher de Dieu son Pere, il est mis comme au dessous non point en ceste essence divine, laquelle reside en luy en toute plenitude, et en laquelle il ne differe point d'avec le Pere ...." (Sermon on I Corinthians 11: 2-3; *CO* 49: 716.)

[3] *Institutes* II, 12, 1; *OS* III, p. 438.

Alongside this predominant use, Calvin expands the meaning of the term Mediator to include the Eternal Son who, even before he was clothed with the flesh, was the only channel between God and fallen, even unfallen, man.

Before the Incarnation Christ was the Mediator between fallen man and God. Commenting on John 17: 12, Calvin speaks of the Mediator's appearing for a time under the form of a servant.[1] Christ was Mediator then so that God's covenant with Eve, Noah, and especially with Abraham might be fulfilled. This is the subject of the main portions of the discussion of Christ and the Old Testament in the *Institutes* II, 7-11. There, the Mediator is said to have been present under signs and figures and most of all under the words of the prophets, as promise.[2] He was also present in the Old Testament period more directly under the form of an angel.[3]

But Calvin also speaks of Christ as the Mediator before the Incarnation even prior to and apart from the Fall. For, "Even if man had remained free from all stains, his condition would have been too lowly for him to reach God without a Mediator."[4]

Calvin's deployment of the term "Mediator" undergoes decisive change as he is forced to clarify his own position in response to the doctrine of F. Stancaro. In contrast with Osiander, Stancaro taught

---

[1] *CO* 47: 382.

[2] Cf. Commentary John 1: 18; *CO* 47: 19-20; John 5: 37-38; *CO* 47: 124; John 5: 45-47; *CO* 47: 128-29; John 8: 56; *CO* 47: 214-15.

[3] Because unbelievers judged only from the appearance of his flesh, Christ reminded them (with his words "Before Arbaham was, I am") that he had something greater and higher than the flesh, perceptible only to faith. What was greater and higher was a heavenly and divine power, which was visible to the Old Testament Fathers before the Incarnation. Some took the "I am" as referring only to the eternal divinity of Christ, but Calvin extends it much further to embrace the power and grace of Christ as Redeemer of the world common to all ages. Even in Abraham's time Christ was acknowledged to be the Mediator by whom God was to be appeased. "Quod tamen saeculis omnibus viguit mediatoris gratia, hoc ab aeterna eius divinitate pendebat. Itaque hoc dictum Christi insigne divinae essentiae elogium continet." (Commentary John 8: 58; *CO* 47: 216.) Calvin here implies a distinction between Christ's efficacy and his divine essence, a distinction, however, not involving a separation since the divine essence is presupposed by the efficacy. This efficacy, this heavenly and divine power, is that by which Christ is effectively Mediator between God and sinful man throughout the ages.

[4] "Quanvis ab omni labe integer stetisset homo, humilior tamen erat eius conditio quam ut sine Mediatore ad Deum penetraret." (*Institutes* II, 12, 1; *OS* III, pp. 437-38.) The 1560 edition leaves out the *sine Mediatore*: "Encore que l'homme fust demeuré en son intégrité, si est-ce que sa condition estoit trop basse pour parvenir à Dieu." (Benoit, *CIB*, II, p. 233.) The title "Emanuel,"

CALVIN'S CHRISTOLOGY

Stencaro that Christ was Mediator only by virtue of his human nature, and in
so teaching he thought, at least for a while, that he had the support of
Calvin.[1] But in a reply to the Polish brethren, Calvin explains the role
of Christ's divinity in his Mediatorship.

> Thus we understand first that the name of Mediator applies to Christ
> not only because he took on flesh or because he took on the office
> of reconciling the human race with God. But already from the begin-
> ning of creation he was truly Mediator because he was always the Head
> of the Church and held primacy even over the angels and was the
> first-born of all creatures. (Eph. 1: 2; Col. 1: 15ff.; Col. 2: 10). Whence
> we conclude that he began to perform the office of Mediator not
> only after the fall of Adam but insofar as he is the Eternal Son of
> God, angels as well as men were joined to God in order that they
> might remain upright. [1]

Calvin here subjects the idea of mediation to two different nuances:
mediation as reconciliation and mediation as sustenance. As reconciler,
the Mediator was ordained because of the Fall to restore the broken
relationship between God and man. As sustainer, the Mediator always
was the way creation was preserved and ordered. The performance of
reconciling mediation acknowledges that, according to the flesh in
which he was manifested, the Son was below and obedient to the
Father. But the performance of sustaining mediation means that the
Eternal Son's full equality of nature with the Father was not diminished just because the Father ordered the universe through him. Thus
Calvin, in the same reply, says:

> It is therefore unthinkingly inferred from the title of Mediator that
> he is inferior to the Father, since these things go well together, that
> the same only-begotten Son of God was both God in one essence
> with the Father and yet was a kind of medium between God and

---

in this second sense, includes the truth that Christ performed the office of
Mediator from the beginning of the world. (Commentary Matthew 1: 23; *CO*
45: 69.) He is the wisdom of God without whom man even before the Fall could
not know God. Calvin uses the tree in the Garden of Eden to symbolize the life
of Christ as the Eternal Word of God, upon leaving whom man fell. (Commentary
Genesis 2: 9; *CO* 23: 38-39.)

[1] "Sed excipimus primum mediatoris nomen Christo quadrare, non solum
ex quo carnem induit, vel ex quo munus suscepit reconciliandi cum Deo humani
generis, sed ab initio creationis iam vere fuisse mediatorem: quia semper fuit
caput ecclesiae, et primatum tenuit etiam super angelos, et primogenitus fuit
omnis creaturae (Ephes. 1, 2; Col. 1, 15 sq. et 2, 10). Unde colligimus non modo
post Adae lapsum fungi coepisse mediatoris officio, sed quatenus aeternus Dei
sermo est, eius gratia coniunctos fuisse Deo tam angelos quam homines, ut
integri perstarent." (*Responsum ad Fratres Polonos*; *CO* 9: 338.)

creatures so that life, which otherwise would have been hidden in God, should pour forth from him. Next we add that although he was predestined Mediator following the alienation of man from God and afterwards exhibited Mediator in another way, indeed as Mediator who would restore the lost race of man to life by expiating sins, nevertheless in this person of the Mediator he was the Head no less of the angels than of men . . . . [1]

Mediator as Head of the angels, and Mediator as expiator of sin: these two form a paradigm for Calvin's understanding of the style in which the Eternal Son mediated for unfallen creation and for rebellious creation. When Calvin uses mediation to refer to Christ's reconciling by expiation, he abides by the traditional use of the term.[2] When he uses mediation to refer to Christ's eternal sustaining of the order of the world, he applies the term in a new way to a function which the tradition held belonged to Christ but which the tradition did not usually describe as mediation.

There is an intimate relation between the "extra Calvinisticum" and Calvin's double use of "Mediator." Christ as Eternal Son mediated the divine ordering of the universe from its beginning; Christ as Eternal Son manifested in the flesh performed the reconciling mediation without the cessation or diminution of his mediation of the divine ordering of the universe. The Eternal Son's ordering of creation according to the Father's will is the more comprehensive category, and his reordering and restoring of rebellious man are special forms and instances of the inclusive office of the Son. It is the same Person who orders unfallen creation and who reconciles rebellious creation.

The Incarnation, according to Calvin, was the consequence of divine initiative and humbleness; it was not the natural result of the coming

---

[1] "Quare inscite ex mediatoris titulo infertur patre esse minorem: quando haec optime inter se cohaerent, unigenitum Dei filium eundem et unius cum patre essentiae fuisse Deum, et tamen fuisse quasi medium inter Deum et creaturas, ut ab ipso vita, quae alioqui erat in Deo abscondita, deflueret. Deinde addimus, quamvis post alienationem hominis a Deo praedestinatus, et tandem exhibitus fuit alio modo mediator, nempe qui perditum genus humanum peccata expiando in vitam restitueret, tamen in hac mediatoris persona non minus angelorum esse quam hominum caput . . . ." (ibid.)

[2] Augustine, Confess. 10, 43, 68; MPL 32: 808; Lombard, Sent. III, d. 19, 7. Max Dominicé is not exactly correct when he says that Calvin teaches in the sense of Augustine "Mediator, non quia deus sed quia homo," and "In quantum homo in tantum mediator." (L'humanité de Jésus d'après Calvin [Paris: Je Sers, 1933], p. 49.) Calvin's teaching is broader than this, and so is Augustine's because since "Mediator" applies to the unity of two natures in one flesh, the divinity has a role in that mediation.

to fulfillment of man's created capacities.[1] Before the movement of
the Eternal Word towards us, there was no human side of Jesus to
which the Word could be added to make One Person; the human
nature of Jesus had no separate existence apart from or prior to the
assumptio carnis. This does not mean, however, as will become clear,
that Calvin detracts from the humanity of Christ or that the dynamic
character of Calvin's Christology derives less from his treatment of
Christ as *vere homo* than from his treatment of Christ as *vere Deus*. For
Calvin the voluntary character of Christ's humility during the whole
course of his obedience, including the act of the Incarnation, must
never cease to be a part of the Church's confession. He was convinced
this voluntary nature of the Incarnation and the Atonement was
ignored by Servetus' denial of Christ's eternal Sonship,[2] and by
Andreas Osiander's doctrine that the Incarnation was a necessary

---

[1] What is at stake anthropologically is this: was man created to provide the
historical receptivity to which the Eternal Son would be added to constitute
the Incarnation; or was man created for freedom in obedience as a creature
standing over against and facing the Creator? Does the *capacitas* for the Incarnation remain in sinful men, or must the Word create for himself that very
capacitas and make his own reception possible?

[2] Servetus taught that Jesus Christ was not eternally the Son of God, but
became such in being begotten by the Holy Spirit in the Virgin's womb. Even
in his last words at the stake, Servetus remained true to his conviction: "O Jesus,
Son of the eternal God, have pity on me." Servetus indeed taught the eternity of
the Word; he could say that this eternal Word could be called Christ and the Son
of God; and he could even say that Christ was *homoousios* with the Father. But all
this was predicated on the notion of the Word's existing eternally as an idea
in the mind of God and becoming successively realized in the visible and material
world. Thus Christ could be said to be eternal in the sense that he was the eternal
idea of man in the mind of God. The Son of God as combination of the Word
and flesh was not eternal, but in speaking about the Word only as the form and
not about the flesh as the matter, one could say the Son of God existed before
the Incarnation. The substance which Christ shared with the Father in some
sense included the flesh which the Word brought down from heaven to be
joined with the flesh from the Virgin's womb. (cf. Roland Bainton, *Hunted Heretic*
[Boston: Beacon Press, 1953], pp. 130-37.)

Calvin insisted, on the contrary, that "... the Church's definition remains
established: he is acknowledged to be the Son of God because the Word begotten
of the Father before all ages took human nature by the hypostatic union." (*Institutes* II, 14, 5; *OS* III, p. 465.)

"Servetus accuses us of making a double Son of God since we say that the
eternal Word, before he was clothed with flesh, was already the Son of God:
as if we were saying something else than that he was manifested in the flesh.
For if he was God before he became man, he did not therefore begin to be a new
God. It is no more absurd that the Son of God was manifested in the flesh and
was the same who by eternal generation always possessed Sonship." (*ibid.*)

part of the act of creation.[1] Calvin believed the voluntary character of the Incarnation was best avowed by a teaching that the majesty, power, and authority which belonged to the Eternal Son of God before the Incarnation were not diminished by his union with the flesh.[2]

---

[1] Osiander, as Calvin understood him, said Adam's creation in God's image means he was fashioned according to the pattern of the Messiah to come, so that man might conform to him whom the Father had already determined to clothe with flesh. From this, Osiander inferred that even apart from the Fall, Christ still would have become man. Because Christ as man had been foreknown in the mind of God, he was the pattern to which men were formed. (*Institutes* II, 12, 6-7.)

Against this, Calvin said we must not enter into such vain speculations (*Institutes* II, 12, 5) but we should acknowledge with Paul that Christ became man to be our Redeemer because of our sinful condition. Admittedly, Adam bore God's image; and admittedly the excellence of Adam above other creatures came from his proximity to the glory of God through the only-begotten Son; and admittedly, even then Christ was the image of God. Calvin also agreed that Christ was exalted to the right hand of God according to his flesh. But where Calvin did not concur with Osiander was in saying that Christ's exaltation applied only to his flesh, since according to his divinity Christ never ceased to be exalted, and in declaring that Christ was always the Head of the angels as well as of men. The Incarnation enabled our exaltation, not his. Calvin specified that in one brief passage (Colossians 1: 14-16) the Apostle Paul taught these two essential facts: through the Son all things were created that he might rule over the angels, and he was made man that he might begin to be Redeemer. (*Institutes* II, 12, 7; *OS* III, p. 446.)

[2] "Et encores qu'il ne se soit point despouillé de sa maieste Divine, si est-ce qu'elle a este chachee pour un temps, et on ne l'a point aperceuë entre les hommes." (Sermon on Isaiah 53: 11; *CO* 35: 664.)

"Quant au mot de Serviteur, nous avons vue ci-dessus que cela ne deroge point a la maieste de nostre Seigneur Iesus Christ: car combien qu'il fust maistre de toutes creatures, si est-ce qu'il a acquis encore un empire nouveau en la personne de Mediateur, et en nostre nature: selon que S. Paul en traitte au 2. chapitre des Philippiens, et nous l'avons desia vue en partie: tant y a qu'il s'est voulu faire serviteur et s'humilier sous ceste condition-la." (*ibid.*; *CO* 35: 665-66.)

"Mesmes que ce qu'il avoit prins de nostre condition n'estoit pas qu'il ne peust maintenir sa maiesté celeste. Tous les deux donc nous sont yci monstrez: car nostre Seigneur Jesus Christ est là en une creche et il est comme reietté du monde ... toutesfois il est magnifié des Anges de Paradis, lesquels luy font hommage." (Sermon on Luke 2: 1-14; *CO* 46:957.) In doing him hommage, the angels look to him who never ceased to be their Head. He "estant ainsi abbaissé pour le salut des hommes, ne laisse pas tousiours d'estre Roy de tout le monde, et d'avoir tout sous son empire." (*ibid.*; *CO* 46: 957.) "... Le Fils de Dieu ne perde rien de sa maieste et de sa gloire, et qu'il n'est pas amoindri en ce qu'il s'est humilié pour nostre salut." (*ibid.*; *CO* 46: 959.) While in the cradle, Jesus Christ had "toute puissance sur les creatures, tant du ciel comme de la terre." (*ibid.*; *CO* 46: 961.) cf. also "... reperies, quomodo unus idemque Christus et suae divinitatis amplitudine coelum terramque excedat, et secundum humanitatem non ubique sit diffusus." (*Responsio ad Sadoleti Epistolam*; *CO* 5: 400.)

Political descriptions of the Incarnation and of God's transcendence

Calvin's adherence to the Eternal Son's sovereign freedom and transcendence even during the Incarnation has caused some historians to charge that his Christology exemplifies the extent to which his thought is governed by an espousal of the philosophical principle *finitum non capax infiniti*.[1] According to this interpretation the "extra Calvinisticum" merely reiterates the notion that finite man and infinite God are separated by immutable remoteness.

Calvin does stubbornly refuse to minimize the distance between God and man, and he agrees with most theologians that God is infinite and man is finite! But Calvin does not seek to fit his Christology into a philosophical principle before knowing the identity of those two natures in the incarnate Lord.[2] The fearsome gulf is between the greatness of the divine majesty and our smallness,[3] between God's power, majesty, and authority and our limitation.[4] The *mysterium tremendum* is most experienced when one gazes on Jesus Christ, in whom the hiatus is bridged. The spirit and motivation for Calvin's Christology are epitomized in his brief words: ". . . ineffabile arcanum, quod Dei filius humanam naturam induerit."[5]

Part of the charge that Calvin works on the basis of the *finitum non*

---

[1] Loofs, *loc. cit.*, *RE*, IV, p. 54; Bauke, *loc. cit.*, *RGG*, I, cols. 1627-28; F. Lau „Christologie," *EKL*, I, col. 767. The most significant contributor to this view is Werner Elert, who sees this principle operating in the Antiochian Christology and characteristic in Reformed Christology. From this, Elert concludes that wherever the principle is at work, one is moving towards or away from Nestorius. (*loc. cit.*, *Zeitschrift für Systematische Theologie*, XVI [1939], pp. 500-504.) Unfortunately, however, those following this interpretation fail to include passages in which Calvin supposedly puts the problem in the context of a philosophical discussion on the mutual exclusiveness of the finite and the infinite.

[2] Berkouwer says it can be shown that the saying *finitum non capax infiniti* does not occur in the writing of Calvin himself. There is nothing to disprove his statement, and his conclusion appears valid: Calvin's is not a philosophical, cosmological theory into which he tries to fit his Christology. (*op. cit.*, p. 282.)

[3] *Institutes* II, 12, 1.

[4] The fault of Sarah's laugh was that she limited the power of God within the bounds of her own sense. (Commentary Mark 1: 22 and Luke 4: 33; *CO* 45: 153.) "Subest igitur antithesis inter immensam Dei virtutem, et inter augustum modulum, quem sibi ex carnis ratione fingebat Sara." (Commentary Genesis 18: 13; *CO* 23: 255.) Calvin's Commentary on Luke 1: 34 is strikingly parallel: many err in limiting the boundless power of God to earthly limits and senses. (*CO* 45: 29.) cf. Commentary Luke 1: 37; *CO* 45: 32-33. The majesty of God would swallow up the whole world were it not mitigated by some mildness. (Commentary Luke 2: 10; *CO* 45: 74.)

[5] Commentary John 1: 14; *CO* 47: 13.

capax infiniti principle is that his thought reflects crudely naive spatial categories. God and man are conceived in quantitative terms so that God, who is boundless, cannot of course be contained within the bounds of human reason or even within the bounds of the humanity he assumed. However, as has already been evidenced, God's boundlessness and transcendence are for Calvin a matter of majesty, power, and authority. "Coming from the Father" means that whatever Christ had was divine.[1] The divine movement was indeed a movement from "heaven" to "earth." But when used to denote whence the descent was made, heaven is not primarily a geographical entity. Those passages of Scripture about God's dwelling in heaven or heaven's being the throne of God do not betoken that he lives in a place "up there." They rather stress the majesty and power and immeasurable essence of God which cannot be comprehended or enclosed by anything earthly. By telling us that God's dwelling place is heaven, the Scriptures, through the prophets and Christ's teaching, remind us that God is far above our ability to grasp him, far above our carnal reason and language.

In rendering an account of God's transcendence, Calvin relies most heavily on political phraseology: majesty, power, authority, glory. Such use of governmental language is of course not original with Calvin; those who see in this practice a preponderance of his legal training overlook the language which was a part of his theological as well as his legal preparation. Tertullian and Augustine, as well as his teachers in jurisprudence, Alciati and l'Etoile, provide linguistic resources for Calvin's theological expression.

The supremacy of political language is manifest in Calvin's account of the Incarnation. If what Gustaf Aulén calls the "classical idea" describes the Atonement in mainly military language,[2] Calvin's words portray the Incarnation in terms suggestive of the political ordering which is the culmination of any successful campaign. This is not to say Calvin does not use other categories; one reason why his thought is so opulent is that it employs a wide variety of cognitive imagery. However, for him, some language must proclaim God's activity towards us, especially as it happened in the person of Christ, and he

---

[1] Commentary John 8: 42; *CO* 47: 207. Calvin's commentary is notable for its lack of explication on "coming down from heaven" in John 6: 33 and 6: 38. All he says about these texts is that the descent was to ratify what the Father had decreed for our salvation.

[2] *Christus Victor*, trans. A. G. Hebert (London: S.P.C.K., 1950), p. 20.

finds the most suitable idiom to be that of political ordering and re-ordering.

He views the Incarnation as a reassertion of Christ's empire over that part of creation which had rebelled. In the Incarnation there was an ordering of the lesser by the greater, of the weak by the powerful, so that the Eternal Son's life and power during the period of the Incarnation were never exhausted by his fleshly Person or by his fleshly accomplishments. Others seek to avoid diminishing Christ's eternal reality during the period of the Incarnation by saying that eternal properties were shared by the humanity, but Calvin feels such a route would bypass the real humanity of Christ. The eternal properties were exercised by Christ during the Incarnation not by the humanity of the One Person but by the divinity of the One Person. In the Incarnation, the Son of God left heaven only in such a way that he continued to exercise his dominion over creation; the Incarnation was the extension of his empire, not the momentary abdication of it.[1]

One of Calvin's important expositions of Christ's eternal dominion over the world is his image of Christ as Head or chief of the angels. Whatever else the Incarnation may have been, it meant that the Eternal Son was incarnate in such a way that he continued to be Head over the angels. The unfallen angels represent creation unaffected by the Fall; they are powers and authorities by which God deals and communicates with men. In always being the Head of the angels, the Eternal Son is always the one through whom God the Father deals with his world. The angels are rational, sinless beings, created by the Son, and sustained in their creation by their Head, the same Son. They are ministers of God, yet always deriving their power from their Creator and Head, the Eternal Son. Not ceasing to be their Head during the Incarnation, Jesus Christ could have summoned them to enable him to escape death at the hands of men, had he not voluntarily been obedient, even unto the death of the cross.[2] Indeed, Christ,

---

[1] See *supra*, p. 73, n. 2; cf. Commentary John 1: 21; *CO* 47: 22, and Commentary Hebrew 13: 8; *CO* 55: 190.

[2] Christ is the Prince and Lord of the angels as well as of men. (Commentary Luke 1: 19; *CO* 45: 20; Commentary Matthew 13: 39; *CO* 45: 370.) It is a firm principle, says Calvin, that God is gracious to both men and angels only insofar as he embraces them in Christ. The angels, unlike us, were never alienated from God so they needed no reconciliation, but they needed Christ as their Head to be united firmly to God. (Commentary Matthew 17: 5; *CO* 45: 488.) Or, as Calvin elsewhere explains at greater length:

being Head of the angels, appeared to the Fathers of the Old Testament as an angel.[1]

Christ was more than the first of many angels, as Calvin carefully points out, just as Christ's role as our Head means he is over us as well as identified with us.[2] The main difference between the angels and Christ is that he alone is the living image of God and the Head of all creatures, and that he alone became truly incarnate. The two angels who were merely in human form in Genesis 18: 16 were not clothed in human bodies in the same manner in which Christ clothed himself with our nature and our flesh.[3] Christ appeared before the Incarnation in the form of an angel but he never really became clothed with angelic nature. Christ in the Incarnation not only bore the appearance of a man but was a real man because he took on man's nature.[4]

The constancy of Christ over the angels even during the period of the Incarnation is a crucial part of the motivation behind the "extra

---

"Dico homines Deo reconciliatos esse, quod ante ab eo essent alienati per peccatum: quod iudicem sensuri erant in suum exitium, nisi intervenisset gratia mediatoris ad iram eius placandam. Genus ergo pacificationis inter Deum et homines fuit, quod per Christum abolitae fuerunt inimicitiae: itaque Deus ex iudice factus est pater. Inter Deum et angelos longe diversa ratio. Illic enim nulla defectio, nullum peccatum: ideoque nullum divortium. Sed tamen duabus de causis angelos quoque oportuit cum Deo pacificari. Nam quum creaturae sint, extra lapsus periculum non erant, nisi Christi gratia fuissent confirmati. Hoc autem non parvum est momentum ad pacis cum Deo perpetuitatem, fixum habere statum in iustitia, ne casum aut defectionem amplius timeat. Deinde in hac ipsa oboedientia, quam praestant Deo, non est tam exquisita perfectio, ut Deo omni ex parte et citra veniam satisfaciat." (Commentary Colossians 1: 20; *CO* 52: 88-89.)

[1] It was Christ who appeared in Judges 13: 8ff as an angel, and was called the eternal God and accepted to be so worshipped. (*Institutes* I, 13, 10.) Already then Christ was descending to earth to perform the office of Mediator. (*ibid.*) Again in Zachariah 2, Christ was the angel who sent the other angel; and Christ was the angel in Isaiah 25: 9 and Malachi 3: 1 (*ibid.*)

[2] The angel who wrestled with Jacob was Christ because he was "vray Dieu" and not an "ange créé." (*ibid.*) Christ and the angels are all ministers, but angels are ministers by nature, Christ by a voluntary submission. Christ was minister in such a way that although he was in our flesh, the majesty of his dominion was undiminished. (Commentary Luke 1: 19; *CO* 45: 20.) Angels, sometimes clothed with real bodies and a human shape (Commentary John 20: 12; *CO* 47: 431) and sometimes glowing with the brightness of the Godhead (Commentary Matthew 28: 2; *CO* 45: 795), were celestial spirits possessing some portion of divinity in their blessed immortality. (Commentary Hebrews 1: 4; *CO* 55: 14.) Yet Christ, the living image of the Father, when appearing to the patriarchs under the form of an angel was always attended by angels over whom he was the Head. (Commentary Genesis 18: 2; *CO* 23: 251.)

[3] Commentary Genesis 18: 16; *CO* 23: 256.

[4] Commentary Hebrews 2: 16; *CO* 55: 33-34.

Calvinisticum": the entire course of the Eternal Son's humiliation, the Incarnation included, was a voluntary act, and the eternal majesty and power which could not be confined within the flesh continued to order all creation, as seen in the case of the angels who otherwise would have been without a Head through whom to be related to the Father. The Incarnation is to be seen, in this context, as a reassertion over the rebelled creature, man, of the empire Christ never ceased to have over the angels. Redemption is the restoration and reformation of man and the world into a proper order. "Now we know that outside of Christ there is nothing but confusion in the world; and though Christ had already begun to erect the Kingdom of God, yet his death was the commencement of a well-regulated condition and the full restoration of the world."[1] The power of "judgment" [2] given to Christ by the Father means the restoration of all things by Christ.

The "Extra Calvinisticum" and the Vere Homo

Calvin never tires of insisting on the reality of Christ's humanity, without which there would be no salvation for us. He chooses to account for Christ's obvious, full humanity by saying that the *Logos*, in freely concealing [3] himself, enabled the fully human character and actions of the Redeemer. As *Deus manifestatus in carne* is an important corollary of the "extra Calvinisticum", so also is Calvin's doctrine of the *kenosis*.

The humanity of the humbled Lord

In his *kenosis* doctrine, Calvin is not talking about a different Christ from the one of whom he speaks in concentrating on Christ the Eternal Son of God. Christ is known as the Eternal Son of God not

---

[1] "Scimus autem extra Christum nihil in mundo nisi confusum esse. Etsi autem iam regnum Dei erigere coeperat Christus, mors tamen eius verum demum status rite compositi exordium et plena mundi instauratio fuit." (Commentary John 12: 31; *CO* 47: 293.)

[2] Commentary John 16: 11; *CO* 47: 360-61.

[3] The Philippist Lutherans were labelled "Crypto-Calvinists" by their stricter brethren; they were accused of being Calvinists at heart but of concealing (*crypsis*) themselves under the guise of Lutherans. There is the intriguing possibility that they could have been labelled "Crypto-Calvinists" also because of their association with the Calvinists who interpreted the *kenosis* as concealment. For Calvin, the Eternal Son in his humility was concealed within and behind the flesh. This Reformed doctrine is in contrast to the opinion enunciated in the "crypto-kenoticist" debate of the 1620's (*supra*, pp. 20-22) to the effect that what was concealed was the humanity's power to be everywhere.

from the way he is in himself but from the way he is among us. Epistemologically, the priority remains with the *Deus manifestatus in carne*; but the incarnate Lord can have this epistemological priority for us only because of his being, in a prior way, eternal God.

> I confess indeed that we may not rightly conceive the Son of God in any other way than as clothed with the flesh. But this did not prevent him, while filling heaven and earth with his divine essence, from supporting his flesh in the womb of his mother, on the cross, in the sepulchre. Indeed then he was not less Son of God in heaven than he was man on earth. [1]

Calvin is so emphatic on the importance of Christ's humanity for the movement of faith and our salvation that it is difficult to understand the criticism that Calvin gives no positive significance to the humanity of Christ.[2] Even in the human nature and servitude of Christ, says Calvin, there was a heavenly power to be considered.[3] The Incarnation was no mere appearance. Christ assumed not just the form of man, as do the angels, but he put on our human nature

---

[1] "Fateor sane non aliter animis concipere Dei filium fas esse, quam carne vestitum. Sed hoc non obstitit quo minus divina sua essentia coelum et terram replens, carnem suam in utero matris, in cruce, in sepulcro gestaret. Tum quoque Dei filius non minus in coelo quam in terra homo fuit." (*Ultima Admon. ad Westph.*; *CO* 9: 171.)

[2] Dominicé argues that Calvin separates too much the two natures of Christ and that the humanity of Jesus as such has no value for Calvin except by its union with the divine nature. (*op. cit.*, p. 48.) The first part of his objection, which is shared by a number of other interpreters, will be dealt with presently. As for the second, it is curious to make the objection against Calvin that he gives no significance to Christ's humanity except in its union with the divine, while at the same time objecting that Calvin separates too much the two natures. For precisely because Calvin endeavors to hold to the unity of the Person, it is a speculative and hypothetical question to speak about the humanity of Jesus apart from its union with the Eternal Son. Of course the humanity of Jesus as such has no value except by its union with the divine nature. In fact, there is no such thing as the humanity of Jesus except in union with the divine nature; but one cannot reverse the statement to say there is no divine nature except by its union with the humanity, again although we may not know what that divine nature is apart from the hypostatic union. It seems to me that Calvin, at least at this point, takes more seriously the value of the *anhypostasis* and *enhypostasis* affirmations than does Dominicé in his implied question. Moreover, when one understands that Calvin is speaking about the One Person of Jesus Christ, one can make the further point that Calvin does assign a special function to the humanity of Christ.
"Christus non tantum, quatenus est aeternus Dei sermo, viva est imago ipsius, sed humanae quoque naturae, quam nobiscum habet communem, insculpta fuit paternae gloriae effigies, ut membra sua in eam transfiguret." (Commentary John 17: 22; *CO* 47: 388.) cf. *Institutes* IV, 17, 2.

[3] Commentary Matthew 3: 16; *CO* 45: 126. cf. *Institutes* IV, 17, 2.

and was really man. He was fatigued by the journey,[1] he did weep,[2] he was in anguish.[3] "If we are ashamed of his fear and sorrow, our redemption will perish away."[4]

The kenosis interpreted as concealment. This full humanity was enabled by the Eternal Son's emptying himself in the sense of freely concealing himself and withholding the exercise of his powers through the flesh to which he was fully joined.[5] The *kenosis* was the concealment, not the abdication, of the Eternal Son's divine majesty.[6] Calvin says that when Paul uses the term *kenosis* (*exinanitio*), he means Christ was brought to nothing (*in nihilum redigi*). "Christ could not indeed abdicate himself of divinity, but he held it hidden for a time lest it appear under the weakness of the flesh. Therefore he laid down his glory

---

[1] Commentary John 4: 6; *CO* 47: 78.

[2] Commentary John 11: 33; *CO* 47: 264-65.

[3] "Into the lower parts of the earth" means the condition of this present life, not purgatory or hell; it means only that from the lofty habitation, Christ descended into our deep grief (Commentary Ephesians 4 : 9; *CO* 51 : 194) This *descensus ad infernum* is in fact the anguish of the man Jesus who felt himself utterly emptied and rejected and who needed to fight fear. (*Institutes* II, 16, 10-12; II, 16, 5.)

[4] Commentary Matthew 26: 37; *CO* 45: 719.

[5] Christ's human torment was genuine as the punishment borne for the enormity of sin. The divine nature was concealed and did not exert its force; but it may be said to have reposed in order to allow an opportunity for making expiation. Christ was really clothed with our human feelings; yet he feared not through constraint but because he voluntarily subjected himself to fear, and all his feelings were regulated in obedience to the righteousness of God. This is to our advantage because we are more ready to follow one who has felt as we feel but who has conquered. (Commentary John 12: 27; *CO* 47: 290-92.) "Caeterum haec quoque pars exinanitionis fuit, non per quam aliquid decederet Christi gloriae, sed tantum ut ad tempus abscondita iaceret." (Commentary Luke 2: 8; *CO* 45: 73.) cf. also Commentary John 8: 16; *CO* 47: 194, and *Genevan Catechism* (1545); *CO* 6: 31-32.

[6] The "form of God" in which Christ was before the Incarnation means, according to Calvin, his majesty. As a man is known when viewed in the form of his face and person, so the majesty which shines forth in God is his form or figure. Or, Calvin takes another metaphor, a king shows himself to be king by his equipage and magnificence: sceptre, crown, robe, attendants, judgment throne, and so forth. Christ before the creation was in the form of God because he had his glory with the Father, as he says in John 17: 5. For in the wisdom of God, prior to his putting on flesh, there was nothing low or abject but there was a magnificence worthy of God. (*CO* 52: 25.) Being such as he was, Christ could have shown himself to be equal with God without doing wrong; but his *kenosis* and humiliation consisted in the fact that "he did not display what he was, nor did he openly take before the eyes of man that which was his by right." (*CO* 52: 25.) The appearance of majesty was laid aside. (*Institutes* II, 14, 3.)

not by diminishing it but by suppressing it before the gaze of men."[1]

Luke's statement that "he grew" refers to Christ's human and not his divine nature.[1] His soul was subject to ignorance, not of necessity as with us, but from voluntary submission, that is, the *kenosis*. Christ received in his human nature, according to his age and capacity, the free gifts of the Spirit so that out of his fullness he might pour them out on us. Those who say that Christ's growth in knowledge was an appearance are too timid, says Calvin.

> One should not imagine that understanding lay concealed in Christ and made its appearance in progress of time. For there is no doubt that God decided to express how Christ, in taking on our flesh, truly and fully fulfilled all that belonged to a brotherly union with men. [3]

On the other hand, Christ exhibited an extraordinary knowledge which Calvin says was due to his divinity, or to the exercise of his divine power, or to the Spirit. Thus, when Christ asked of the crowd, "Who touched me?" he knew by virtue of his divinity whom he had cured: the same woman he had intentionally drawn to him by his Spirit.[4] Often, Calvin attributes this special knowledge not just to

---

[1] "Non potuit quidem Christus abdicare se divinitate: sed eam ad tempus occultam tenuit, ne appareret sub carnis infirmitate. Itaque gloriam suam non minuendo, sed supprimendo in conspectu hominum deposuit." (Commentary Philippians 2: 7; *CO* 52: 26.) Calvin's exegesis preserves the ethical bent of the Philippians 2: 5ff. passage. He says Paul is recommending the exercise of humility from the example of Christ. But then, in a typical fashion, Calvin points out the differences between the humility of Christ and the humility to which we are exhorted after Christ's pattern.
"Humilitas Christi fuit, e summo gloriae fastigio se deiicere ad infimam ignominiam: nostra humilitas est, nos falsa opinione non efferre. Cessit ille suo iure: a nobis tantum hoc requiritur, ne plus nobis sumamus quam oportet . . . . Quam igitur absurdum est, quum filius Dei ex tanta altitudine descenderit, nos, qui nihil sumus, efferri superbia?" (*CO* 52: 25; cf. also *Institutes* II, 13, 2.)

[2] Commentary Luke 2: 40; *CO* 45: 103-104.

[3] Commentary Luke 2: 40; *CO* 45: 104. The man Jesus was ignorant about the date of the *parousia*; he was not merely hiding a knowledge belonging to his humanity by virtue of its union with the divine. (Commentary Matthew 24: 36; *CO* 45: 671-72.) Christ was a real man, taught by his own experience to help the miserable. (Commentary Hebrews 4: 15; *CO* 55: 54-55.)

[4] Not with his human sight but through his divine sight, Christ was aware of Nathaniel under his tree. (Commentary John 1: 48; *CO* 47: 35.) He knew from the beginning that some of his hearers would not believe; but this knowledge was peculiar to his divinity. (Commentary John 6: 64; *CO* 47: 160.) Calvin seems to concede that Christ knew the time of his death which had been foreordained and determined in the purpose of God. (Commentary John 7: 1; *CO* 47: 164.)

Christ's divinity but to his divine Spirit, or explicitly to the Holy Spirit.[1] Christ, by his divine Spirit, penetrated the hidden parts of the human heart.[2]

When Calvin describes the source of Christ's extraordinary knowledge, he often does so with the words "divine Spirit," "divine power," "the power of his divinity," or simply, "his Spirit." In this fluidity of language, another corollary of the "extra Calvinisticum" is uncovered: the relation between Christ and the Holy Spirit, whose proceeding is *Filioque*.

Calvin's "Spirit-Christology." One of the strengths of Calvin's Christology and of his Pneumatology is his representation of the person and work of Christ in constant reference to the Spirit, and the reality and work of the Spirit in constant reference to Christ. Calvin's Christology is of course a "Spirit-Christology" in the sense that it is so much a *Filioque-Christology* he never loses sight of the role of the Holy Spirit in the Incarnation.[3] But his is not a Spirit-Christology in the sense that, instead of a doctrine of the hypostatic union,

---

This was the same kind of knowledge Christ exhibited when he appeared as one of the three angels who visited Abraham. He revealed himself to be the chief of the angels in that while his back was turned he detected that Sarah laughed within herself. (Commentary Genesis 18: 13; *CO* 23: 254-55.)

[1] Mark 7: 24 tells that Christ went into the house "that no one should know it, but he was unable to hide it." Calvin says,

"Loquitur autem Marcus pro communi carnis sensu: etsi enim spiritu suo divino praeviderat Christus, quid futurum esset, quatenus tamen patris minister erat ac legatus, sese intra vocationis sibi iniunctae fines humanitus continuit: ideo non potuisse dicitur, quod secundum hominem volebat." (Commentary Mark 7: 24; *CO* 45: 456.)

[2] Commentary Matthew 9: 4; *CO* 45: 246. Mark's account adds to Matthew's in pointing out, says Calvin, "Christum divino suo spiritu illuc [what lies hidden within the hearts] usque penetrasse." (*CO* 45: 246.) Similarly, Christ discerned the hearts of those trying to trip him on the question of the allegiances due to God and Caesar. In that passage once again Christ discerned "quia Deus erat"; he exhibited his "divinitas"; he knew "quia spiritus eius cordium erat cognitor." (Commentary Matthew 22: 18; *CO* 45: 601.) When Peter denied him the third time Christ, according to Luke's account, turned and looked at him. Says Calvin, that was no ordinary look:

"... sed in respiciendo Petro oculis suis adiunxisse arcanam spiritus efficatiam, atque adeo gratiae suae radiis in cor eius penetrasse. Quare sciamus, quoties lapsus fuerit quispiam, ei non esse poenitentiae initium nisi a Domini adspectu." (Commentary Matthew 25: 75; Luke 22: 61; *CO* 45: 745.)

[3] In his excellent work on the Holy Spirit in Calvin, Krusche says: "Wird man sagen müssen, dass Calvins Christologie stark pneumatologisch akzentuiert ist, so muss man andererseits auch sagen, dass seine Lehre vom Geist eine starke christologische Akzentuierung erhält ..." (*op. cit.*, p. 151.)

he teaches the man Jesus was animated by the Holy Spirit. Christ's existence and ordering reality beyond the flesh are in large measure to be accounted for Pneumatologically. Part of the force of the "extra Calvinisticum" in Calvin's thought is that it makes Pneumatology integral to Christology and so affords a Christology more properly Trinitarian than would otherwise be the case. Calvin so gives content to the *Filioque* provision that it serves not to buttress a subordination or devaluation of the Spirit to the Son, but to underscore that the Son is never effectively active in creation or redemption without the Spirit. What the incarnate Lord accomplished was never without the transforming presence of his Spirit. He who redeems is the same who sends his Spirit; he who sanctifies is the same who makes redemption to be appropriated by men, the gracious objects of redemption.

According to Calvin, it is through the Holy Spirit that the humanity assumed by the Eternal Son was sanctified for the office to be accomplished by the *Deus manifestatus in carne*. It was not because he was engendered without sexual intercourse that Jesus Christ was exempt from original sin, but because he was sanctified in his birth by the Holy Spirit and so his generation was without blemish, even as was generation before the Fall.[1]

In contrast to the prophets who went before him, Christ alone was given the Spirit without measure,[2] and he alone received the Spirit in order to bestow him on all others.[3] Christ's uniqueness was that he had poured out on him by the Father an unlimited abundance of his Spirit.[4] Christ received the Spirit not as the Eternal Son but according to his manifestation in the flesh.[5]

---

[1] *Institutes* II, 13, 4. We are sanctified even by Christ's human nature; not that it had a holiness of its own, but because God poured upon it a perfect fulness of holiness. (Commentary Hebrews 2: 11; *CO* 55: 28.) Before his Baptism, Jesus was indeed indwelt by the Holy Spirit; but with the Baptism he was clothed with a new power of the Spirit not so much for his own sake as to perform the office of Redeemer for others. The appearance of the Holy Spirit on that occasion was a reminder that nothing carnal was to be expected in Christ: he came from heaven as a divine man in whom the power of the Holy Spirit reigned; so even as a servant and according to his human nature here was a heavenly power. (Commentary Matthew 3: 16; *CO* 45: 126.)

[2] Commentary Luke 1: 15; *CO* 45: 15.

[3] *Ibid.*

[4] Commentary John 3: 34; *CO* 47: 74-75.

[5] The power of Christ's Spirit, which came from the Father to renew men (Commentary Matthew 12: 48; *CO* 45: 350), was received according to Christ's humanity. The Spirit of the Father's love flowed into the human nature. (Commentary Luke 19: 41; *CO* 45: 576.) This anointing with the Holy Spirit equipped the

There is no clear indication as to the identity of the divine power of Jesus to which Calvin gives so much weight. Is that power the efficacy of the Second Person which makes itself experienced beyond the confines of Christ's flesh, or is it in fact the Holy Spirit himself? Calvin has no set phrase for denoting the divine power at Jesus' disposal. He usually restricts his descriptions to the effect of that power, sometimes calling it the divine Spirit of Christ, the power of the Holy Spirit, Christ's divine or secret power, or Jesus Christ's spiritual power.[1]

The "extra Calvinisticum" and Christ's redemptive obedience as prophet, king, and priest. The full humanity of Christ is absolutely indispensable

---

humanity with gifts to accomplish the office of the Redeemer. What Calvin says about the gifts of God in the nativity applies as well to the further gifts of the Holy Spirit at the Baptism:

". . . Il y ait beaucoup de choses qui nous pourroyent desbaucher, et pour le moins esblouir les yeux pour n'appercevoir point la gloire celeste qui lui a este donnee de Dieu son Pere: je di mesme en ceste nature humaine qu'il a prise de nous. Car entant qu'il est Dieu, il ha tout de soy-mesme (comme il en est parlé au 17. ch. de S. Jehan), mais selon son humanité il ha receu de don gratuit tout ce qu'il nous a apporté, afin que nous puisions de sa plenitude, et que nous trouvions en luy tout ce qui est desirable, et ayons tout nostre repos et contentement en luy seul." (Sermon on the Nativity; *CO* 46: 960-61.)

[1] In the Institutes, Calvin says that Paul speaks not of a heavenly essence but of "the spiritual power which is poured out from Christ to make us alive." (*Institutes* II, 13, 2; *OS* III, p. 451.) As will be shown in the section on the work of Christ, Calvin speaks of Christ's assembling the multitudes by the power of his Spirit, of his preparing the hearts of his hearers by the power of his Spirit, of his discerning the inward thoughts of men by his divine power, and especially of his performing miracles by his divine power. But Calvin objects to the question: could not Christ have drawn down the Holy Spirit while he was on earth? His very attitude to the question implies that for him Christ did not draw down the Holy Spirit while he was on earth. (Commentary John 16: 7; *CO* 47: 358.) In the same chapter Calvin makes a distinction between Christ's essence and power, and between Christ's "hidden and intrinsic power as it is called" and "that office which he has been appointed to exercise towards us." (Commentary John 16: 15; *CO* 47: 364.)

According to Krusche, the power of Christ by which he was generally present and maintained creatures alive was "His Spirit." (*op. cit.*, p. 128.) He detects in Calvin's thought two manners of the Spirit's working, one in the universe and order of nature, the other in the renewal of fallen nature. These do not correspond to a difference (not in Calvin) between the Spirit of God and the Spirit of Christ, but to the difference Calvin speaks of between the Spirit of the Eternal *Sermo* and the Spirit of the Mediator. (*op. cit.*, p. 127.) Krusche points, however, to the way in which Christ, whether as Eternal Word or as Mediator in the flesh, was never separated from his Spirit. *Filoque* said of the Eternal Word refers to the Spirit's world-ordering function, and *Filioque* said of the Mediator in the flesh refers to the Spirit of regeneration. (*op. cit.*, pp. 128-29.)

because it constitutes the instrument of Christ's redemptive obedience. What is saving in Christ's teaching, miracles, and death is not simply that they occurred, but that they occurred voluntarily. The heart of the reconstituting act is the free obedience of the Second Adam which displaces the willful disobedience of the first Adam, and frees the members of the Second Adam for new obedience in place of their inherited disobedience. That the whole course of Christ's obedience, the act of the Incarnation being but the first and continuing stage, was a voluntary submission, is an affirmation guarded by the "extra Calvinisticum." For that doctrine points to the fact that throughout his humility in the flesh, Christ was not compelled to become incarnate or to adhere to his whole course of obedience. The redemptive activity of the incarnate Lord was a free movement of the Eternal Son. In order to satisfy the requirements of the Father's majesty, the sacrifice had to be freely given. The restoring character of Christ's obedience is manifest especially in his work as priest; but it is equally operative in his prophetic and reigning powers. The *triplex munus* scheme is not a vehicle to help Calvin delineate three different functions of Christ; it sets forth three aspects of the ministry of the one redeeming Mediator. And the central fact about that office, the thread which ties the *triplex munus* together much more than later orthodoxy is wont to acknowledge, is the obedience of the one who is the subject and the active executor of these functions.[1]

---

[1] It is only in the 1559 edition of the *Institutes* that this emphasis on the obedience of Christ in relation to his redemptive work receives full expression. Then it is introduced as a sort of shorthand expression for Calvin's understanding of Christ's total redemptive act. Its most concise formulation is found in the *Institutes* II, 16, 5:

"Iam ubi quaeritur quomodo abolitis peccatis dissidium Christus inter nos et Deum sustulerit, et iustitiam acquisierit quae eum nobis faventem ac benevolum redderet: generaliter responderi potest, toto obedientiae suae cursu hoc nobis praestitisse." (*OS* III, pp. 485-86.) Indeed Christ from the time he took on the person of the Servant in order to free us began to pay the price of liberation. But Scripture, which should define more certainly the mode of salvation, ascribes this as peculiar and proper to Christ's death. The Apostles' Creed passes in right sequence, says Calvin, from the birth of Christ to his death and resurrection, in which the sum of perfect salvation consists.

"Neque tamen excluditur reliqua pars obedientiae qua defunctus est in vita: sicuti Paulus ab initio ad finem usque totam comprehendit, quod seipsum exinanierit, forma servi accepta, et Patri fuerit obediens usque ad mortem: nempe mortem crucis (Philip. 2. a. 7). Et sane in ipsa quoque primum gradum occupat voluntaria subiectio: quia ad iustitiam nihil profuisset sacrificium nisi sponte oblatum." (*ibid.*, p. 486.)

The "extra Calvinisticum" functions, in observing the office of prophet,[1] to fortify the accomodation character of Christ's teaching. Christ's accomodation to his hearers reflected, and was a part of, the Son's humility. He could be the prophet recorded in the New Testament, he could instruct as the New Testament states, because in this prophetic act the Eternal Son of God accomodated himself, freely and voluntarily, to the condition of his listeners. "He taught with authority" means that his authority, the boundless power at his command, enabled him to call Israel to repentence in ways comprehensible to the true Israel but not to the false.

Particularly in the Commentary on John's Gospel, Calvin expresses the accomodating character of Christ's self-testimony.[2] This is notably true of those passages which might be taken in a subordinationist sense. When Christ said the Father was greater than he, he was speaking *per concessionem* to his hearers.[3] The way in which Christ accomodated himself was by referring whatever was divine in him to the Father. He said "I do nothing of myself" to conform to the capacity of his hearers.[4] Still, his accomodation could take the form of being an open proclamation of his divinity; or again, he could be content to sustain the character of a man, and yield to the Father the whole glory of divinity.

> Because the majesty of Christ could not be apprehended in its height, the power of God which appeared in his flesh gradually raised the rough and slow senses of men to that height. For since he wanted entirely to be ours, it is not surprising if by various ways he should accomodate himself to us. [5]

This indicates how much, for Calvin, the teaching function was a continuation and part of the *exinanitio*. For, as he puts it, "On all

---

[1] A look at what Calvin says about the boundless power of the Son and the prophetic office will indirectly substantiate the contention that the prophetic office is much more integral to Calvin's thought than J. F. Jansen admits it to be. (*Calvin's Doctrine of the Work of Christ* [London: J. Clarke, 1956], pp. 51-54.) At any event, it must be taken seriously that this *triplex munus* formulation, though not an expanded version of it, appears already in the 1539 edition of the *Institutes*.

[2] Cf. Commentary John 14: 24, 14: 30; *CO* 47: 333-34, 337.

[3] Commentary John 7: 16; *CO* 47: 169-70.

[4] Commentary John 8: 28; *CO* 47: 200.

[5] "Quia enim non poterat Christi maiestas in sua altitudine apprehendi, Dei virtus, quae in carne eius apparuit, ad illam altitudinem gradatim subvexit rudes et tardos hominum sensus. Nam quum totus esse noster voluerit, non mirum est si variis modus se nobis accommodet...." (Commentary John 11: 41; *CO* 47: 269.)

occasions when it was necessary for him to perform the office of teacher, his deity rested and was somehow concealed, that it might not hinder what belonged to him as Mediator."[1]

The most salient exception to this rule was the transfiguration. On that occasion Christ deliberately allowed his glory to be seen, but only in part and only by three of the disciples at that, as a testimony to the fact that when he would later become subject to death it would be of his own free will.[2]

As king also, Christ performed as teacher: the mighty wonder-worker was the teacher, and vice versa. It is essential, according to Calvin, to keep miracles and doctrine together. This is so because it aids in distinguishing false spirits from true ones. Here is an expression of the correlation Calvin maintains between the Word and the Spirit. The Word corresponds to Christ's doctrine, while the Spirit corresponds to the power displayed by the wonders Christ wrought. The testimony of the Holy Spirit is self-authenticating, yet if we are to guard against error there should be an unbroken connection between doctrine and signs.[3]

The bond between Word and Spirit, between doctrine and miracle, is seen in Calvin's appraisal that as Christ taught by his mouth he also inflamed his hearers inwardly by his Spirit.[4] It was Christ's ordering action, by his secret power, which made room for his doctrine, and which prepared the sphere in which his doctrine was to be

---

[1] Commentary Luke 19: 41; *CO* 45: 576.

[2] "Clarum enim est, nihilo fuisse difficilius Christo corpus suum a morte eximere quam ornare coelesti gloria. Docemur itaque morti fuisse obnoxium, quia voluit: crucifixum fuisse, quia se obtulit. Nam eadem illa caro, quae in cruce immolata in sepulcro iacuit, quum iam prius coelestis gloriae particeps fuisset, immunis esse potuit a morte et sepulcro. Quin etiam docemur, quamdiu accepta servi forma versatus est in mundo Christus, et sub carnis infirmitate latuit eius maiestas, nihil ei fuisse detractum, quia sponte se exinanivit: nunc autem resurrectio velum illud sustulit, quo virtus eius tecta ad tempus fuerat." (Commentary Matthew 17: 1ff. and parallel passages; *CO* 45: 485.)

[3] Commentary Matthew 24: 23; *CO* 45: 663.

[4] Commentary Luke 24: 32; *CO* 45: 809. It was the same Christ who was the minister of the external words and who penetrated the disciples' hearts to teach them by his secret power. (Commentary Luke 24: 45; *CO* 45: 817.) Calvin can also say that the risen Lord who formerly performed the office of teacher toward his disciples without, however, making much impact on them, subsequently taught them inwardly by "his Spirit" (which seems to be used in this context synonymously with "his secret power"). (*ibid.*; *CO* 45: 816.) This last raises a problem, for Calvin elsewhere says explicitly that when he taught, Christ initially inflamed his hearers by his Spirit; so that apparently his teaching ministry always bore this feature.

received or rejected.[1] This is not the same as saying the Spirit brought the heavenly doctrine before the Word arrived so that in coming the Word received assent. For even this would break too much the conjunction between the external Word and the inward, ordering activity of the secret power of Christ's Spirit.[2]

Christ's divinity is to be judged from his works, and Calvin is fond of John 5: 17 as an example of this. Christ was free and able to do the work of healing on the Sabbath because he was the Lord of the Sabbath: "My Father is working still, and I am working." This means that Christ had the power to heal and forgive, and to govern the world and sustain all things along with the Father.[3] Here once again appears Calvin's thought that Christ was able to effect these things because of the divine power united to but extending beyond the flesh.[4]

The reality of the divine efficacy beyond the flesh is a pronounced feature of Calvin's treatment of the ministry of Jesus. In some passages

---

[1] Cf. Commentary Matthew 26: 47; *CO* 45: 728. While he was speaking, the divine power of Christ inwardly tormented those who came to capture him in the garden.

[2] As Calvin sees it, this is the reason, according to the Johannine account, Christ first cleansed the temple even before beginning to teach. For it seems to be a disorderly and improper method to apply the hand for correcting vices without first applying the remedy of doctrine. But since the time was now at hand for him only to carry out the office given him by the Father, Christ wished to take possession of the temple as proof of his divine authority. And something extraordinary had to be done to awaken sluggish minds to what he would teach. Since he wished to restore the purity of doctrine, he had to show himself to be the Lord of the temple. Besides, Calvin adds, there was no other way to restore the spiritual use of sacrifices but by removing the abuse of them. (Commentary John 2: 12; *CO* 47: 43.)

[3] *Institutes* I, 13, 12 (already 1539); *OS* III, pp. 124-25. The miracles testify to Christ's divinity because they show he had power in himself; and because he was able to give power to his disciples to resuscitate the dead. (*Institutes* I, 13, 13; *OS* III, p. 125.) Christ was more eminent in miracles than others because he was the author of the miracles, both of those he did and of those others did. He employed his own name, his own authority, his own power in performing his miracles. (Commentary John 15: 24; *CO* 47: 352.)

[4] The demoniacs were drawn to Christ for example, by a secret exercise of his rulership. (Commentary Mark 5: 6; *CO* 45: 269.) It was the divine power hidden under the flesh that did the healing of the lame man. (Commentary John 5: 19; *CO* 47: 112.) It was by his Spirit that Christ drew to him the woman whom he knew he had cured and whom he willingly cured (despite his question: "Who touched me?"). (Commentary Matt. 9: 20; *CO* 45: 257.) Christ by his Spirit moved the events of men during his time on earth. The enlarged crowds present in Jerusalem the last week of Christ, beyond those usually on hand for such a feast, were drawn there by the secret instinct of the Spirit. (Commentary John 12: 12; *CO* 47: 281.)

Calvin employs this teaching even in such a way as to dwindle the necessity of Christ's bodily presence during his earthly ministry. Here the "extra Calvinisticum" provides unsteady and soft terrain for theological movement. Calvin can stress Christ's spiritual presence after the ascension; but it is something else again so to stress his spiritual presence even before the ascension that his physical proximity to his contemporaries becomes a matter of indifference.[1] Is the Word when accompanied by the bodily presence not more efficacious than when it is without the bodily presence?[2] Nonetheless, Calvin's teaching on this point instructs us encouragingly that the disciples of the first century had no particular advantage over us: Christ can be as mightily present with us by his Spirit as he was bodily present with them with his Spirit.[3]

---

[1] When Christ slept (according to the demands of human nature) "his divinity watched over him," Calvin says of the Matthew 8:23 episode. Yet the entire event was arranged by the secret providence of God. The disciples were rebuked because they attached too much importance to the bodily presence of their Master. They ought to have believed that the divinity of Christ would not be oppressed by carnal sleep and they ought to have had recourse to his divinity. They should have relied on his divine power and without so much alarm expected the assistance which they asked. (Commentary Matthew 8:23, 25; CO 45:264-65.) In the same way, Mary erred in saying "Lord, if you had been here our brother Lazarus would not have died": for if she had had proper faith, she would have been assured that Christ's efficacy did not depend on his bodily presence. "Neque enim Christi virtus, quae coelem et terram replebat, restringi ad corporalem eius praesentiam debuit." (Commentary John 11:32; CO 47:264. cf. Commentary John 11:21; CO 47:261.)

[2] Calvin says that Christ could just as well have healed Simon's mother-in-law by a movement of his will; but he found it advantageous to heal her by a touch of his hand as an outward sign. (Commentary Mark 1:29; CO 45:155.) By his word alone, Christ might have healed the leper, but the stretched out his hand as a sign of his condescension. (Commentary Matthew 8:3; CO 45:232.) He could have healed the man who was deaf and had a speech impediment by a single movement of his will, but he healed him by putting his hands on him as an advantageous outward sign. (Commentary Mark 7:32; CO 45:461-62.)

The centurion was praised because he was satisfied with the bare Word. He asked no bodily presence but believed that the Word possessed efficacy to cure his servant. "Atque hinc colligi potest generalis regula: quamvis salutem nostram Deus in carne Christi perfici voluerit, et sacramentis quotidie obsignet, eius tamen certitudinem ex verbo petendam esse." (Commentary Matthew 8:10; CO 45:237.) This is an illuminating conjunction of two uses of the term "the Word." It is used first as the promise spoken by Christ and heard as voice by the centurion; it is used second to mean again Christ's promise to be present, but as it comes to us in the Church. By contrast with the centurion, the ruler mentioned in Matthew 9:18 was to be criticized because he ascribed to Christ no power except through his touching the Person. (CO 45:256.)

[3] This is what Kierkegaard is also saying in a different way and context with his category of our contemporaneity with Christ.

The "extra Calvinisticum" influences Calvin's judgment of Christ's priestly office, which he esteems to be the principal office of Christ. This principal office may be briefly but clearly stated: in taking away the sin of the world by his death he reconciled men to God. Christ conferred other benefits on us indeed, but the main one, on which the others depend, is that by appeasing the wrath of God, he makes us to be reckoned just and pure. From this flow all the streams of blessing: by not imputing our sins God receives us into favor.[1]

Christ's human suffering, the suffering of an expiatory victim, is an essential part of his office as priest.[2] When Calvin says one of the reasons Christ suffered was to learn obedience,[3] he means in part that Christ had to learn the trials without which genuine obedience was not possible. In the Incarnation the Eternal Son put on real human feelings so that he might be merciful and therefore be a faithful high priest. Yet the Son of God had no need of experience to know the emotions of mercy. It was for us that he experienced this; we could not otherwise have been persuaded of his mercy. Since Christ never ceased to have dominion over all things he had the power not to be obedient. His temptation in the Garden of Gethsemane was all the greater than any temptation we know; for we do not have such dominion and our routes of escape are more limited. Our disobedience rests in our use of what power of escape we do have; Christ's obedience rested in his refusal to use the unlimited powers of escape at his disposal in order to take up what we have attempted to evade.[4]

---

[1] Commentary John 1:29; *CO* 47:25. As Calvin can say that Jesus Christ the Mediator was the ladder joining heaven and earth (Commentary Genesis 28:12; *CO* 23:390), so he can also apply the ladder figure to the cross. The cross was the ladder by which we ascend to heaven in such a way that since Christ is now ascended we ought to be led from the contemplation of the cross to heaven, that death and reparation of life may be found to agree. (Commentary Matthew 26:29; *CO* 45:709.) The cross is a splendid chariot of Christ. (Commentary Luke 23:16; *CO* 45:757.)

[2] "Victimam enim expiatricem fieri oportuit Dei filium, et peccati reatum sustinere, ut essemus iustitia Dei in illo." (Commentary Colossians 1:20; *CO* 52:88.)

[3] The ultimate reason for Christ's suffering was that he might be consecrated as priest for our salvation, whereas the proximate reason was that he might learn obedience. (Commentary Hebrews 5:7; *CO* 55:61-63.) This obedience involved real courage on the part of Christ, a genuine decision in which fear had to be overcome in favor of obedience. (Commentary John 13:3; *CO* 47:306.)

[4] Christ's sacrifice was voluntary. (Commentary John 12:12; *CO* 47:281.) Christ ministered in such a way that nothing was diminished from the majesty of his dominion. "Praeterea sic minister est Christus, ut nihil illi ex imperii maiestate

The humanity of the risen and ascended Lord

The "extra Calvinisticum" and its corollary that the efficacy of Christ's Spirit extends beyond Christ's flesh function to protect Calvin's assertion of the full humanity of Christ not only before the resurrection but also after it in Christ's risen and ascended state.[1]

The occasion for the intense Christological debate of the sixteenth and early seventeenth centuries was the nature of the humanity of the living Lord of the Church. More specifically, the question was about the manner in which Christ, the risen and ascended Lord, communes with us in the Lord's Supper: according to what kind of humanity and to which kind of bodily nature can Christ be present with his Church in the bread and wine? The issues were hotly discussed because the Reformers took seriously the Lordship of Christ over his Church and the character of the communion of the Head with his members. The two great interrelated issues—how can the bread and wine be the body and blood of Christ, and how are the two natures related in the One Person to enable the Real Presence—were facets of the larger question: what is the character of the Lord's communion with believers, his Lordship over the Church, and over the world?

The controlling concern for Calvin is how the efficacy and power of Christ's work and person can become real for us, so that we may be a part of his ordering and restoring work. It is by being joined in faith to Jesus Christ, the Lord of the Church and the world, that this happens. What safeguards our union with the risen Lord is fervently and carefully affirmed by Calvin. What threatens either the union (such as the making of Christ's presence in the Eucharist merely, or even overly, symbolic) or the Lordship (such as a Christology which in deifying Christ's humanity offers a Lord who is not the One who

---

decedat etiam in carne." (Commentary Hebrews 1:14; *CO* 55:20.) A voluntary subjection took nothing away from Christ's glory. "Ideo Christus considerare eum iubet, quid susceptae servi personae conveniat, quia voluntaria subiectio nihil derogat eius gloriae." (Commentary Matthew 3:14; *CO* 45:125.) Because he never ceased to be the Eternal Son of God, Christ's death was by his own free will. While the prophets predicted the death of Christ, says Calvin, Christ was sitting on the invisible throne of glory as the eternal wisdom of God; so he was liable to death only insofar as he submitted himself to it. (Commentary Matthew 17:3; *CO* 45:486.) cf. Commentary Matthew 17:1; *CO* 45:485, and Matthew 17:9; *CO* 45:490: ". . . etiam quo tempore exinanitus fuit, deitatem tamen suam illi integram stetisse, licet abscondita esset carnis velo."

[1] Dominicé's neglect to treat the humanity of the ascended Lord is remarkable. Unlike Dominicé, Calvin does not imply that the humanity of Jesus ends with the completion of his obedience unto death.

suffered on the cross and is not Lord of our undeified flesh) is rejected with patience and impatience, theological calm and polemic heat. "Ordering communion with Christ": this is what Calvin is intent above all on preserving. The dynamics of this communion, through which the Lord orders our lives, in word and sacrament but beyond them as well, is the movement of the Holy Spirit.

The reason Christ's ascended humanity is so important is that since the Incarnation we are always (I Corinthians 15:28 possibly excepted) related to God only through that same Person. Christ's resurrection and ascension do not mean his humanity was deified, somehow relinquishing that which made it human. Rather, by the resurrection Christ's victory was sealed. In the ascension, Christ withdrew his bodily presence that he might be present with the faithful in a far richer way, through the Holy Spirit; and by the ascension Christ, clothed with our flesh, ascended to the position of government and control over all things. The *sursum corda*, as Calvin understands it, joins these facts of salvation: by being bound to the exalted Christ through the Holy Spirit, we in our new humanity are also exalted alongside Christ [1] to a new position of power in an ordered creation.

The risen humanity. Calvin's interpretation of Christ's post-resurrection appearances in his body is striking in his emphasis on the concrete reality and locality of Christ's humanity. The men on the road to Emmaus failed to recognize him not because the figure of his body had changed. He was as he always had been; but "the eyes of the beholders were restrained," as Luke says.[2] On the other hand, the men recognized him when he broke bread because their eyes were opened.[3]

Even more pointed is Calvin's interpretation of Christ's appearance in the midst of his disciples after the doors were shut in the house

---

[1] Cf. Commentary John 14:2; *CO* 47:322. Christ's ascension here is not private, to enable him to dwell in heaven alone; his members are beneficiaries of that ascension.

[2] Commentary Luke 24:16: *CO* 45:803.

[3] This teaches, says Calvin:

". . . nullam fuisse in Christo metamorphosin, ut formarum varietate hominum oculos luserit (sicuti Proteum suum fingent poetae), sed videntium oculos potius errasse, quia velati essent. Sicuti paulo post non evanuit ab iisdem oculis, quia per se invisibile fuerit eius corpus, sed quia Deo vigorem suum subtrahente obtusa fuit eorum acies." (Commentary Luke 24:31; *CO* 45:809.)

where they had taken refuge after the crucifixion. Calvin does not even mention that this might refer to Christ's capacity for passing through closed doors because of the nature of his glorified humanity. He says simply that the incident took place late at night when doors are closed, and it was at this time that Christ came to the disciples.[1] Christ called the disciples to verify by their senses that a body and not a shadow was before them. He distinguished bodily man from spirit, as if to say: "Sight and touch will prove me to be the real man who formerly moved about with you: because I am still clothed with that flesh which was crucified and which bears the marks of the crucifixion."[2] Since his body was palpable it differed from spirit, and even today this distinction between flesh and spirit holds good; from the words of Christ, it is necessary to uphold it as perpetual.[3]

This passage from Luke argues against the doctrines of transubstantiation and the bodily ubiquity of Christ. One can claim that it does not apply to Christ's ascended state since he still bears wounds here but in heaven must exist whole and unhurt. But, says Calvin, it is not a matter of what Christ's condition was on appearing, but of what he testified to regarding the true nature of his flesh.[4]

The ascended humanity. Calvin believes that Christ's humanity did not change, nor was it relinquished by his ascension. Christ's ascension depended precisely on the perpetual union between his divine nature and his human nature. For Christ was not exalted as God: he had never ceased as God to occupy the position of dominion over all. He was exalted according to his manifestation in the flesh.[5]

Christ's humanity is real and is the same as he possessed on earth, the only difference being that his flesh no longer bears with it the

---

[1] Commentary Luke 24: 36; *CO* 45: 811.

[2] Commentary Luke 24: 39; *CO* 45: 812-13.

[3] "Ergo hodie quoque discrimen istud carnis a spiritu manere necesse est, quod perpetuum esse ex Christi verbis statuere licet." (*ibid.*; *CO* 45: 813.)

[4] "... facile discutitur hoc cavillum, neque enim hoc tantum agitur, quali habitu apparuerit Christus, sed quid testetur de vera carnis suae natura." (*ibid.*)

[5] *Institutes* II, 13, 2. cf. also:

"*Dies carnis*, nemini dubium est hic accipi pro praesenti vita. Unde sequitur, carnis nomine non substantiam notari, sed qualitatem. Quemadmodum 1. Corinth. cap. 15, 50, caro et sanguis regnum Dei non possidebunt. Desipiunt ergo fanatici homines qui nunc Christum somniant carne sua exutum, quia dicatur superasse dies carnis. Aliud enim est, esse verum hominem, tam etsi beata immortalitate praeditum: aliud esse obnoxium humanis aerumnis et infirmitatibus quas sustinuit quamdiu in mundo versatus est, nunc vero in coelum receptus deposuit." (Commentary Hebrews 5: 7; *CO* 55: 61.)

bondage of human hardship and weakness, and apparently [1] it is not touched, at least in the same way as before, by the affections.[2] The ascension means that (1) Christ's bodily presence really left us, and (2) he now fills all things by his virtue and his grace, and extends the power of his empire over the whole world.[3]

Here is exactly the concern operative in the doctrine of the "extra Calvinisticum": the reality of the efficacy and power of the Son's working also beyond the flesh.[4] To say that Christ's power to govern is everywhere diffused does not mean that Christ is ubiquitous in his human nature.[5]

When it comes to the geography involved in the ascension, Calvin is anxious to ward off certain ideas, and he is satisfied with a negative statement regarding the exact locale of the ascended Christ. In ascending, Christ went beyond the created world.[6] The ascension was a movement from one place to another,[7] but saying that Christ ascended

---

[1] According to the Commentary on Matthew 9: 36; *CO* 45: 262.

[2] "Etsi autem nunc in coelum receptus non eosdem retinet affectus, quibus obnoxius esse voluit in hac mortali vita, curam tamen ecclesiae suae non abiecit, quin respiciat palantes suas oves, imo gregem suum crudeliter a lupis fugatum et discerptum colligat." (*ibid.*)

[3] "Ergo Christi in coelos ascensu praesentiam carnis sic nobis ablatam esse dicimus, ut virtute gratiaque sua omnia impleat, ut vim sui imperii extendat per totum orbem, nec solum ut praesenti auxilio nos tueatur, sed etiam ut vere in nobis habitet, imo carne sua et sanguine animas nostras pascat." (*Ultima Admon. ad Westph.*; *CO* 9: 197.)

[4] "Alia enim ratio est corporis, quod in coelum receptum est: alia virtutis, quae ubique est diffusa." (*Genevan Catechism* [1545]; *CO* 6: 36.) It is by his power which is everywhere diffused that Christ is present with us. And it is by this power that he governs all things. For, being seated at the right hand of the Father, to him is given the dominion of heaven and earth that he might govern all things. (*ibid.*) "To go to the Father" (John 16: 5) is nothing else than reception into the heavenly glory in order to possess the highest governance. (*CO* 47: 357.) cf. also Commentary John 16: 28; *CO* 47: 372. The ascended Christ governs the whole world, but especially the pious. (Commentary Mark 16: 19; *CO* 45: 828.) According to Calvin, Stephen saw Christ reigning in that very flesh in which he had been abased. (Commentary Acts 7: 56; *CO* 48: 168.)

[5] "Nam quod certo loco continetur, id non obstat, quin virtutem suam exserat per totum mundum. Quare si illum gratiae suae efficacia sentire praesentem cupimus, in coelo quaerendus est: quemadmodum se illinc patefecit Stephano." (*ibid.*) As to his being contained in a place, Calvin goes on, "Fateor quidem, proprie loquendo, hoc est philosophia, nullum supra coelos esse locum. Sed hoc mihi satis est, perversum esse delirium, Christum alibi quam in coelo, et supra mundi elementa, locare." (*ibid.*; *CO* 48: 168-69.)

[6] He must not be imagined as dwelling among the spheres in order to count the stars. (Commentary Ephesians 4: 10; *CO* 51: 195.)

[7] *Institutes* IV, 17, 27.

to a place beyond the world implies only that the Kingdom of God cannot be conceived in other than ordinary terms.[1] One thing is clear: when Christ is placed above the heavens or in the heavens, all that surrounds the earth, all that lies beneath the sun and stars and beneath the whole frame of the visible world, is excluded.[2]

---

[1] Commentary Ephesians 4: 10; *CO* 51: 195.

[2] Christ, superior to all elements, dwells beyond the world, not in a hut somewhere among the planets. (*Secunda Defensio contra Westphalum*; *CO* 9: 79.) The "right hand of God" is everywhere, so that the Kingdom of Christ extends everywhere. (Commentary Ephesians 1: 20; *CO* 51: 158.) The "all things" of "fills all things" applies properly to the Church, his body. (Commentary Ephesians 1: 23; *CO* 51: 160.)

Ronald S. Wallace has interpreted Calvin as teaching that the whole humanity of Christ, while remaining in heaven, yet exerts its virtue on earth and can even be said to be active on earth. (*Calvin's Doctrine of the Word and Sacrament* [Edinburgh: Oliver and Boyd, 1953], pp. 231-233.) Wallace's interpretation merits brief re-examination.

1. He discusses Calvin's use of the *totus-totum* distinction, and he rightly links this distinction to Lombard and Augustine. He seems, however, to take *totus* as standing for the whole humanity rather than for the whole Christ, as Calvin does (*supra*, p. 31ff.).

2. Wallace cites Calvin's explanation of the *communicatio idiomatum* in the *Institutes* II, 14, 2 and seems to take it for granted that the crucial *dabat* (". . . propter duplicis naturae unionem alteri dabat quod erat alterius") means that the human nature has essentially communicated to it the properties of the divine nature.

3. From Calvin's *Final Admonition to Westphal*, Wallace cites the place where Calvin says:

"I confess indeed that we may not [*sane* omitted in translation] conceive the Son of God in any other way than as clothed with flesh. But this did not prevent Him, while filling heaven and earth with His divine essence, from wearing His flesh in the womb of His mother, on the cross, in the sepulchre. Though then Son of God He was, nevertheless man in heaven as well as on earth." (p. 232.) The difficulty with Wallace's interpretation appears only with this last sentence, a translation of admittedly ambiguous Latin: "Tum quoque Dei filius non minus in coelo quam in terra homo fuit." (*CO* 9: 171) The context, however, suggests it should be translated instead: "Indeed then he was not less Son of God in heaven than he was man on earth"; because Calvin goes on immediately to say, "If anyone should infer from this that his flesh was then in heaven, he absurdly confuses all things by reasoning and finally reaches the point that, snatching away the nature of flesh from Christ, he also robs him of his office of Redeemer." ("Si quis tamen inde inferat carnem eius tunc in coelo fuisse, insulse ratiocinando omnia confundet: ac tandem eo perveniet, ut Christo eripiens carnis naturam simul eum spoliet redemptoris officio." (*CO* 9: 171.)

4. Wallace refers also to a passage from Calvin's 1561 work against Heshusius. It seems to escape Wallace's notice that Calvin is arguing rhetorically here; he is saying in effect: if we adopt Heshusius' position we are led into the absurdity of saying that independently of the use of the Supper, the flesh of Christ dwells essentially in believers because they possess the presence of his deity. This is

just the opposite from what Wallace's translation leads one to believe. Because the context is so crucial, the following translation has on the left side, in brackets, the parts omitted by Wallace which restore the sense of the passage. On the right side is Wallace's translation (p. 231). Calvin is saying that Heshusius:

["... means the human nature of Christ is not ubiquitous or in many places as is the divine nature. Here I ask, since Christ's dwelling in the faithful is perpetual how will he deny that Christ dwells bodily regardless of the celebration of the Supper? For most clearly it seems to me we should reason thus: If]

"It is unlawful to dissever the flesh of Christ from His divinity. Wherever the divinity dwells, the flesh also dwells corporeally. But the deity of Christ always dwells in believers as well in life as in death; therefore so dwells the flesh ...

["Let Heshusius resolve this 'antistrophon' if he can and I will gladly handle the rest.]

"I again repeat, as the divine majesty and essence of Christ fills heaven and earth, and this is extended to the flesh; therefore independently of the use of the Supper, the flesh of Christ dwells essentially in believers, because they possess the presence of His deity."

["Now let him shout that those who do not attribute the same qualities to each nature tear asunder the indivisible person of Christ. For I submit this: that it follows that the substance of the flesh is by no means more to be found in the bread than in the sole power of faith."]

("... sed tamen vult humanam Christi naturam non minus ubique vel pluribus locis esse quam divinam. Hic quaero, quum perpetua sit habitatio Christi in fidelibus, cur neget extra coenae usum habitare ipsum corporaliter. Ego enim optime colligere mihi videor: Si nefas est distrahere carnem Christi a divinitate, ubicunque habitat divinitas, etiam corporaliter habitat caro. Atqui semper tam in vita quam in morte habitat in fidelibus Christi deitas: ergo etiam caro. Diluat hoc antistrophon, si potest, Heshusius, et reliqua facile expediam. Iterum repeto: Quia coelum et terram implet divina Christi maiestas et essentia, id ad carnem extenditur: ergo extra coenae usum caro Christi in fidelibus essentialiter habitat, quia potiuntur deitatis praesentia. Clamet nunc eos divellere indivisibilem Christi personam, qui non easdem utrique naturae qualitates attribuunt. Nam hoc posito, sequetur nihilo magis reperiri sub pane carnis substantiam, quam in sola virtute fidei.") (*De vera participatione Christi in Coena*; *CO* 9: 509.)

This ascension is not the exalted position which Christ, as Eternal Son of God, never ceased to occupy. Just as the *exinanitio* consisted in the voluntary subjection of the Son to take on our condition yet without relinquishing his place of dominion, so the ascension was the exaltation not of Christ as Son of God but as he was manifested in the flesh. Just as he was made low not for his sake but for ours (he did not have to earn the position of dominion), so he was exalted on account of his body by which he entered the sanctuary bearing what is ours.[1] God the Father appointed Christ "haeredem omnium, per quem etiam saecula condidit" (Hebrews 1: 2) only according to his being manifested in the flesh, not according to his eternal divinity.[2]

The humanity when God is all in all. Calvin takes with full seriousness I Corinthians 15: 28, in which Paul says Christ will deliver up the Kingdom to the Father and God shall then be all in all. He acknowledges that the difficulty of this passage stems from an apparent conflict between it and the doctrine of the eternity of Christ's reign (II Peter 1: 11). Calvin begins his interpretation with a reminder that all power was handed over by the Father to Christ inasmuch as he was manifested in the flesh.[3] God, in doing so, however, never ceased to be the Ruler: "Deum quidem agnoscimus rectorem, sed in facie hominis

---

Wallace, usually quite careful in his fine study, is not at all justified, on the basis of these passages, in drawing the conclusion that, "It is quite obvious from such passages that Calvin would not have much difficulty in arguing further that Christ can be man on earth, even though His manhood is now confined in its entirety to heaven." (p. 232.) What is obvious, on the contrary, is that for Calvin the manhood of Christ, insofar as the flesh is its most obvious feature, remains in heaven after the ascension, and until his return in judgment; but that the One Person, the one Mediator, the *Deus manifestatus in carne*, is present with us by his divine essence and by virtue of his Spirit. Though Christ remains bodily absent from us, yet we are properly said to be given life by his flesh because he is present with us through his divine energy which is everywhere diffused. "For when by the secret grace of the Spirit he penetrates to us, it is not necessary, as we said elsewhere, that he himself descend corporeally." (*Secunda Defensio contra Westphalum*; *CO* 9: 76.)

[1] Commentary Hebrews 9: 11; *CO* 55: 109-10.

[2] Commentary Hebrews 1: 2; *CO* 55: 11. Did not Christ fill all things before his ascension? Calvin replies:

"Certe sua divinitate, fateor: sed virtutem sui spiritus non ita exserebat, nec in ea suam praesentiam exhibebat, sicut adita regni possessione, Johan. 7, 39. Nondum spiritus datus erat, quia Iesus nondum erat glorificatus. Et 16, 7, Expedit vobis ut vadam. Nisi enim abiero, paracletus non veniet. Denique sicut tunc coepit sedere ad dexteram patris, coepit etiam implere omnia." (Commentary Ephesians 4: 10; *CO* 51: 195-96.)

[3] Commentary I Corinthians 15: 27; *CO* 49: 549.

Christi."[1] At the very end, though, Christ will return the Kingdom which he received, so that we may cling completely to God.[2]

Does this not imply that the Eternal Son did not always have dominion over all things, that he had that dominion only by virtue of his having become incarnate and glorified? And finally does it not imply that we shall at the end be united to God the Father directly and not through the Eternal Son?

No; Christ's being given all dominion according to his manifestation in the flesh means for Calvin only that the rulership which eternally belongs to the Eternal Son and which was extended for a while (the period between the ascension and the end) to the humanity he assumed, will again be restricted to him as Eternal Son, not that as Eternal Son he ever ceased or ever will cease to have dominion over all things.

> But in this way he will not abdicate his reign but will transfer it in some way from his humanity to his glorious divinity, because then there will appear a means of approach from which our weakness now keeps us back. In this way, therefore, will he be subjected to the Father: because, when the veil has been removed we will see God openly reigning in his majesty; and no longer will the humanity of Christ hold us back from a nearer vision of God. [3]

This last sentence recalls the fact that the flesh of Christ is still necessary, until the final things mentioned in I Corinthians 15: 27-28, not only to draw us near to God, but to prevent us from being overwhelmed and utterly destroyed by his majesty. Sin holds us back from a closer vision of God, but so also does our creaturely weakness before the Creator's majesty. In this final stage we will not be absorbed into the deity, nor will there cease to be a distinction between the Persons. That is, τὰ πάντα will not be folded back up into the Godhead, nor, of course, will the unity and distinction of the Persons of the Godhead cease to be.[4]

---

[1] *Ibid.*

[2] *Ibid.*

[3] "Neque hoc modo regnum a se abdicabit, sed ab humanitate sua ad gloriosam divinitatem quodammodo traducet: quia tunc patebit accessus, quo nunc infirmitas nostra nos arcet. Sic ergo Christus subiicietur patri: quia tunc remoto velo palam cernemus Deum in sua maiestate regnantem: neque amplius media erit Christi humanitas quae nos ab ulteriore Dei conspectu cohibeat." (Commentary I Corinthians 15: 27; *CO* 49: 549.)

[4] Calvin introduces this I Corinthians 15: 27-28 passage to explain in part what Christ meant when he said, "The Father is greater than I." (John 14: 28) "Regnat certe Christus non in humana tantum natura, sed quatenus Deus est manifestatus in carne. Quomodo igitur regnum exuet? nempe quia divinitas,

It is noteworthy that Calvin never says, even in describing the meaning of this final state, that Christ will *relinquish* his humanity: he says only that Christ will tranfer his reign from his humanity to his divinity. One may think this entails the virtual surrender of the humanity,[1] since the humanity of Christ has then no further soteriological function, and since Calvin has all along judged the nature of Christ's Person by the soteriological criterion. But Calvin himself does not choose to follow this logic, any more than he chooses to say that our humanity, including our spiritual bodies, will be abandoned at the end. Indeed, our being in proper order again is the antithesis of losing our humanity: restored and perfected humanity is the condition for right relation to God. Man will remain man; he will not become God.[2]

CONCLUSION

The "extra Calvinisticum" is not an exclusive mark distinguishing the Christology of Calvin from other Christologies of the one Catholic Church; indeed, to achieve a distinctive Christology was not exactly Calvin's fondest wish! Rather, the doctrine sustains the correct Catholic interpretations of the Biblical witness to Christ, while leaving them stamped from the special pressure to which Calvin subjects them. His impress is that he keeps in the foreground the assertion that the Incarnation was not the Eternal Son's abdication of his universal empire but the reassertion of that empire over rebellious creation. This continuity of gracious order over creaturely attempts at discontinuity depends on the identity of the Redeeming Mediator in the flesh with the Mediator who is the Eternal Son of God by whom, and with whose Spirit, all things were created according to

---

quae nunc in sola Christi facie cernitur, tunc palam in se conspicua erit." (Commentary John 14: 28; *CO* 47: 336.) Christ indeed pointed out to the disciples that their highest goal ought to be to go to the Father: "Gaudendum, inquit, erat, quod redeam ad patrem, quia haec ultima est meta, ad quam tendere vos oportet." (*ibid.*) But this comparison between the Father and himself was made not in reference to his divinity but to his manifestation in the flesh.

[1] "Notons qu'il arrive à Calvin d'enseigner qu'après le Jugement dernier le Christ céleste *déposera* en quelque sorte *son humanité*, afin de nous apparaître dans toute la pureté de sa divinité." (Ganoczy, *op. cit.*, p. 91, n. 133.)

[2] Nor, strictly speaking, will he ever become an angel. He will become like the angels. They are spiritual and incorporeal creatures who may, by exception, take on the form of men, but it is not their created nature to do so. Man is a spiritual and corporeal creature, materially corporeal in this world and spiritually corporeal in the next, who may, by exception, exist without the body.

the Father's will. Just as he uses "Mediator" in this twofold sense, Calvin also takes "Christ" to refer both to the Eternal Word and to Jesus.

Contrary to common opinion, the "extra Calvinisticum" is not governed by the philosophical principle *finitum non capax infiniti*, but by imagery and language drawn from political life. Further, while it does encourage Calvin's occasional minimization of man's need for Christ's bodily presence even before the resurrection and ascension, it surely does not shake loose the Church's confession of the One Person. The fact is that the "extra Calvinisticum" is a medium for professing the unity of the person of Jesus Christ without displacing mystery with speculation, and it is a way of accounting for the freedom of Christ's obedience which is his redemptive work.

CHAPTER FOUR

THE SO-CALLED EXTRA CALVINISTICUM AND
CALVIN'S DOCTRINE OF THE KNOWLEDGE OF GOD

THE PROBLEM OF NATURAL THEOLOGY
IN THE INTERPRETATION OF CALVIN

To what extent is Calvin's knowledge of God, and therefore his
theology, grounded upon the unique character of God's revelation
in the Incarnation? This is the question which the doctrine of the
"extra Calvinisticum" raises for the problem of the knowledge of
God in Calvin's thought. The difficulty is this: if the "extra Calvinisticum" involves an implicit distinction between the *logos ensarkos* and
the *logos asarkos*, is not God's full revelation of himself exclusively in
Jesus Christ jeopardized, and is not the way opened to a natural
theology alongside and complementary to revealed theology? [1]

The validity and limitations of the Barth-Brunner framework of investigation

The problem of the knowledge of God in Calvin has elicited a
remarkable amount of careful attention in recent Calvin studies. The
special interest in this area has been a normal consequence of the
renowned debate between Karl Barth and Emil Brunner about natural
theology. [2] The systematic-theological discussion involved extensive
historical and theological judgments. Both parties were caught in a
certain amount of semantic ambiguity, [3] but in their historical critiques,

---

[1] See judgments of Barth and Niesel, *supra*, pp. 2-3, van Buren, *supra*, p. 3,
and Schweizer, *supra*, p. 2, n. 2.

[2] Emil Brunner, *Natur und Gnade* (4th and 5th ed.; Zürich: Zwingli Verlag,
n.d.); Karl Barth, *Nein! Antwort an Emil Brunner*, Theologische Existenz heute,
Heft 14 (München: Chr. Kaiser Verlag, 1934). Brunner's 1935 version is an
expansion of the original 1934 pamphlet which drew Barth's response.

[3] Brunner accused Barth of misunderstanding him; yet Brunner fostered
misunderstanding by using the term "Wortfähigkeit" (p. 11) (which could mean
either man's capacity for the Word or man's power of speech), by distinguishing
between the material and the formal image of God in man (pp. 10-11), and by
insisting on the term "Ergänzung" (p. 25) (which implied not only that nature
is a complementary source of our knowledge of God but that the knowledge
of God we have from Christ complements what we know of God from nature).
Barth, for his part, did not help matters by refusing to treat the very question
of natural theology as anything but an abyss to be side-stepped, and an abstract

it must be said that while Brunner was a more polite disputant, Barth was usually more accurate and certainly more vivid.[1] When it came to the specific question of interpreting Calvin on the knowledge of God, Brunner as well as Barth had a valid point. Barth, seeing the "deutschen Christen" fortifying themselves with an appeal to natural theology,[2] knew it was not time for a return to a "right" natural theology.[3] He concentrated on those passages in which Calvin stresses the Christological character of our knowledge of God. By "natural theology" Barth meant a systematic discourse about God based on something other than revelation in Jesus Christ, and this he did not find in Calvin. Brunner, with as much political ineptitude as missionary concern, chose the years following 1929 to insist that of course the Christian message can be heard by man only if some natural capacity for the Word remained in him after the Fall. He concentrated on those passages in which Calvin suggests the possibility of a natural theology. By "natural theology" Brunner seemed usually to mean God's objective revelation of himself in nature, not the subjective appropriation received through Christ in Scripture. Barth understood Calvin's *duplex cognitio Dei* to be the knowledge of God derived from nature and through Christ.[4] Brunner spoke of the same twofold knowledge of God but did not identify it as Calvin's *duplex cognitio Dei*.[5]

This debate constituted a watershed on either side of which subsequent contributions tended to fall.[6] What remain the two best

---

speculation which is not the Christian theologian's business. As he put it, rejection of natural theology is not part of the Creed, but it is a hermeneutical rule forced on the exegetical theologian by the Creed itself and by revelation himself. (pp. 11-12.)

[1] Brunner was roundly called to task by Barth for his sweeping characterization of Roman Catholic natural theology.

[2] *Op. cit.*, pp. 8-9.

[3] *Ibid.*, p. 7.

[4] *Ibid.*, pp. 41-42.

[5] *Op. cit.*, pp. 12-14.

[6] Peter Barth, taking up his brother's part, and with careful documentation, made it quite clear that for Calvin God is known in a saving way from nature only when he is known first through Christ witnessed to in Scripture. (*Das Problem der natürlichen Theologie bei Calvin*, Theologische Existenz heute, Heft 18 [München: Chr. Kaiser Verlag, 1935], pp. 25-26.) He objected that Brunner used "natural theology" to mean a theology of the first article of the Creed (p. 4) and rejected Brunner's use of the term "Ergänzung" (p. 18). Gunter Gloede, on the other hand, took up Brunner's side, attempting, not always successfully, to mean by "Calvin's natural theology" what Calvin says we know of God from nature seen through the spectacles of Scripture. (*Theologia Naturalis bei Calvin* [Stuttgart: Kohlhammer, 1935], pp. 10ff.) Pierre Maury's brief but admirably

studies of Calvin's doctrine of the knowledge of God, Edward A. Dowey, Jr.'s *The Knowledge of God in Calvin's Theology*,[1] and T. H. L. Parker's *Calvin's Doctrine of the Knowledge of God*,[2] also reflect the division established by the Barth-Brunner debates. These two Calvin scholars may not be called Brunnerian and Barthian, but certainly in their interpretations of Calvin one is more receptive to the insights of Brunner and the other to those of Barth. Dowey argues that the structure of Calvin's *Institutes* conforms to Calvin's conception of the *duplex cognitio Dei*, according to which the *duplex cognitio* is not the one supplied by nature on the one hand and revelation on the other but is supplied by our knowledge of God the Redeemer, known only through the Scriptures, and of God the Creator, known through Scriptures and the world.[3] Parker does not think that the *Institutes* is patterned after this *duplex cognitio* scheme, but rather that the *duplex cognitio* which the *Institutes* reflects is the knowledge of God and of ourselves. He feels that although Calvin is sometimes guilty of not making Christ the starting point of all theology, he is not a natural theologian with an apologetic program.[4]

It is a vain hope to want to elude entirely the framework of the Barth-Brunner debate. The issues there raised cannot ultimately be

---

clear treatment of the problem demonstrated the tenuousness of speaking about a natural theology in Calvin, since for Calvin God's revelation in nature becomes appropriated only when the Christian has confronted God in Scripture; only Jesus Christ himself, and not even the most zealous missionaries, can prepare rebellious humanity to receive the Word. ("La Théologie naturelle chez Calvin," *Bulletin de la Société de l'Histoire du Protestantisme Français*, LXXXIV [Avril-Juin, 1935], pp. 267-279.

[1] *Op. cit.*

[2] 2nd. ed.; Grand Rapids: Wm. B. Eerdmans, 1959 [first publ., 1952].

[3] Although Dowey's conclusion about the structure of the *Institutes* is not shared by this present discussion, his creative treatment of the issues has been useful.

[4] Parker attends more closely to the Trinitarian implications of Calvin's thought than Dowey does, but he still does not see how thoroughly it informs Calvin's doctrine of the knowledge of God. He correctly demures from Dowey's view of the structure of the *Institutes*, but his study, though excellent, is less detailed than Dowey's. Parker's worry about an alliance between natural theology and a misconstrued apologetic task of theology applies less to Dowey than to the work of Kenneth S. Kantzer, whose subject is the knowledge of God the Creator in what he calls the apologetic discourses of the *Institutes* (*Calvin's Theory of the Knowledge of God and the Word of God*, Ph. D. thesis, Harvard University, 1950, pp. 26, 51). Kantzer treats the knowledge of God the Creator without including the knowledge of God the Redeemer (pp. 26-27), so that no Christological content is even indicated for Calvin's doctrine of common grace (pp. 313-344).

reduced to semantics,[1] nor have they been fully digested or resolved by contemporary theology. Calvin's answers to the questions put to him in that cadre may after all have had a salutory effect on the present-day Church. However, because his thought is inevitably colored when it is required to respond precisely to questions asked in any epoch, an endeavor must be made to enter a new stage of inquiry.

The place of the "extra Calvinisticum" in further research into Calvin's doctrine of the knowledge of God

Part of such a movement beyond the Barth-Brunner framework is to admit that the question is no longer: "Does Calvin teach a natural revelation and hold that there is a natural knowledge of God?"; it is rather: "In what senses does Calvin speak of the knowledge of God and what kind of natural revelation does he teach?" For it is clear that Calvin teaches a natural revelation in a certain sense, and it is equally clear that in another sense he teaches that our knowledge of God is limited to what we have through Christ.

This chapter undertakes to discern the variety of ways in which Calvin expounds both positions, and to see how, if at all, the diverse teachings are systematically related in his thought. This discloses that the doctrine of the "extra Calvinisticum" lies close to the heart of the strengths and the ambiguities inherent in Calvin's doctrine of the knowledge of God.[2]

The "extra Calvinisticum" functions in Calvin's doctrine of the knowledge of God to bind closely together the two aspects of the *duplex cognitio Dei* (*cognitio Dei creatoris et redemptoris*), to emphasize the basic unity of the act of knowing in this twofold fashion, and above all to emphasize the unity of the God thus known. More briefly put, it marks the Trinitarian character of our knowledge of God. It does so by helping Calvin to insist on the Christological character of our knowledge of God without either making the Father and the Spirit subordinate in revelation or sacrificing the decisive role which the revelation of God in the flesh has for Christian theology. In this way

---

[1] Even after the necessary task of semantic criticism has been helpfully accomplished by Dowey. (*op. cit.*, p. 247ff.)

[2] It cannot be claimed that an analysis of the function of the "extra Calvinisticum" will escape the distorting impact which is an inevitable part of every hermeneutical act, no matter how objective the interpreter may try to be. But what such an analysis will do is to call attention to one permanent feature of Calvin's thought, the neglect of which has given a somewhat more twisted view of Calvin's doctrine of the knowledge of God than is necessary.

it serves as a constant reminder that creation, redemption, and sanctification are the interpenetrating spheres forming the context which is presupposed by the Church's knowledge and service of God.

THE KNOWLEDGE OF GOD ONLY THROUGH CHRIST

A repeated affirmation of Calvin's is that we know God only through Christ.[1] Those who conceive the naked majesty of God outside of Christ (*extra Christum*) have an idol instead of God.[2]

Superfluous and ungrateful character of all "theologia extra Christum"

Calvin is not saying merely that there is no knowledge of God apart from Christ. His Christological accent is rather that since God has fully revealed himself in Jesus Christ it is unnecessary or ungrateful to seek him elsewhere. This is different from saying that God does not reveal himself elsewhere. Whether or not God reveals himself outside of Christ is of secondary, because of abstract, importance to Calvin; the point is that God has revealed himself fully in Christ and that is all men need for salvation and the enjoyment of the blessings of God. When Christ said he is "the Way", it amounted to an assertion that whoever obtains Christ wants nothing and whoever is not satisfied with Christ alone strives for something beyond perfection.[3] Men who acknowledge that the happiness of man lies in God alone go wrong if they go on to seek him elsewhere than in Christ and in so seeking tear him, as it were, from his true and solid divinity.

---

[1] God is not to be sought in his unsearchable height but to be known insofar as he manifests himself in Christ. (Commentary II Corinthians 4: 6; *CO* 50: 53.) Commenting on Hebrews 1: 3, where it is said that Christ is the brightness of the glory of the Father, Calvin says what is meant is that the glory of the Father is invisible until it shines forth in Christ. The intent in that verse is not so much to show what likeness the Father has to the Son as to build up our faith: "... ut discamus, non aliter Deum nobis patefieri quam in Christo. Tam enim in Dei essentia immensus est fulgor, ut oculos nostros perstringat donec irradiet nos in Christo. Unde sequitur, nos caecutire ad lucem Dei, nisi in Christo nobis affulgeat. Haec vere utilis est philosophia, ex serio fidei sensu et experimento discere Christi excellentiam." (*CO* 55: 12.) God is known alone in Christ in the sense that only in him did God, who had remained invisible before, become visible. "Cognitio enim Dei ianua est, qua in bonorum omnium fruitionem ingredimur. Ergo quum se Deus nobis per solum Christum patefaciat, hinc etiam consequitur, omnia a Christo petenda esse." (Commentary John 1: 18; *CO* 47: 19.)

[2] Commentary I Peter 1: 3; *CO* 55: 210.

[3] Commentary John 14: 6; *CO* 47: 324.

all *theologia extra Christum* is not only confused and empty but also inane, false, and spurious. For, even if the philosophers sometimes make excellent sounds, still they have only that which is passing and mixed up with perverse and erroneous things."[1] To be valid, Law and antiquity must be shown to witness to Christ. That Christ is the one door means that the Law has authenticity as preparation for the Gospel and as such is not in opposition to it, and that apart from Christ there is only destruction and horrible confusion.[2]

This concentration on the unnecessary, ungrateful character of seeking a knowledge of God outside Christ appears in an interesting combination in Calvin's commentary on the second chapter of Colossians. Since God is found entirely in Christ, those who seek him elsewhere desire something more than God[3]. They who are not satisfied with Christ alone detract from the glory of God by desiring something above his perfection, and are ungrateful because they seek elsewhere what they already have in Christ.[4]

That God is known only through Christ in this sense applies not only to the Church of the New Covenant but to all men since the Fall. The men and women of the Old Testament knew God only through Christ, as the one to whose future manifestation they looked forward but also as the eternal Word through whom God revealed himself in their own times. It is in this sense that God was never known by God cannot be possessed in any other way than in Christ. "Wherefore

---

[1] "Summa porro huius sententiae est, quisquis potitur Christo, nihil illi deesse: ideoque ultra ultimam perfectionem eniti, quisquis eo uno contentus non est." (*ibid.*) "Quare omnis extra Christum theologia non modo confusa est ac inanis, sed etiam delira, fallax et adulterina. Nam etsi philosophis praeclarae interdum voces effluant, nihil tamen habent nisi evanidum et perversis etiam erroribus implicitum." (*ibid.*; *CO* 47: 324-25.)

[2] "In summa, testatur Christus doctrinas omnes, quibus ab eo mundus abductus fuerat, totidem fuisse mortiferas pestes, quia extra ipsum nonnisi exitialis et horrenda sit dissipatio." (Commentary John 10: 8; *CO* 47: 238.) All who leave Christ and, like the giants, attempt to rise to heaven, are without a right knowledge of God (*recta Dei notitia*), since he is the image of the Father. (Commentary John 8: 19; *CO* 47: 195.)

[3] "Porro quum dicit, plenitudinem deitatis habitare in Christo, nihil aliud sibi vult quam totum Deum in ipso inveniri: ut aliquid Deo melius ac praestantius appetat, qui solo Christo non est contentus. Summa est, quod Deus in Christo se nobis plene atque in solidum exhibuerit. ... Deus enim saepius se exhibuit hominibus, sed in parte. In Christo autem totum se nobis communicat. Alias etiam se manifestavit, sed in figuris, aut virtute et gratia. In Christo autem essentialiter nobis apparuit." (Commentary Colossians 2: 9; *CO* 52: 104.)

[4] *Ibid.*

the Patriarchs except in Christ.[1] To be sure, the Fathers of the Old Testament knew God but only partly since he concealed from them his secret glory and remained invisible until he became visible in his manifestation in the flesh.[2] Christ was always the means of knowing God. He was exhibited to the Fathers under the Law as the object toward which they should direct their faith.[3] Christ appeared in the Old Testament ceremonies in the same image in which he now appears in full splendor to us.[4] The felicity and well-being of the Church, even the Old Testament Church, was always founded on the person of Christ.[5] What we receive in the sacraments today the Jews of the Old Testament also received in their sacraments, namely, Christ with his spiritual gifts.[6] The Fathers of the Old Covenant both had and knew Christ through whom they were joined to God and made sharers of his promises.[7]

The marks of saving knowledge of God through Christ alone

The knowledge of God which we and all men since the Fall share only through Christ is a saving knowledge, as distinguished from the knowledge of God which all men do indeed have but which renders them without excuse.

This saving knowledge of God is not just intellectual assent to revealed truth, or speculation which flutters in the brain,[8] or is frigid.[9] It is also and above all "pious" faith in the constancy of God's good disposition towards us in Christ.

> By the knowledge of God I mean not only that by which we conceive that some sort of God exists but also grasp what it belongs to us to know of him, what is useful for his glory, finally what is expedient. For, properly speaking, we say there is no knowledge of God where there is no religion or piety. [10]

---

[1] "Deum ergo nonnisi in Christo patribus olim fuisse cognitum." (Commentary John 1:18; *CO* 47: 19.)

[2] *Ibid.*

[3] *Institutes* II, 6, 2; *OS* III, p. 323.

[4] *Institutes* II, 9, 1; *OS* III, p. 398.

[5] *Institutes* II, 6, 2; *OS* III, p. 321.

[6] ". . . Christum scilicet cum spiritualibus suis divitiis." (*Institutes* IV, 14, 23; *OS* V, p. 281.)

[7] *Institutes* II, 10, 2; *OS* III, p. 404.

[8] *Institutes* I, 5, 9; *OS* III, p. 53.

[9] *Institutes* I, 2, 2; *OS* III, p. 35.

[10] "Iam vero Dei notitiam intelligo, qua non modo concipimus aliquem esse Deum, sed etiam tenemus quod de eo scire nostra refert, quod utile est in eius gloriam, quod denique expedit. Neque enim Deum, proprie loquendo, cognisci dicemus ubi nulla est religio nec pietas." (*ibid.*, p. 34.)

Calvin goes on in the same subparagraph to explain what he means by the piety which is indispensable in the knowledge of God: "I call *pietas* that love of God and awe in his presence which a knowledge of his benefits brings about."[1] Calvin defines the knowledge of God by referring to the role of faith in that knowledge, and in turn defines faith in reference to this special kind of pious knowledge: "Now we have a correct definition of faith if we say it is a firm and certain knowledge of the divine benevolence towards us, which, being founded on the truth of the freely given promise in Christ, is by the Holy Spirit revealed to our minds and countersigned on our hearts."[2]

Such knowledge is distinguished from false knowledge of God not only by being marked with *pietas* but also by being sure and unconfused.[3] Knowledge is necessary to faith to differentiate it from erroneous opinions; but the certainty with which the truth of God impresses itself on us is not the same as with the learning of human sciences: it is special to that act by which the Holy Spirit testifies to its truth.[4] By referring the certainty, sureness, and clearness of our knowledge to the special testimony of the Holy Spirit, Calvin makes room for the important qualification that even Christians in this life are often beset by testings and doubt, struggling through which is part of their continual growth in grace and the knowledge of God.[5]

Sound doctrine is a mark of this true knowledge of God for Calvin, who lays great stress on the importance of right doctrine because it

---

[1] "Pietatem voco coniunctam cum amore Dei reverentiam quam beneficiorum eius notitia conciliat." (*Institutes* I, 2, 1; *OS* III, p. 35.)

[2] "Nunc justa fidei definitio nobis constabit si dicamus esse divinae erga nos benevolentiae firmam certamque cognitionem, quae gratuitae in Christo promissionis veritate fundata, per Spiritum sanctum et revelatur mentibus nostris et cordibus obsignatur." (*Institutes* III, 2, 7; *OS* IV, p. 16.)

[3] "Addimus, [that the knowledge of faith is] certam ac firmam, quo solidior persuasionis constantia exprimatur. Nam ut dubia et versatili opinione non est contenta fides, ita nec obscura perplexaque conceptione: sed plenam et fixam, qualis de rebus compertis et probatis esse solet, certitudinem requirit." (*Institutes* III, 2, 15; *OS* IV, p. 25.) cf. Commentary Ephesians 3:12: a nude and confused knowledge of God should not be held as faith, but one which is directed to Christ to seek God there. (*CO* 51:183.) cf. also Commentary John 3:33; *CO* 47:73.

[4] "*Credendi* verbum priore loco ponitur, quia rectae intelligentiae initium est fidei obedientia, imo fides ipsa vere mentis oculus est. Verum continuo post notitia subiicitur, quae fidem ab erroneis falsisque opinionibus discernit. Credunt enim Turcae et Iudaei et papistae, sed nihil norunt neque tenent. At fidei annexa est cognitio, quia nobis certo et indubie constat Dei veritas: non qualiter apprehenduntur humanae scientiae, sed dum eam cordibus nostris spiritus obsignat." (Commentary John 6:69; *CO* 47:163.)

[5] Cf. *Institutes* III, 2, 17; *OS* IV, p. 27 and *Institutes* III, 2, 18; *OS* IV, p. 29.

serves to nourish the community of faith. The true use of doctrine, he says, is "to join us together that we may grow to perfect manhood, to the measure of maturity."[1] Doctrine is not divisive in character but serves the unity of the Church by which believers are nourished to maturity. Philip's doctrine was at many points simple and immature, yet was a means of bringing Nathaniel to Christ: so the principle aim of doctrine is that somehow those who hear it might arrive at Christ.[2]

KNOWLEDGE OF GOD EXTRA HANC CARNEM
SED NON EXTRA CHRISTUM

When Calvin says that men know God only through Christ, he means primarily but not exclusively the man Jesus Christ. Calvin does not say we have no knowledge of God *extra hanc carnem*; he says we have no knowledge of God *extra Christum*. *Christus* may refer in a secondary sense to the Eternal Son of God *extra carnem* as well as in a primary sense to the *Deus manifestatus in carne*.[3] Calvin's doctrine of the knowledge of God is exclusively Christological only in the sense that a saving knowledge of God is available through Christ alone, who as the Eternal Son of God cannot be isolated from or known without his manifestation in the flesh, but who is not restricted to that flesh.

There are not two Christs here, nor are there two *logoi*. There is one Christ, the Eternal Son or the Eternal Word, whom we know to have been God who was to become manifest in the flesh, even the same Eternal *Sermo* by whom men of the Old Testament knew God. There are not two different *logoi* at the source of our knowledge of God, the *logos ensarkos* and the *logos asarkos*. There is one eternal *Logos* who is *ensarkos* as *Deus manifestatus in carne* and is *asarkos* only in the sense that after the Incarnation the Word was joined to the flesh, not restricted to it but not separated from it. That is, the *Logos* after the Incarnation existed also beyond the flesh but was not separated from it. God is revealed fully only through Christ in the flesh, so that the *Deus manifestatus in carne* remains the way by which we understand and know more completely than the Old Testament faithful the mean-

---

[1] "Hic enim verus est doctrinae usus, nos coaptare ut adolescamus in virum perfectum, in mensuram plenae aetatis." (Commentary Hebrews 5: 12; *CO* 55: 66.)

[2] "Videmus ergo hoc in doctrina esse praecipuum, ut quoquomodo ad Christum perveniant qui nos audiunt." (Commentary John 1: 45; *CO* 47: 33.)

[3] See *supra*, pp. 67-78.

ing of the signs and figures in which Christ, not yet manifested in the flesh, showed himself. Christ's work beyond the flesh is understood only through his work in the flesh. The *Deus manifestatus in carne* remains epistemologically the prior and the ultimate criterion.[1]

The priority of the Deus manifestatus in carne

The *Deus manifestatus in carne* maintains his priority because he is the only all-sufficient source of our knowledge of God, the ultimate criterion by which the knowledge gained elsewhere is determined to be knowledge of God and not knowledge of an idol, and the *datus* by whom other *data* are interpreted and appraised for their place in the saving knowledge of God.

For Calvin, however, Christological knowledge of God even in the strictest sense, namely, knowledge gained by gazing nowhere else but at the *Deus manifestatus in carne,* is never a knowledge of God restricted to the flesh. It is always a knowledge of God who was free to unite himself to the flesh he assumed and never left off what belonged to him eternally. Even in this strictest sense of Christological knowledge of God, it is not possible for our knowledge to be limited to what is learned from the flesh of Christ, because the one there present is the Jesus Christ promised in the Old Testament and manifested in the New, the one whose boundless power was never restricted to the flesh. The Christ to whom the Scriptures of the Old and New Testaments witness is he whose power, including his power to reveal God, was not restricted to the flesh, even in the Incarnation. His manifestation in the flesh not only made clear the meaning of his manifestation under signs and symbols in the Old Testament, but his Old Testament manifestation prepared the way for and helped to make recognizable his manifestation in the flesh.[2]

Theologia crucis et gloriae

Does this not mean that Calvin's is a *theologia gloriae*, since it does not start and end with what we know of God in the humiliated flesh

---

[1] Calvin is speaking of the *Deus manifestatus in carne* when he says: "Quod si nunc postremum loquutus est Deus, huc usque progredi convenit: quemadmodum etiam quum eo perveneris, sistendus est gradus." (Commentary Hebrews 1:1; *CO* 55:10.)

[2] See *supra*, pp. 67-69; cf. Dowey's comment: "There is no redemptive knowledge of God, whether patriarchal, prophetic, or apostolic, apart from the mediatorial office of Christ." (*op. cit.*, p. 10.) cf. also Wallace, *op. cit.*, pp. 62-65.

of his Son? Otto Ritschl has termed Calvin the theologian of glory [1] in the sense that much of Calvin's thought is a response to his unceasing awe in the presence of the glory of God's greatness and mercy and eternal counsel. With this, Ritschl has called attention to an important aspect of Calvin's thought, but in doing so he has used the term *theologia gloriae* differently from the way it is customarily used (including in Luther's Heidelberg Disputation), which is in opposition to *theologia crucis*. Taken Ritschl's way, Luther's theology is also a *theologia gloriae*. For Luther, God's glory was indeed revealed in his humility in Christ, but it was his glory that he was so revealed. To do justice to Calvin's thought one would have to say that in a different way his theology is one of the cross as is Luther's. Both men are one in their rejection of *theologia gloriae* when that term refers to a speculative theology not taking as its starting point the particularity of God's revelation in Jesus Christ. Both men confess that we can know God only as he revealed himself to us, that we can know only the *Deus ad nos*, never the *Deus in se*. Both men confess that we know God fully only as Immanuel. Both hold to the unity of God's redemptive movement into the human predicament in the person of Jesus Christ: the Incarnation, death, and resurrection are held together.

But, whereas Christ's humility and condescension are the preoccupation of Luther, Christ's obedience is determinative for Calvin. Luther lays more weight on the cross as a part of the decisive act which was the Incarnation; Calvin lays more stress on the Incarnation as a condition of Christ's obedience in his passion. This means that Calvin can never say in exactly the same way as Luther that " . . . ego nullum nec in coelo neque in terra Deum habeo aut scio extra hanc carnem, quae fovetur in gremio Mariae Virginis."[2]

Luther is able to be more strongly paradoxical in making such an affirmation than either Calvin or even Lutheran orthodoxy.[3] With

---

[1] *Dogmengeschichte des Protestantismus*, III (Göttingen: Vandenhoeck & Ruprecht, 1926), pp. 169-173.

[2] *Supra*, p. 24, n. 1.

[3] Erich Vogelsang points to a fundamental tenet of Luther's Christology: the *Gleichformigkeit* of Christ and of the Christian by virtue of the fact that both pass through temptation. (*Der Angefochtene Christus bei Luther* [Berlin and Leipzig: de Gruyter, 1932], pp. 100ff.) What happened to Christ on the cross happens to us in our own setting. But Christ was both the tested one of God and the God who does the testing, an affirmation which can never be made of us. "Der menschlich Angefochtene ist zugleich der göttlichen Anfechtende, d.h. im Zorn der Liebe Helfende. Der von Gott am Kreuz Gerichtete wirkt zugleich als der Richter das gleiche Gericht an dem Menschen, das er selbst getragen hat." (p. 103.)

its particular Lutheran version of the communicatio idiomatum, Lutheran orthodoxy could contend it was basing its theology and its knowledge of God exclusively on *haec caro* because it taught that the divine majesty was communicated to the flesh. In looking to *haec caro*, one was seeing a created being partaking of the attributes otherwise peculiar to God.[1] This solution is subject to the query, "Is this not the old *theologia gloriae* returned through the back door, insofar as it at least raises a question about the identity of such a majestic or divine flesh with that flesh 'quae fovetur in gremio Mariae Virginis' ?" Luther was spared the task of evolving in detail a doctrine of the *communicatio idiomatum*, so that in affirming his knowledge of God only as *haec caro* he moves less quickly into the sphere of ontological consideration than into the dialectic of the *Deus absconditus-Deus revelatus*: it is precisely in this lowliness of the flesh that God revealed himself.

Concealment and revelation of God in the flesh

Calvin is never able to work with exactly the same *Deus absconditus-Deus revelatus* paradox as Luther.[2] Whereas Luther insists that we know God revealed in his hiddenness in the flesh, Calvin says this also but moves on quickly, perhaps too quickly, to say that God is revealed in Christ when he overtly displays the effects of his boundless

The interesting aspect of Vogelsang's observation is that precisely this language about what Christ does as God and then what he does as man is customarily the object of Lutheran orthodox criticism against Reformed Christology. Vogelsang insists, and rightly so, that Luther's doctrine does not endanger the unity of the person of Jesus Christ: such language about Christ who obeys and commands or who is tempted and tests others has an ethical thrust and does not imply too sharp a separation of the two natures.

[1] *Supra*, pp. 20-21.

[2] "Necesse enim est, ut Deus, cum se nobis revelat, id faciat per velamen et involucrum quoddam et dicat: Ecce sub hoc involucro me certo apprehendes." (*WA* 42, p. 12.) "Itaque cum versaris in loco Iustificationis et disputas de inveniendo Deo qui iustificat seu acceptat peccatores, Ubi et quomodo is querendus sit, Tum prorsus nullum Deum scito extra istum hominem Iesum Christum; hunc complectere et toto corde in eo haere omissa speculatione Maiestatis. Scrutator enim Maiestatis opprimitur a gloria. Ego expertus scio, quid dico." (*WA* 40[1], p. 78.) Scripture leads us first to Christ as to a man, then to a Lord over all creatures and finally to a God. (*WA* 10[1: 2], p. 297.) Yet the balance of his teaching is expressed in his saying that ". . . denn die menscheytt were keyn nutz, wenn die gottheyt nit drynnen were, doch widderumb will unnd mag gott nit fundenn werden denn durch und ynn disser menscheyt . . ." (*WA* 10[1:1], p. 208.) cf. Philip Watson, *Let God be God* (London: Epworth Press, 1958 [first pub. 1947]), p. 102ff.

power. For Calvin, when the divinity hidden by the flesh breaks out into open manifestation, there God is disclosing himself to those who are at the same time moved by the Holy Spirit to receive this manifestation of divine glory.

Calvin does say that God's glory is revealed precisely in his humility and condescension.[1] But his more characteristic interpretation is that during the course of Christ's earthly ministry the divinity of Christ alternately was concealed behind the flesh as a veil and was manifested through the flesh.[2] The divine majesty of Christ was not so concealed by the lowliness of the flesh that it did not send forth rays of its brightness in many ways.[3] Calvin takes the veil of the temple as descriptive of the flesh of Christ behind which is the majesty of his divinity.[4] The low condition of Christ and his flesh, wherein he differed from no one, prevented men from submitting to his divine power; but now with the power of the Spirit displayed in the resurrection, the veil is drawn aside and men are called to behold his heavenly glory.[5] The majesty of God which is invisible to us shines in Christ.[6] Or, revelation takes place when the majesty of God shines brightly in Christ.[7]

The revelation really took place as the flesh directed men beyond itself to something higher, behind, or beyond it. "Because the splendor of God was so unmistakable before their [the shepherds'] eyes and reverence for the Word was so fully engraved on their minds, by the

---

[1] Cf. Parker, *op. cit.*, p. 81ff.

[2] Christ's divine identity was for a time hidden by his lowliness and humanity: "... ad tempus non resplenduit divina gloria, sed tantum in vili et abiecta conditione apparuit humana species..." (*Institutes* II, 13, 2; *OS* III, p. 451.) See *supra*, pp. 80-81. Kratz has called attention to this feature of Calvin's thought, asking the question what is the relation of the concealment of the Son of God in the flesh to his revelation in the flesh? He concludes the relation between the divinity and the humanity in Christ, according to Calvin, is to be discussed not so much in terms of ontology as in terms of historical revelation. The relation between the two natures is, according to Calvin's treatment, not simply statically accomplished with the Incarnation but is realized afresh in each successive historical moment, either when the human side of Christ is more apparent and the Son of God more concealed, or when the divine side of Christ shows forth through miracles and powerful deeds. (*loc. cit.*, *Evangelische Theologie*, XIX [1959], p. 212.)

[3] Commentary John 6: 41; *CO* 47: 148.

[4] Commentary Hebrews 10: 20; *CO* 55: 129.

[5] Commentary John 6: 62; *CO* 47: 158-59.

[6] Commentary John 14: 13; *CO* 47: 328.

[7] Commentary Mark 5: 15; *CO* 45: 271.

exaltation of their faith they easily rose above whatever was inglorious or contemptible in Christ."[1] Since Christ was the lively image of the Father, we should first look on him; he descended that we might do so and that, beginning with him, we might ascend. We must begin with Christ's humility and not fly to God's incomprehensible divinity.[2] We must start with Christ's lowliness and so avoid the dangers attendant upon a *theologia gloriae*; but we are promptly referred further, beyond the humanity, to the divinity.[3] Thus, in the act of revelation there is for Calvin a reflection of the *sursum corda*. Our hearts are lifted up, by way of the Holy Spirit's use of the flesh of Christ, to the acknowledgement of God's power and goodness. We then acknowledge not the bare majesty of God but the "rays of the brightness of his glory." The fullness of the Godhead which dwelt bodily in Christ was, according to Calvin's interpretation, the fullness of God's "righteousness, goodness, wisdom, power, in short, his entire self."[4]

Visibility and invisibility of God's revelation in the flesh

This relation between concealment and revelation in Christ is paralleled by what Calvin has to say regarding the role of the body and the invisible reality. Here again there is evidence of a certain depreciation of the bodily presence in the act of revelation.[5] Seeing Christ in the body was a *sine qua non* of revelation, but the appropriation of revelation took place on a different level. In teaching this, Calvin takes cognizance of the fact that the contemporaries of Jesus responded variously to his presence. Some saw him in the flesh, saw the wonders he performed, and even heard his doctrine—but did not repent and believe. Commenting on John 20: 29, Calvin remarks that the unbelievers who saw Christ in the flesh were not more blessed on that account than those who did not see him in the flesh; believers who never beheld Christ with their eyes enjoy blessedness also. What counts is that we behold spiritually in Christ what is heavenly and

---

[1] Commentary Luke 2: 16; *CO* 45: 79.

[2] Commentary John 14: 1; *CO* 47: 321-22.

[3] Christ the man gently takes us by the hand to lead us to the Father so that he who was terrifying and alarming may be reconciled by Christ and made friendly to us. (Commentary I Timothy 2: 5; *CO* 52: 270.) cf. also Calvin's statement of faith's movement from Christ-man to Christ-God, Commentary John 20: 28; *CO* 47: 444. cf. Parker's section "By Christ-Man to Christ-God", *op. cit.*, p. 88ff.

[4] Commentary Colossians 1: 15; *CO* 52: 85.

[5] See *supra*, pp. 88-89.

divine.[1] Calvin thinks it was effrontery for Thomas to wish to touch
and feel before believing.[2] Thomas unfortunately needed to be drawn
to faith by the experience of the senses, which is altogether at variance
with the nature of faith. Faith cannot flow from a mere knowledge of
events but has its origin in the Word of God. Christ commends
faith on this ground, that it acquiesces in the bare word and does not
depend on carnal views or human reason. Indeed, we ought to honor
God by viewing his truth as self-authenticating. Faith fixes its anchor
in heaven, rising above those things which are visible in this world.
Faith is not of a right kind unless it be founded on the Word of God
and rise to the invisible Kingdom so as to go beyond all human capacity.[3]

What makes Calvin's exegesis of John 20 perplexing is that it seems
to go against his explicit teaching elsewhere that faith must mount
from Christ's body and must not start anyplace but with the lowliness
and meekness of Christ. It is one thing to argue that Christ's bodily
presence is not essential to those who are not the first-century contemporaries of Christ and another to suggest that his bodily presence
was not essential to those who were his chronological and geographic
contemporaries.[4]

Election and the subjective side of revelation

This relation of the concealment and the revelation in Christ
accompanies Calvin's view of the relation between election and revelation. His conception is governed by the Biblical account of the
obvious disparity of human response to the Gospel and Christ's
presence. The majesty of God was equally shown to all around Jesus;
empirically the display was evident to all, but it had a different effect
on the elect and the reprobate.[5] The asset of Calvin's position is that

---

[1] *CO* 47: 445.

[2] Commentary John 20: 26; *CO* 47: 443. It was a sign of Martha's weakness
in faith to suggest that by Christ's bodily presence her brother Lazarus would
have been spared death. (Commentary John 11: 32; *CO* 47: 264.)

[3] Commentary John 20: 29; *CO* 47: 445.

[4] We in fact have an advantage over Christ's pre-Pentecostal contemporaries:
"Non versatur quidem in terris Christus, nec eum gestamus inter ulnas, sed in
evangelio divina eius maiestas clare et palam refulget, et se illic nobis quasi facie
ad faciem, ut inquit Paulus (2 Cor. 3, 18), conspicuum exhibet: neque amplius
in carnis infirmitate, sed in magnifica virtute spiritus, quam in miraculis, in
sacrificio mortis suae, in resurrectione exseruit." (Commentary Luke 2: 30;
CO 45: 90.)

[5] Commentary Matthew 28: 4; *CO* 45: 796.

he does not take refuge in attributing a non-material, non-empirical character to these events of salvation history. He does not argue that the elect were deluded into thinking they were seeing something which was not really happening in an objectively verifiable way, while only the unbelievers were seeing clearly, but not to their salvation. Rather, Calvin relies on the view that during the life of Jesus Christ in Nazareth the Word and Spirit were so joined that only those moved by the Holy Spirit believed that Jesus, even after they saw his power demonstrated, was the Messiah of God. Of course only those so moved perceived, in the face of his humility when his power was not openly manifest, his true identity. The revelation was real enough, an unmistakable and concrete exhibition of divine power; but the revelation never became revelation for anyone of Jesus' chronological companions except by the work of the Holy Spirit. Thus, many saw the miracles but only some were moved to believe; and some believed on the power of the Word alone, its effects unseen. Some were even deliberately prevented from beholding the operation of the divine power and so did not believe. Their senses were deadened and the manifestation of power served only to confirm their unbelief, rebellion, and alienation from God.[1]

The problem of these and similar passages is the same one inherent in the mystery of election. Election is a gracious thing, and the mystery about God's will is ultimately for Calvin the mystery of God's graciousness to some of those who deserve condemnation. It is man's self-imposed darkness, not God's cruelly arbitrary will which makes revelation not universally received and responded to in belief. The Word of God, Calvin says in commenting on Matthew 13: 11, is by its nature always bright, and it is the darkness of men which smothers its brightness for them. Yet the Lord conceals the mysteries from the

---

[1] When he met the disciples on the road to Emmaus, Christ's body was not visibly different after the resurrection than it had been before. The disciples on the road failed to recognize him not because his body was visibly different but because he "restrained their eyes," as on other occasions he had restrained the eyes of some not to see or to see differently on different occasions. (Commentary Luke 24: 16; *CO* 45: 803-804.) The same applies to the text "he disappeared from before their eyes." (Luke 24: 31.) The reason some saw and did not believe, or heard and did not follow, was that God hardened the hearts of some and blinded the eyes of others. (Commentary John 12: 40; *CO* 47: 297.) Christ was not continually assuming new shapes like Proteus but was sometimes recognized by his friends and sometimes not, because it is in the power of God who gave eyes to men to lessen their sharpness of vision whenever he thinks proper. (Commentary John 20: 14; *CO* 47: 431-32.) cf. *supra*, p. 92.

perishing sometimes by speaking in a dark manner and sometimes by striking their senses with dullness.[1]

Yet one wonders if Calvin does not put in question the priority of revelation and therefore the weight of the revelation of God in the particular person of Jesus Christ. What seems to be too readily determinative for him at this point is a will of God to which Christ's revelation is subject, and a will which is discoverable by us outside the *Deus manifestatus in carne*. From Immanuel we can know that the will of God is all-powerful and that by the Holy Spirit we are freed to obey it as God's desicion to restore the world and reconcile men to himself. But why it is a twofold, eternal decision of salvation or damnation for each individual, and why the particular revelation in Christ should hasten men to their predestined end—this is seemingly not known from the incarnate Lord. Here is where Calvin unfortunately advances too boldly, in spite of the pastoral context and reverence for the mystery which persistently characterize his treatment of the doctrine of predestination.

Revelation and the Word joined to the Spirit

What has been said about the revealing character of Christ's bodily presence for his first-century contemporaries and the work of the Holy Spirit applies in a more general way to the relation between the Word and the Spirit in the act of God's revelation to all generations. The saving knowledge of God which we have fully only through Christ is gained solely through his Word joined to his Spirit.

Just as Adam's Fall was defection from the Word of God as command, so redemptive revelation comes through the Word and only through the Word. God wishes to be adored in his Word, so that when his Word is despised, all reverence for him is shaken off. "But as God does not manifest himself to men otherwise than through the Word, so neither is his majesty maintained nor does his worship remain secure among us any longer than while we obey his Word."[2]

The Word for Calvin may mean the Eternal Son, although the term he prefers for this is *Sermo, not Verbum*.[3] Or simply, the Word of God

---

[1] Commentary Matthew 13: 11; *CO* 45: 357-58. cf. Commentary Matthew 13: 14; *CO* 45: 360-61.

[2] "Atqui ut non aliter se hominibus manifestat Deus quam per verbum: ita neque aliter eius maiestas consistit, nec salvus manet eius inter nos cultus, quam dum obedimus eius verbo." (Commentary Genesis 3: 6; *CO* 23: 60.)

[3] Commentary John 1: 1; *CO* 47: 3.

is the efficacious doctrine of God whether as Gospel or Law.[1] The
Word is also the message the prophets spoke about God's purposes,
it is the doctrine and message which Jesus preached during his earthly
ministry, and it is the preaching of the Church from the pulpit in
an exposition of Scripture. Calvin emphasizes the priority of hearing
over seeing as a means of receiving revelation. Faith is not conceived
by beholding heaven and earth but by hearing the Word; men may
be made inexcusable without the Word, but they are led to a saving
knowledge only as the Word directs them.[2] Thus Calvin says that
although Christ did not need to speak in order to heal the girl, he
raised her by his voice in order to accustom people to attend to his
doctrines.[3]

The Word is also and especially for us the Scriptures of the Old
and New Testaments; especially for us, in the sense that our knowledge
of the Word as *Sermo* and the Word as spoken by the prophets, apostles, and Jesus Christ can be derived from no other source than the
Scriptures. The teaching of the Fathers, the mutual instruction and
admonition of fellow members in the body of Christ, can be sources
of right doctrine, but only insofar as they confirm Scripture.

> This, then, ought to be taken for grated: in order for true religion
> to shine brightly among us, there has to be a teaching from the heaven-
> ly doctrine; nor can anyone succeed in having the slightest taste of
> right religion except the one who will be a disciple of Scripture. [4]

---

[1] Commentary Hebrews 4: 12; *CO* 55: 51.

[2] Commentary Acts 14: 17; *CO* 48: 327-28.

[3] Calvin warns against allowing miracles to interfere with doctrine. (Commentary Mark 1: 45; *CO* 45: 233.) Signs and miracles are not necessary because
God has included all we need to know in his Word: "Denique proprium Dei
munus est, nos ad se trahere, qui vult efficaciter per verbum suum operari."
(Commentary Luke 16: 30; *CO* 45: 413.) In raising Lazarus, Christ addressed
the dead man and made himself to be *heard*. (Commentary Luke 7: 14; *CO* 45:
239.) cf. Commentary Luke 4: 21; *CO* 45: 142.
This accentuation of doctrine over miracles also provides some of the impetus
behind Calvin's preference for the Fourth Gospel as a basis for interpreting the
others. The object of the Synoptics is to embrace the history of our Lord's
actions, John's his doctrine. (Commentary Mark 14: 26; *CO* 45: 711.) cf. the
Argumentum to the Commentary on John: while the object of all the Gospel
writers is the same, to point to Christ, the Synoptics are more rich in their narra-
tive of his life and death, while John concentrates more on the doctrine by which
the office of Christ, together with the power of his death and resurrection, is
unfolded. (*CO* 47: VII-VIII.)

[4] "Sic autem habendum est, ut nobis affulgeat vera religio, exordium a caelesti
doctrina fieri debere, nec quenquam posse vel minimum gustum rectae sanaeque
doctrinae percipere, nisi qui Scripturae fuerit discipulus; unde etiam emergit
verae intelligentiae principium, ubi reverenter amplectimur quod de se illic

Christ is known rightly only from the Scriptures.[1] Yet Calvin acknowledges that men may contrive ways from Scripture for not coming to Christ.[2] He says the Word is self-authenticating [3] but only insofar as the Holy Spirit is self-authenticating.[4]

The only way to discern Jesus Christ from the false "christs" is through the Scriptures as they are expounded in the life of the congregation of the faithful.[5] Of themselves, the Scriptures do not lead men to Christ any more than Christ himself, apart from the efficacy of his Spirit, made believers of all who saw and heard him during his earthly ministry. The Spirit inwardly draws men, just as it was only

---

testari Deus voluit. Neque enim perfecta solum, vel numeris suis completa fides, sed omnis recta Dei cognitio ab obedientia nascitur." (*Institutes* I, 6, 2; *OS* III, p. 63.) cf. also *Institutes* I, 13, 21 and Commentary John 20: 29; *CO* 47: 445, on the truth of God being self-authenticating.

[1] Commentary John 5: 39; *CO* 47: 125. cf. "Quare ut nobis hodie Christus per evangelium pateat, Mosen et prophetas tanquam anteambulones in medium prodire necesse est." (Commentary Luke 24: 27; *CO* 45: 806.)

[2] Commentary John 7: 41; *CO* 47: 184.

[3] Commentary Hebrews 6: 18; *CO* 55: 80.

[4] "Si excipiant, hoc modo everti ac in nihilum redigi miracula, quibus tam legis quam evangelii sancita fuit autoritas: respondeo, certam spiritus notam illis insculptam fuisse, quae dubitationem et errandi metum fidelibus eximeret." (Commentary Matthew 24: 23; *CO* 45: 663.) "Maneat ergo hoc fixum, quos Spiritus sanctus intus docuit, solide acquiescere in Scriptura, et hanc quidem esse ἀυτόπιστον, neque demonstrationi et rationibus subiici eam fas esse: quam tamen meretur apud nos certitudinem, Spiritus testimonio consequi." (*Institutes* I, 7, 5; *OS* III, p. 70.) "Huc summa redit, Spiritum sanctum vinculum esse, quo nos sibi efficaciter devincit Christus." (*Institutes* III, 1, 1; *OS* IV, p. 2.)

[5] Oberman has called attention to the way in which *sola scriptura* for the Reformers was not set over against "the single exegetical tradition of interpreted Scripture" (which he designates "Tradition I"). ("Quo Vadis, Petre? The History of Tradition from Irenaeus to *Humani Generis*," The Dudleian Lecture 1962, *Harvard Divinity Bulletin*, XXVI [July, 1962], p. 11.) Instead, Scripture interpreted within the context of this Tradition I is opposed by the Reformers to "the two-sources theory which allows for an extra-biblical oral tradition" (which he designates "Tradition II"). (*ibid.*) The importance of this is that it undermines the all too familiar view projected onto the Reformers' teaching that Scripture is opposed to tradition, a position certainly not shared by Calvin. Calvin draws on the tradition as a confirming source for his interpretation of Scripture. (*supra*, pp. 26-60.) The community within which Scripture speaks in a saving way has as one of its ministries the prophetic-doctoral one. Robert W. Henderson argues that Calvin never drew a clear distinction between the prophetic and doctoral offices, although the prophetic office was especially for making the will of God known and the doctoral office was especially for taking care that sound doctrine was propagated for the sake of pure religion within the Church. (*The Teaching Office in the Reformed Tradition* [Philadelphia: Westminster Press, 1963], p. 31.) In any event, the prophetic-doctoral ministry in the Church ". . . rested squarely on the prophetic-doctoral office of Christ himself. . . ." (*ibid.*)

by the action of the Holy Spirit that the prophets and apostles were chosen as special witnesses of God's actions and were guided in the transcribing of their witness. The Scriptures are the means of this particular vivifying revelation for us when the Holy Spirit graciously uses them to point to Christ, who is the image in whom the Father is fully revealed.

The breadth and variety of meaning Calvin gives to the affirmation that we know God only through Christ is now evident. To recapitulate briefly: Calvin holds that God is known fully only in Christ in the sense that he does not need to be searched for elsewhere, that such a knowledge involves sound doctrine and pious reliance on God's disposition towards us, that the knowledge so described applies not to man as created but as sinner, and that the Christ spoken of here is known to be our Redeemer only from the Scriptures of the Old and New Testaments. Further, on the grounds of the particular revelation of God in Jesus Christ known from Scripture which speaks to us by the witness of the Holy Spirit in the community of the faithful, Calvin suggests there is a revelation of God which is united to but not restricted to what is known from Christ's humanity. That is, there is a knowledge of God through Christ whose source is not exclusively the flesh of Christ.

THE DUPLEX COGNITIO DEI AND THE DOCTRINE OF THE TRINITY

Now, does Calvin propound another knowledge of God, not originating in the Christ witnessed to in the Scriptures of the Old and New Testaments, and if so, how?

Does this question mean that at last, and with a sigh of relief, this study moves away from the knowledge of God based on his revelation in Christ to a knowledge of God based on his revelation in creation? It comes as no surprise that the answer to this question depends on what one means by "revelation." If one means God's self-disclosure in non-Scriptural ways which can be appropriated by sinful men as an alternative source of saving knowledge, the answer must still be *no* in Barth's sense. If one means God's self-disclosure through the marks of justice and ordering power in creation, no matter how utterly incapable sinful men are, lacking Scripture, of appropriating this self-disclosure, then the answer must be *yes* as with Brunner.

Or again, does this transition mean that the discussion now leaves

off the knowledge of God in Christ to turn to the knowledge of God from nature? Once more, the answer must be qualified. It is *yes* only if one takes the *duplex cognitio Dei* the way both Barth and Brunner took it when they posed the question in an *either* Christ *or* nature form. The answer is *no* if one sees that the "extra Calvinisticum" functions in Calvin's thought not to abolish but to mitigate the implied either-or. For the bald either-or rests on the assumption that the *cognitio redemptoris* is a knowledge of the Redeemer which does not presuppose and include a knowledge of the Father and the Spirit.

Calvin's *duplex cognitio Dei*, however, is the knowledge of the one God as he reveals himself in his creative and redemptive activities; he does not envisage a *cognitio creatoris* which is not Christological-Pneumatological. The two facets of our knowledge of God are not *creatoris et Christi* but *creatoris et redemptoris*, because for Calvin Christ is not only the redemptive Word of God but also the creative Word of God, just as the Spirit is not only regenerative but also creative.[1] And, equally important, Calvin for the same reasons does not envisage a *cognitio redemptoris* which does not presuppose the *cognitio creatoris*.

The doctrine of the Trinity and the structure of the Institutes

The "extra Calvinisticum" points to this overlapping in Calvin's thought of the *cognitio creatoris* and the *cognitio redemptoris*, which might otherwise be taken as being too isolated from one another, notably if one were to judge from the titles of the first two books of the *Institutes*. Dowey's study carries an illuminating insight to the effect that Calvin relates the knowledge of God as Creator and the knowledge of God as Redeemer in terms of "the way in which the idea of law spans the two orders of the knowledge of God ...."[2] This present investigation explores another road, one which Dowey in fact mentions as a possibility,[3] but one which leads further than he suspects: the relation between the doctrine of the Trinity and Calvin's Christology. Here, it is found that the "extra Calvinisticum" functions to bolster the two related facts: (1) that the *duplex cognitio Dei* is one act of knowing in a twofold movement, even as *cognitio* is singular not only grammatically but also in the actual experience of the Church;

[1] Cf. Krusche, *op. cit.*, pp. 128-29.
[2] *Op. cit.*, p. 222.
[3] *Ibid.*

and (2) that since the one act of knowing which can be analyzed in a twofold fashion is given its unity by the unity of the one thus known, this knowledge of God is fully Trinitarian not only in presupposition but in result.

That Calvin's thought is not consistently Trinitarian in structure can be argued on the grounds of his perpetual admonitions that classical terminology is ultimately insufficient for expressing the mystery of God's nature, on the interpretation of him by some of his contemporaries, and on the book titles of the 1559-60 editions of the *Institutes* which suggest a binitarian rather than a trinitarian knowledge of God.

In 1537 Caroli accused Calvin of not holding to the doctrine of the Trinity because he and Farel avoided the classical terms "trinity" and "persons" and had refused Caroli's demand that they sign the Athanasian Creed with its anathemas, even though they were willing to sign the Nicene and Apostles' Creeds. Although Calvin easily purged himself of this charge before a Synod at Lausanne (1537), and although he could point to his acceptance of the terms in the 1536 *Institutes*, the ministers of the Church of Strasbourg asked for a precise statement of his position on the doctrine when accepting him as the minister of the French-speaking Church in that city.[1] Calvin's point even at that early date in his theological development of the doctrine was that he preferred Biblical language to terms such as *ousia-natura* and *hypostasis-persona*. Calvin never gave up his reservations about classical terminology.[2] However—and it is in this sense that one must speak about a development in Calvin's doctrine of the Trinity—he became increasingly convinced of the immense usefulness of the accepted classical terminology for guarding against the heresies propagated by those who, under the program of restricting themselves to Biblical language, threatened the Biblical witness to the Triune God of which the classical language, for all its weaknesses, was a faithful interpreter.[3] A certain refreshing restraint always marks

---

[1] See the *Confessio de Trinitate propter calumnias P. Caroli*, signed by Calvin, Farel, and Viret and approved by Capito and Bucer of Strasbourg and Myconius and Grynaeus; *CO* 9: 703-10. For a treatment of the incident, see Schaff, *op. cit.*, VII, pp. 350-52, and Emil Doumergue, *Jean Calvin*, IV (Lausanne: Georges Bridel, 1910), pp. 96-97.

[2] *Institutes* I, 13, 5.

[3] "Dic consubstantialem, detraxeris versipelli larvam, et tamen nihil addis Scripturis . . . Dic in una Dei essentia personarum Trinitatem: dixeris uno verbo quod Scripturae loquuntur, et inanem loquacitatem compresseris." (*Institutes* I, 13, 5; *OS* III, pp. 115-16.)

Calvin's attitude to the doctrine. When it comes to this doctrine, he says, humble submission to Scripture more than theological acumen is called for to avoid, above all, audacious speculation about God's inner being.[1] Unleashed Trinitarian speculation was always distasteful to Calvin, but his experience in controversy over the years demonstrated to him that in addition to being empty and signifying the haughtiness of man, anti-Trinitarian speculation brought heretical tendencies jeopardizing the soteriological impact of the Biblical witness. Of the classical terms, Calvin says he could wish them buried, "if only this faith were agreed on among all: that Father and Son and Spirit are one God, yet the Son is not the Father, nor the Spirit the Son, but that they are distinct in property."[2] When Calvin wishes to describe the distinction of the Persons, he says, "To the Father is attributed the beginning of acting, and the fountain and wellspring of all things; to the Son, wisdom, counsel, and the ordered disposition of all things; but to the Spirit is assigned the power and efficacy."[3]

There is still the possibility that Calvin's doctrine of the Trinity remains formal and is never integrated into his thought as a whole. Such might be surmised from the titles given to the books in his final edition of the *Institutes*: there is "De Cognitione Dei Creatoris" and "De Cognitione Dei Redemptoris," but no "De Cognitione Spiritus Sancti." Even if it be decided that the *duplex cognitio* scheme and not the three articles of the Creed provides the primary instrument for structuring the final edition of the *Institutes*, still the subject of Books III and IV is generally the work of the Holy Spirit, as the subject of Book I is generally God the Creator and of Book II generally the Redeemer. The Holy Spirit is not for Calvin only the means of our knowledge of God: he is also the subject of our knowledge of God, along with the Father and the Son. Books III and IV should be seen as serving in part to elaborate the content of our knowledge of the Holy Spirit from a consideration of his offices.[4]

---

[1] *Institutes* I, 13, 21; *OS* III, pp. 136-37.

[2] "Utinam quidem sepulta essent, constaret modo haec inter omnes fides, Patrem, et Filium, et Spiritum esse unum Deum: nec tamen aut Filium esse Patrem, aut Spiritum Filium, sed proprietate quadam esse distinctos." (*Institutes* I, 13, 5; *OS* III, pp. 113-14.)

[3] ". . . Patri principium agendi, rerumque omnium fons et scaturigo attribuitur: Filio sapientia, consilium, ipsaque in rebus agendis dispensatio: at Spiritui virtus et efficacia assignatur actionis." (*Institutes* I, 13, 18; *OS* III, p. 132.)

[4] It is true, as Dowey points out, that in Book I Calvin does not begin discussion of his Christology proper, for he specifically mentions that in Book I

The *duplex cognitio Dei* in its fullest and most cohesively systematic
sense connotes two planes along which the one act of knowing the
Triune God occurs. One is the special history of God's covenantal
purposes recounted in the Scriptures, where God revealed himself
fully only in his Son's manifestation *in carne* but also through the
Mediator even before the Incarnation. The other is the general
history of God's purposes for the entire world, whose meaning becomes known salutarily when seen in the light of the special covenantal
history. In this second sphere God still reveals himself only through
the Mediator, but is revealed through the sustaining, not the reconciling ordering of the Mediator joined with his creative Spirit.[1]

Only in a general sense can it be said that the subject of one movement of this *duplex cognitio Dei* is the Redeemer and the subject of the
other the Creator. For redemptive history implies the right ordering
of creation by God the Creator, as world history implies the right
ordering of creation to a redemptive end by God the Redeemer who
is known from Scripture to have dominion over all. Thus, in knowing
the Redeemer we know one who is the image of the Father; and as
the one who makes visible the invisible Father, the Redeemer is
correctly said to be of one substance with the Father.[2] Calvin says all
divine revelations are rightly called the Word of God, so that we
ought above all to esteem that substantial Word as the source of all
revelations which is liable to no variation, and is God himself.[3]
"Since the beginning of the world God has held no intercourse with

---

he is not yet speaking of Christ as Redeemer. (*Institutes* I, 13, 9; *OS* III, p. 119.)
Dowey is further correct in stating that the doctrines of the Trinity, providence,
and creation are learned only from Scripture, according to Calvin's discussion
in Book I. However, strictly speaking, it is not accurate to say, "Yet they [these
doctrines] concern only the Creator . . ." As Dowey himself goes on to explain,
if man had not fallen, the *doctrine* of the Trinity would not have been known
"but God himself in his eternal Tri-unity" would have. Dowey extends himself
a bit too much in claiming the doctrine of the Trinity" . . . does not include
Calvin's Christology. Nor is it meant to establish the divinity of Christ, but
rather of the Eternal Son or Wisdom of God who became incarnate in Christ
and of the Spirit." (*op. cit.*, p. 127.) This judgment rests on the assumption that
"Christ" is an exact equivalent, for Calvin, of the Eternal Son's manifestation
in the flesh as "Redeemer."

[1] *Supra*, pp. 67-73.
[2] Commentary Colossians 1: 15; *CO* 52: 84-85.
[3] "Ergo ut omnes divinitus profectae revelationes verbi Dei titulo rite insig-
niuntur, ita verbum illud substantiale summo gradu locare convenit, oraculorum
omnium scaturiginem, quod nulli varietati obnoxium, perpetuo unum idemque
manet apud Deum, et Deus ipse est." (*Institutes* I, 13, 7; *OS* III, p. 118.)

men save through the agency of his eternal wisdom or Son."[1] Even if man had not fallen he could not have reached God without a Mediator. Calvin carefully does not say that before Christ the ancients knew God through the Eternal Word; instead, he says that before Christ *was manifested*, the ancients knew God through the Eternal Word.[2] It is this identity but not absolute congruence of Christ in the flesh and the Eternal Word which Calvin interprets I Peter 1: 11 as meaning when it says that the ancient prophets as much as the apostles spoke by the Spirit of Christ.[3]

So it appears that Calvin is, after all, discussing his Christology already in Book I, though the major Christological section remains in Book II. Otherwise, his discussion of the Eternal Son would be of a relatively abstract concept, not immediately fathomable because not known through the manifestation in the flesh. As the "extra Calvinisti-cum" serves to underline this relation of identity but not congruence of the Eternal Son with the Redeemer, it functions not to provide the basis for an abstract discussion of the Eternal Son or Word but for a consideration of the identity of the Eternal Son of God and the Redeemer with the one God. The doctrine of the "extra Calvinisticum" as it appears in Calvin is not an attempt to apply some notion of the Eternal Word or Son derived from, say, an extra-Biblical source, and still fit in God's particular redemptive action. The methodological order is exactly the opposite. The "extra Calvinisticum" as it appears in Calvin takes as granted that the Redeemer is graciously related to us, that he can be Redeemer only because of his identity with the eternal God, and then seeks to extract the implications of this eternal identity for our apprehension of God in the created world and in the Scriptures.[4]

---

[1] "Sic habendum est, nullam abusque mundi initio Dei communicationem fuisse cum hominibus, nisi intercedente aeterna eius sapientia vel filio." (Commentary Galatians 3: 19; *CO* 50: 216.)

[2] "Quia vero nondum manifestatus erat Christus, necesse est Sermonem intelligere ante secula ex Patre genitum." (*Institutes* I, 13, 7; *OS* III, p. 117.)

[3] *Ibid.*

[4] Dowey makes this point in passing but does not see its expansion in Calvin's thought via the "extra Calvinisticum." He recognizes that the *cognitio creatoris* presupposes the *cognitio redemptoris* and vice versa; he does not, however, call attention to the extent to which this is integral to Calvin's thought and how it is made operative partly by the "extra Calvinisticum." (*op. cit.*, p. 46.)

Revelation through the Word and Spirit in the works of God

God's exclusive revelation of himself in his Word applies not just to his redemptive but also to his creative Word. The creative Word reveals God through the *opera Dei*; even Adam's knowledge of God before the Fall through the works of God was a knowledge through the Word by whom, through whom and with whose Spirit all things were created. The Christological content of the knowledge of God the Creator is the revelation of God through the Word in the *opera Dei*. A passage from Calvin's Genesis commentary merits quotation in extenso:

> ... The invisible Kingdom of Christ occupies all things and his spiritual grace is diffused through all things. Yet this does not prevent us from applying our senses to the consideration of heaven and earth, for thence we may seek the things which confirm us in the true knowledge of God. For Christ is that image in which God makes conspicious to us not only his heart but also his hands and feet. I call his heart that secret love with which he embraced us in Christ: by his hands and feet I understand those works which are displayed before our eyes. Just as soon as we depart from Christ, there is nothing either crass or insignificant in which we are not necessarily deceived. [1]

With this, Calvin proposes that even in the knowledge of God which we have from the created order we are deceived in departing from Christ because he is the image in which God presents to us the very means by which he is known from the created order. However, the knowledge of God derived from nature is a confirmation of the true knowledge of God which we have when we are first instructed by Christ in his school.[2]

Calvin does not stop with this warning that our knowledge of God from creation serves only as a confirming knowledge. He goes on to the positive exhortation that because creation is the work of God, its fruits should be studied and enjoyed. We are to receive a "pious

---

[1] "... invisibile Christi regnum omnia occupat, et spiritualis eius gratia per omnia diffusa est. Verum hoc non obstat quominus sensus nostros ad coeli terraeque considerationem applicantes, inde etiam petamus quae nos in vera Dei notitia confirment. Christus enim imago est, in qua non modo pectus suum nobis Deus conspicuum reddit, sed manus quoque et pedes. Pectus appello arcanum illum amorem quo nos in Christo complexus est: per manus autem et pedes, quae oculis nostris exposita sunt opera intelligo. A Christo simulatque discessimus, nihil est tam crassum vel minutum, in quo non hallucinari necesse sit." (Commentary Genesis, *Argumentum*; *CO* 23: 10-11.)

[2] "... sursum, inquam, et deorsum nihil reperiemus quod nos ad Deum usque attollat, donec in sua schola nos Christus erudierit." (*ibid.*; *CO* 23: 10.)

delight" from the manifest and obvious works of God in this "most beautiful theater" of the world.[1] Calvin's delight in creation as a source of confirming knowledge of God is missed too easily in a theology which sets Christological knowledge in virtual opposition to the knowledge of God from creation.

The works of God not only confirm our knowledge of him, according to Calvin, but they also demonstrate how the whole man is involved in the act of knowing God. Reference to God's works combats the notion that true knowledge of God is a purely intellectual matter, since through his works God impinges upon us to make himself known by his effects and to make his will and even his presence felt.

> We are not invited to a knowledge of God which flies about in the head because it is content with empty speculation, but we are invited to the knowledge of God which will be solid and fruitful if it is rightly received by us and takes root in our hearts. For the Lord is manifested by his powers. When we feel their drive within us and enjoy the benefits, we are necessarily more affected by this knowledge than if we should imagine a God of whom nothing would penetrate to our senses. [2]

God's works are not only those redemptive effects of Christ upon us when joined to him by the Holy Spirit, or the creating and sustaining activity constantly exhibited in the external world. The works of God are also those signs of his creation which confront us when,

---

[1] "Interea ne pigeat in hoc pulcherrimo theatro piam oblectationem capere ex manifestis et obviis Dei operibus. Est enim hoc (ut alibi diximus) etsi non praecipuum, naturae tamen ordine primum fidei documentum, quaquaversum oculos circunferamus, omnia quae occurrunt, meminisse Dei esse opera: et simul quem in finem a Deo condita sint, pia cogitatione reputare." (*Institutes* I, 14, 20; *OS* III, p. 170.) cf. Commentary Genesis 2: 3; *CO* 23: 33 and *Institutes* I, 5, 5, and *Institutes* I, 5, 1: we contemplate God in the symmetrical arrangement of the world as in a mirror.

[2] *Institutes* I, 5, 9; *OS* III, p. 53. The tie in Calvin's mind between powers and works of God is indicated by alternative words in earlier editions of this passage, words which are here in parentheses within the 1559 text: "Atque hic rursus observandum est, invitari nos ad Dei notitiam, non quae inani speculatione contenta in cerebro tantum volitet, sed quae solida futura sit et fructuosa si rite percipiatur a nobis, radicemque agat in corde. A suis enim virtutibus [1541: oeuvres; 1560: vertus] manifestatur Dominus: quarum vim quia sentimus intra nos, et beneficiis fruimur, vividius multo hac cognitione nos affici necesse est quam si Deum imaginaremur cuius nullus ad nos sensus perveniret." God is not to be sought as by audacious curiosity we try to sound out his essence, ". . . sed ut illum in suis operibus contemplemur quibus se propinquum nobis familiaremque reddit, ac quodammodo communicat." (*ibid.*)

considering our own nature, we discover conscience and a sense of the divine. Such marks of our being created by God, such witnesses to God in ourselves as his creatures, remain in some form even after the Fall.[1] Just as other works of God in the external world, they are sources of our knowledge of God only by confirming what is known through the Holy Scriptures. But as confirming sources they are not to be disdained: they occasion rejoicing and awe at the wonder of God's gracious, creative will. It is in this sense that Calvin can speak of man as a microcosm of the world, in which the message of God as found in the external world is contained in miniature.[2]

Extra-Scriptural Knowledge of the Natural Order, and the Saving Knowledge of God

Thus far, this discussion has centered on the knowledge of God granted to the community of the faithful through the Scriptures and from the created order when read through the spectacles of Scripture. The knowledge of God as Redeemer and Creator thus described is not two knowledges. It is one knowledge of God inevitably comprised of two elements, available to the community of the faithful. For when the Church reads its special history in the Bible, its reception of the Word is informed by its experience in the world. This experience is essential as the Word addresses the historical condition of the Christian and not some proleptic condition of men and the Church. When the Church looks at the world, both outside its fellowship and within, it sees the theater of God's glory; that is, it sees the context in which it has lived and in which it continues to live, all the while attending to the special history told in the Scriptures.

Because of the Fall, knowledge of God from nature apart from the aid of Scripture is not saving. Adam before the Fall had no need of Scripture; he knew God from the ordering of the world. Even in his original state as created, man knew God only through the sustaining agent of the world, the Mediator with his Spirit. Had man continued in this original knowledge of God, it would also have been saving, although Adam's knowledge of God was not complete and although

---

[1] The *sensus divinitatis* persists even in the impious. (*Institutes* I, 3, 3; *OS* III, p. 39.) cf. also "Manet tamen semen illud quod revelli a radice nullo modo potest, aliquam esse divinitatem: sed ipsum adeo corruptum, ut non nisi pessimos ex se fructus producat." (*Institutes* I, 4, 4; *OS* III, p. 44.)

[2] *Institutes* I, 5, 3; the philosophers who called man a microcosm were correct. (*OS* III, pp. 46, 47.)

he would have grown in it.[1] But man rebelled, with the result that the original possibility of knowing God in a saving way from the world is a hypothetical one: "si integer stetisset Adam."[2] God continues to reveal himself objectively in the world and nature despite the Fall, although even this revelation of God in nature is not as full as before the Fall, since nature itself has been disrupted in some measure, just as redemption is in some measure cosmic. Nonetheless, the revelation of God is there, in nature, with sufficient clarity and force so that it is man's blindness, incurred through rebellion, which keeps nature from being a source of saving knowledge of God apart from Scripture. The responsibility for ignorance of God is thrown on man by God's works in nature and history. They render man inexcusable before God [3] and excite the believer to wonder and praise at the beauty and majesty of God's providential ordering.

The unbeliever can observe these works of God as well as the believer. Indeed, he may learn more about how they function to maintain the order of the world,[4] and his knowledge may itself become one of God's ways for governing the world. In this very restricted sense the unbeliever's knowledge of the *opera Dei* is a saving knowledge: not that he is saved by this knowledge but that this knowledge is effective in maintaining the world which is both the context and in some sense the object of redemption.

However, such knowledge is not saving as is knowledge marked by *pietas*. It does not signify participation in the membership of the faithful community.[5] For the believer also, such knowledge helps to maintain the order of God's creation; but for him such knowledge brings with it joy and thanksgiving in seeing these works as signs of God's steadfastly ordering love. Moreover, the believer can distinguish between a right and a wrong use of the created order, between

---

[1] In this respect Calvin reflects a portion of the traditional teaching about the relation between the original creation and man as perfected according to God's intention. Adam was created without blemish but not fully matured in his relation to God: Irenaeus distinguished between man, created unblemished but as *paidos* in the image of God (that is, in the Son) and man reaching maturity as Christ recapitulates the original creation, completing what man was created to complete but failed to because of his rebellion.

[2] *Institutes* I, 2, 1; *OS* III, p. 34.

[3] ". . . praecisa est omnis tergiversatio." (*Institutes* I, 5, 15; *OS* III, p. 59.)

[4] E.g., Calvin's appreciation of Galen, *Institutes* I, 5, 2.

[5] However, Calvin insists such human reason does not even tend towards an understanding of God's true identity or of his will towards us. (*Institutes* II, 2, 18; *OS* III, p. 261.)

what conforms to God's restoring will and what does not. And further, he is able confidently to rely on God's just ordering, no matter how thwarted God's will might appear to be in historical events.[1]

The pious knowledge of God does not interfere with a clear knowledge of him on the basis of his works in nature and history or with his use of knowledge so gained to sustain his world. The Christian is encouraged to engage in those sciences which God makes available to all men.[2]

CONCLUSION

Calvin is not preoccupied with the questions: "Without God's revelation in Jesus Christ, the *Deus manifestatus in carne*, can we know God?" and "How would we know God if we were not blinded by sin?" These are too hypothetical, because God is in fact known where he wills to be known perfectly, from his manifestation in the flesh of Jesus Christ. Unless one choose to reject God's perfect gift, there is no need to look elsewhere.

The "extra Calvinisticum" functions to remind us that salutary knowledge from Christ as witnessed to in the Scriptures of the Old and New Testaments when illumined by the Holy Spirit in the community of the faithful, derives not from his flesh alone. For the Christ witnessed to in Scripture is precisely the Eternal Word through whom and with whose Spirit believers of the Old Testament knew God, and who, even in the Incarnation, was not confined to the flesh. When Calvin says that men know God only through Christ, he means primarily but not exclusively the man Jesus Christ. Calvin does not say that we have no knowledge of God *extra hanc carnem*; he says we have no knowledge of God *extra Christum*. *Christus* may refer in a secondary sense to the Eternal Son of God *extra carnem* as well as in a primary sense to the *Deus manifestatus in carne*.[3] Calvin's doctrine of the knowledge of God is exclusively Christological only in the sense that a

---

[1] Calvin clearly recognizes that the just ordering of history is not obvious to all and that the faithful are often terrified and confused by events. Yet they know God regulates all. (*Institutes* I, 17, 1; *OS* III, pp. 202-03.)

[2] In commenting on Paul's words about the wisdom of the world (I Corinthians 1: 20), Calvin says the point Paul is making is not that man's reason and the liberal sciences (*doctrinae liberales*) should be abandoned and thrown down but that all of man's learning and wisdom *extra Christum* does not enable him to acquire spiritual wisdom. (*CO* 49: 325.) As regards Scripture, for Calvin, "Comprehensibility is a matter not only of illumination of the Spirit but also of sound learning." (Dowey, *op. cit.*, p. 34.)

[3] *Supra*, pp. 67-78.

saving knowledge of God is available through Christ alone, who as the Eternal Son of God cannot be isolated from or known without his manifestation in the flesh, but who is not restricted to that flesh.

Because the Redeemer is the same Eternal Word, by whom all things were made with his Spirit according to the Father's will, creation and redemption are not competing sources of revelation. The Trinitarian character of Calvin's doctrine of the knowledge of God, supported by the "extra Calvinisticum," subjects to critical scrutiny the either-or framework of considering the knowledge of God from creation and in Christ. Nature, illumined by Scripture, reveals the work of the one God, the Spirit no less than the Father and the Son. Even if it be decided that the *duplex cognitio* scheme and not the three articles of the creed provides the primary instrument for structuring the final edition of the *Institutes*, still Books III and IV of that edition serve to elaborate the content of our knowledge of the Holy Spirit from a consideration of his offices. The *duplex cognitio Dei* in its fullest sense connotes two planes along which the one act of knowing the Triune God occurs. One is the special history of God's covenantal purposes recounted in the Scriptures, where God reveals himself fully only in his Son's manifestation in the flesh but also through the Mediator even before the Incarnation. The other is the general history of God's purposes for the entire world, whose meaning becomes known salutarily when seen in the light of the special covenantal history. In this second sphere God still reveals himself only through the Mediator, but is revealed through the sustaining, not the reconciling, ordering of the Mediator joined with his creative Spirit.

CHAPTER FIVE

THE SO-CALLED EXTRA CALVINISTICUM
AND CALVIN'S ETHICS

COALESCENCE OF KNOWLEDGE AND OBEDIENCE

Calvin's thought allows for no discontinuity between the knowledge and the service of God. There can be a true knowledge of God only where there is *pietas*, and the content of this *pietas* is the joyful reverence and trust of freely obedient creatures under and before the Creator.[1] This free submission consists, according to Calvin, of the dynamic life of the Christian community as it is continually being conformed to its Head, Jesus Christ.[2] The Christian life is described by Calvin in various ways. But the reality is the same: it is the new life in the Church and in the world into which men are brought through faith in Christ and through the power of his Spirit.

There is a direct correspondence, in Calvin's thought, between the character of man's knowledge of God and knowledge of himself. Just as there is a knowledge of God only as he comes to man, so there is a knowledge of man only within the patterns of human relations. And, just as, apart from the specific redemptive revelation, there is a knowledge of God only which leaves man without excuse, so apart from awareness of membership in the community of forgiveness and sanctification, there is a knowledge of the Christian only which re-

---

[1] Wisdom is mainly a composed sobriety in compliance to God. " ... quum praecipuum sapientiae caput sit composita in Dei obsequium sobrietas." (Commentary Genesis 3: 5; *CO* 23: 59.)

[2] That knowledge is true which leads believers to conform to Christ; conformity to Christ means believers do not put themselves forward at the expense of their brethren, are not slow and cold in the duties of live, and so in this way bear the cross of Christ. Christ tells his disciples that those are blessed who know and do his will.

"Neque enim vera cognitio dici meretur, nisi quae fideles eousque adducit, ut se capiti suo conforment. Vana potius imaginatio est, dum Christum et quae Christi sunt extra nos conspicimus. Hinc collige, donec se quis fratribus suis subiicere didicerit, eum nescire, sitne Christus magister. Quum autem nemo se omni ex parte fratribus impendat, multi etiam lente et frigide se in caritatis officiis exerceant, hinc apparet quantum a plena fidei luce adhuc distemus." (Commentary John 13: 17; *CO* 47: 310.)

veals him as one bearing the marks of the height of created order from which, through sin, he is inexcusably delinquent. Man's knowledge of God and his knowledge of himself can never be separated: in knowing God rightly man knows himself as the object of God's creative, redemptive, and regenerative activity, and in not knowing God rightly he knows himself incompletely and as being rebellious. This second self-knowledge is confused but sufficient to make man conscious of his predicament.

In Calvin's own words, the *duplex cognitio hominis* is the knowledge of our original condition and our spoiled condition after the Fall. "... The knowledge of ourselves is double, namely, as we were formed in our first origin, and then into what condition we fell by the demise of Adam."[1] But Calvin indeed describes man as redeemed and sanctified [2] and if one pays insufficient attention to his words about Christian knowledge within the community of redemption and sanctification, one furthers the erroneous characterization of Calvin as a theologian preoccupied with man's fallen condition. For, in man's original condition Calvin sees the state which the sanctified life increasingly approximates but never perfectly achieves, at least in this life, and in the fallen condition he sees the servitude from which the Redeemer has freed man.

Calvin can delineate the Christian life with a fully Trinitarian exposition because his Christology does not in effect pose the problem of the ethical life in such terms that Christocentric life, life in the Spirit, or life in properly ordered creation become alternatives. As the "extra Calvinisticum" functions in the doctrine of the knowledge of God to emphasize the Trinitarian character of that knowledge, so it also underlines the Trinitarian presuppositions of the ethical act.

LIMITATIONS AND UTILITY OF PARALLELS BETWEEN CHRISTOLOGICAL AND ETHICAL DISCOURSE

A word of caution is necessary regarding the legitimacy of drawing parallels between Christological affirmations and ethical thought. If

---

[1] "... quales nos prima origine simus conditi, et qualis nostra conditio esse coeperit post Adae lapsum ..." (*Institutes* I, 15, 1; *OS* III, p. 173.)

[2] The best route to a knowledge of the image of God into which man was created is via a knowledge of the reparation of its corrupted nature. "Id [imago Dei] vero non aliunde melius quam ex reparatione corruptae naturae cognosci potest." (*Institutes* I, 15, 4; *OS* III, p. 179.) Man, leaving the reign of God by sin, lost the spiritual gifts, but recuperates them by the grace of regeneration and it is Christ who restores him into this state. (*Institutes* II, 2, 12; *OS* III, pp. 254-55.)

a one-to-one ratio existed between the Church's Christological language and dogma and its ethical discourse and formulation, Christian ethics as a theological discipline would be a relatively simple matter. One could, for example, take the four Chalcedonian adverbs as descriptive of how the Church is in but not of this world: without confusion, without change, without division, without separation.

"*Extra Calvinisticum*": *a guard against the Analogia Unae Personae as a method for ethical discourse*

Precisely because of the "extra Calvinisticum" such a simplified approach is impossible for Calvin. His interpretation of the ascension makes the difference between the person of Christ and the Church unmistakably clear. The One Person is far removed from us according to his human nature, but is present in his divine majesty and through the Holy Spirit. The incarnate Lord unites himself to his Church and remains Lord over her, but the Church is not the extension of the Incarnation. When Calvin talks about the knowledge of God which conforms us to the Head of the Church, his immediate reference is to the crucified, risen, and ascended servant Lord of those who know and hearken to his commandment to love one another. The Christian life is a conformity to Christ in his redemptive obedience; it is not a duplication of his unique Person. We are one with the Son of God, not because he conveys his substance to us but because, by the power of his Spirit he imparts to us the life and all the blessings which he has received from the Father.[1] The key to Calvin's conception of Christ and the Church in the sphere of ethical action is the remark that "... what was experienced by him who is the Head of the whole Church must happen to us who are members of it."[2] "Above all, we ought not to avoid the cross by which the Son of God himself was trained from his earliest infancy."[3] Obedience ought to be the foundation of all we do.[4]

---

[1] Commentary John 17: 21; *CO* 47: 387. cf. Commentary John 17: 26; *CO* 47: 391.

[2] "... idem, quod ipse expertus est, qui commune est ecclesiae caput, nobis qui membra sumus, accidere oportet." (Commentary Matthew 26: 22; *CO* 45: 701.)

[3] Commentary Matthew 2: 13; *CO* 45: 97.

[4] "Sit igitur fundamentum omnium quae aggredimur obedientia. Monemur etiam, quibus causam Christi agere propositum est, non semper ita dextre se gerere, quin aliquid vitii obrepat: quo magis sollicite rogandus est nobis Dominus, ut nos in singulis actionibus gubernet spiritu prudentiae." (Commentary John 18: 10; *CO* 47: 395.)

The warning about direct transference of Christological language to the sphere of ethics applies, perhaps especially, to the "extra Calvinisticum." The Son *etiam extra carnem* maintains his special union with the flesh of Jesus, and does not somehow exchange that special union for one with the Church as the body of Christ. There is only one hypostatic union between God and man, the One Person Jesus Christ. The Church is joined to that One Person by the Holy Spirit, but it can never be said of the Church in this world what must always be said of Christ's humanity, that it is "yet without sin."

Therefore, the "extra Calvinisticum" is no help for those who are intent upon finding an axiom for compressing the expansive ambiguities of ethical decision. It cannot be loaded with material to brace up some universal ethic, say one based on natural law, from which to derive a Christian ethic. Nor can the "extra Calvinisticum" prepare a place for injecting, from non-Biblical resources, new content into the Church's knowledge of God's will gained from Scripture.

Similarities between the "extra Calvinsticum" and descriptions of Christ's special and universal Lordship

Where the "extra Calvinisticum" does find a parallel is in Calvin's teaching about the Lordship of Christ. The confession that the *Logos* is united to the flesh but exists *etiam extra carnem* corresponds to the relation between Christ's Lordship over the Church and his Lordship *etiam extra ecclesiam*. It functions to inform man's knowledge of himself in the Church and in the world, as either a willing or a reluctant subject of the creating, redeeming, and sanctifying God.

It is through the kingdom of Christ that God reigns.[1] All power in heaven and earth is committed to him, who exercises it by his Spirit.

---

[1] Christ is exalted to the right hand of the Father ". . . quia consortem opsum imperii sui fecerit, quia per ipsum omnem suam potestatem exerceat." (Commentary Ephesians 1: 20; *CO* 51: 158.) *Regnum Dei* and *Regnum Christi* mean practically the same thing in Calvin's usage. cf. Karlfried Frölich, *Gottesreich, Welt und Kirche bei Calvin* (München: Ernst Reinhardt, 1930), pp. 5, 94. There is a difference of connotation, however, between "kingdom of God" and "kingdom of Christ" which corresponds to the difference between "Son" and "God" as set down by Calvin in *Institutes* I, 13, 6. When God is mentioned simply and indefinitely, the term belongs not only to the Father but also to the Son and to the Spirit; whenever the Father is compared with the Son, the special property of each distinguishes the two. "Kingdom of heaven" is a closely-related term, referring to Christ's actual, though often concealed, reign over the elect and the angels. This is not the same as "kingdom *in* heaven," for the locus of the "kingdom *of* heaven" is not just heaven. Those who think the kingdom of God means heaven are mistaken, says Calvin. The kingdom of God is rather the spiritual life begun

Christ reigns particularly over the Church and generally over all mankind. His reign over the Church involves voluntary obedience from the faithful through the exercise of his gifts of grace and the secret operation of the Spirit where the Gospel is communicated. His reign over all men compels them, even against their will, to serve his purposes now and will finally drag them before his seat of righteous judgment. Christ has been given command over all men by the Father, but not to give life indiscriminately to all; he gives that only to those who know him in a saving way, who are incorporated into his body by faith and who are made partakers of divine adoption and heirs of heaven, namely, the elect. "The reign of Christ is extended to all men, but it is saving only for the elect who, with voluntary obedience, follow the Shepherd's voice. The others he forcibly compels to obey, until finally he entirely destroys them with his rod of iron."[1]

CHRIST'S REIGN OVER THE FREELY OBEDIENT CHURCH

The sceptre of the Word

The kingdom of Christ is, above all, for Calvin, that spiritual and heavenly reign exercised by Christ over his people through the Gospel. The Gospel is like a sceptre to govern believers whom the Father has made his subjects.[2] The arm of the Lord, or the power of his rule, is the "doctrine of the Gospel" which is available to all; but it is saving only for those who have been elected to receive the witness of the Holy Spirit.[3] ". . . By the preaching of the Gospel, the kingdom of God is set up and established among men, and in no other way does God reign among men. Whence also it appears how miserable the

---

in this world and increasing daily according to the incessant advances of faith. (Commentary John 3: 3; *CO* 47: 54.) The Church militant, when obedient to Christ, may be called the kingdom of heaven. However, "kingdom of heaven," unlike "kingdom of God" and "kingdom of Christ," does not extend to God's reign over those forced, despite their will, to serve his purposes, and it always carries the connotation of invisibility insofar as its actuality in this world is concerned.

[1] "Ergo regnum Christi ad omnes quidem homines extenditur, sed nonnisi solis electis est salvificum, qui voluntario obsequio sequuntur vocem pastoris: alios enim parere sibi violenter cogit, donec tandem sceptro ferreo penitus eos conterat." (Commentary John 17: 2; *CO* 47: 376.) Christ fills the offices of king and pastor for the godly who submit willingly and obediently; still he rules and breaks the ungodly with his rod of iron and already executes judgment among the nations even before the final judgment. (*Institutes* II, 15, 5; *OS* III, p. 479.)

[2] Commentary John 5: 24; *CO* 47: 115.

[3] Commentary John 12: 38; *CO* 47: 297.

human condition is apart from the Gospel."[1] We are delivered from the reign of Satan only by the Gospel.[2] The special purpose of Christ's reign over his people is that they have life and happiness (*felicitas*); he erects his kingdom for the express purpose of bestowing on all his people perfect happiness.[3]

When Calvin says Christ rules by the sceptre of his Gospel, he means a great deal more than that the Church is a forum where the message is repeated and heard. Christ rules by his Gospel when the Church is thereby renewed, which means that an inward quickening to newness of life takes place in the elect.[4]

Justification and sanctification of the freely obedient subject

The kingdom of Christ is the kingdom including those who are justified and sanctified. Both justification and sanctification flow from

---

[1] ". . . eius praedicatione *regnum Dei* erigi in terra et constitui, nec alio modo Deum regnare inter homines. Unde etiam apparet, quam misera sit absque evangelio hominum conditio." (Commentary Mark 1: 14; *CO* 45: 139.)

[2] Commentary Luke 10: 18; *CO* 45: 315.

[3] Commentary Matthew 9: 35; *CO* 45: 262. cf. "Regnum enim Dei inter homines nihil aliud est quam restitutio ad beatam vitam, adeoque vera et aeterna felicitas." (Commentary Matthew 3: 2; *CO* 45: 111.) cf. also Commentary Matthew 6: 21; *CO* 45: 205, where the relation between the *summum bonum* and *felicitas* is discussed. Also, ". . . regnum Dei est iustitia, pax et gaudium in Spiritu sancto." (*Institutes* II, 15, 4; *OS* III, p. 476.) "Iustitia et salus perfectaque felicitas in eius resurrectione fundata est. Ergo evangelium solennis est promulgatio de filio Dei in carne exhibito, ut perditum mundum instauret, ac homines restituat ex morte in vitam. Nec abs re bonus vocatur ac laetus nuntius, quando in eo continetur perfecta felicitas: finis enim est, ut regnum Dei in nobis inchoans, abolita carnis corruptione, spiritu renovatos in coelestem gloriam deducat. Qua ratione saepe regnum coelorum nuncupatur, et instauratio beatae vitae per Christum allata, interdum regnum Dei . . ." (Harmony of the Gospels, *Argumentum*; *CO* 45: 2.)

The relation between Christ's rule through the Gospel and through human felicity needs to be noticed. On this subject, Georgia Harkness writes, "If the whole scheme of things exists not for man's benefit but for God's glory, it follows that the way any individual treats himself or his neighbor will be of minor consequence in comparison with the way he honors God. If the chief end of man is to glorify God and enjoy him forever, the first of Christ's two great commandments will overshadow the second, and the Decalogue the Sermon on the Mount." (*John Calvin, the Man and His Ethics* [New York: Henry Holt, 1931], p. 84.) This evaluation sets the honoring of God over against relations with other men in a way foreign to Calvin. Calvin is very Augustinian at this point, and he draws a parallel between free obedience to God, involving the reorientation of affections, and *felicitas* sought by men as the highest good. Calvin does not easily separate the glorification of God and the enjoyment of his benefits, the Ten Commandments and the Sermon on the Mount.

[4] Commentary Luke 17: 20; *CO* 45: 424.

faith, when by faith is meant a firm reliance on God's love for us in Christ.

Sanctification and justification can never be separated—any more than Christ by whose righteousness we are clothed to be justified, can be separated from his Spirit by whom we are made holy, or any more than Christ can be torn asunder.[1] Even in analysing the Christian life with regard to these two aspects, Calvin grants no priority of chronology. He places only a degree of emphasis, when considering the question of the certainty of salvation, on the free act of God in not imputing our sins to us because of Christ's sacrifice.[2] On the other hand, in the *Institutes*, Calvin treats regeneration first and then justification in order to stress the fact that the faith which enables free justification by God's mercy is not without good works.[3] From our fellowship with Christ we receive a twofold grace, "namely, that by his sinlessness we are reconciled with God and for a judge in heaven we now have a propitious Father, and also that sanctified by his Spirit we are intent upon an innocent and pure life."[4]

Calvin's special doctrine of double justification affords a particularly

---

[1] *Institutes* III, 11, 6; *OS* IV, p. 187.

[2] "Nondum tamen satis liquet, cur et quomodo vitam nobis conferat fides: an quia spiritu nos suo regenerat Christus, ut vivat in nobis ac vigeat Dei iustitia, an vero quia sanguine eius purgati a peccatis gratuita venia iusti apud Deum censemur. Certum quidem est haec duo semper coniuncta esse, sed quia hic de salutis certitudine agitur, tenenda praecipue est haec ratio, nos ideo vivere, quia Deus peccata non imputando gratis nos amat." (Commentary John 3: 16; *CO* 47: 65.)

[3] *Institutes* III, 11, 1; *OS* IV, p. 182.

[4] "... nempe ut eius innocentia Deo reconciliati, pro iudice iam propitium habeamus in caelis Patrem: deinde ut eius Spiritu sanctificati, innocentiam puritatemque vitae meditemur." (*Institutes* III, 11, 1; *OS* IV, p. 182.)

Poenitentia for Calvin means the conversion after which, leaving aside the perversity of this world, we return to the way of the Lord; the effect of this repentence depends on our regeneration, which consists of two parts: mortification of the flesh and vivification of the spirit "qua hominis natura in suam integritatem instauratur". (*Catechism* [1538]; *CO* 5: 336.) Calvin can turn the relation of repentence and regeneration around and say that "... la regeneration consiste en penitence. Car penitence, à proprement parler, n'est autre chose que de renoncer à nous mesmes, pour estre nouvelles creatures à vivre selon Dieu." (*Contre la secte phantastique et furieuse des libertins*; *CO* 7: 202.) "... Il y a deux choses requises pour nostre salut: c'est d'un costé que Dieu nous accepte comme iustes, et nous advouë mesme pour ses enfans: L'autre, c'est que nous soyons conduitz sous sa main, que nous soyons maintenus et garantis par sa vertu invincible." (Second Sermon de Melchisedec; *CO* 23: 655.)

interesting means for relating sanctification and justification.[1] His doctrine is that one justification takes place when the sinner is accepted into the household of God and the other takes place graciously and repeatedly during the believer's growth in sanctification. In the first justification the works of the sinner play no part, and in the second the works of righteousness are considered to be the fruits of faith. In the second, acceptation means that God receives the adopted man as a new creature along with the gifts of the Spirit.[2] "For the faithful after God calls them are approved by God, even with respect to their works, because it is not possible that the Lord should not love and embrace the good things he has effected in them by his Spirit."[3]

It is not the case, as Niesel says it is, that Calvin's use of this doctrine of double acceptance, or double righteousness, is the product of Calvin's "polemic with Roman Catholics" [4] or that "he refuted the Scripture proofs of Roman theologians" with this doctrine.[5] It was, in fact, one point of contact between Calvin and the doctrinally reforming Roman Catholic theologians like Gasparo Contarini whom he met in discussion at the Conference at Ratisbon (1541). There, agreement on the article of justification was achieved precisely by the use of a doctrine of double justification.[6] Where the Roman Catholic theologians distinguished between justification by the inherent justice of Christ and justification by the imputed justice of Christ, and where the object of both was the person and not the works, Calvin said the

---

[1] Wallace gives a thorough documentation of the way in which justification and sanctification are for Calvin the double benefits which we receive from Christ by faith. (*Calvin's Doctrine of the Christian Life* [Edinburgh: Oliver and Boyd, 1959], pp. 23-27.) cf. also pp. 302-03, where he extensively cites places where Calvin says our works as well as our persons are justified. Wallace, however, misses the point that this is Calvin's own version of the doctrine of double justification and that it serves to relate the two benefits of faith, justification and sanctification.

[2] *Institutes* III, 17, 5; *OS* IV, p. 257.

[3] ". . . post suam vocationem Deo fideles approbantur, operum quoque respectu: quia Dominus non amare et osculari non potest, quae per Spiritum suum in illis efficit bona." (*ibid.*)

[4] *Op. cit.*, p. 135.

[5] *Ibid.*, p. 136.

[6] *CR* 4: 200. Later, at Trent, Girolamo Seripando made great but unfortunately vain efforts to get a wide and official consensus on one version of the doctrine of double justification. (His influence is behind Chapter Seven of the second decree proposal on justification [*CT* 5: 423], and his questions were submitted to the theologians in a revised form on October 15, 1546 [*CT* 5: 523].) He succeeded only in saving Contarini and others of similar persuasion from being condemned as holding a Lutheran doctrine in their espousal of double justification.

justice by which both men and works are rendered acceptable to
God is the justice of Christ which is imputed to them. Again, the
intimate connection between the work of the Holy Spirit and the
work of Christ in Calvin's thought came to light: in accepting men
and their works on the basis of the righteousness of Christ imputed
to them, God is also simply accepting the goodness of the gifts of his
own Spirit.

The Law as a guide for the freely obedient subject

In Calvin's thought there is no separation between the Law and
the Gospel, even to the extent of saying that the special reference of
justification is the Gospel and the special reference of sanctification is
the Law. The Law has its functions of condemning unrighteousness
outside Christ [1] and of being an instrument of civil justice. But it is
to be joyously received by believers as a great gift; it continues to
serve the life of the community freely under the rule of Christ. "Moses
taught beautifully that the Law which for sinners can only bring
about death, ought to have a better and more excellent use in the
saints." [2] The use of the Law as a guide for believers is, according
to Calvin, its principal one, that is, to lead those in whose hearts the
Spirit of God already rules and flourishes. [3] The sacred tie between
Law and Gospel must be maintained, since the Gospel is nothing else
than a fulfillment of the Law. The Commandments are the rule of life
which is unchangeable; therefore that error is to be rejected which
says that the deficiencies of the Law are supplied by Christ. Christ is
not a new legislator who adds anything to the eternal righteousness
of his Father, but he is a faithful expounder of the Law. [4] The transition
to the New Testament brings some appearance of change with respect
to ceremonies, but even this goes only as far as their use and not their
meaning. "So far as doctrine is concerned, we should not imagine
that in Christ's coming there is an abrogation of the Law. For since
it is the eternal rule of devout and holy living, it must be as unchangeable as the justice of God which it embraces is constant and one." [5]
Where Luther would say Christ is no new Moses and mean that Christ

---

[1] *Institutes* II, 7, 3-7. In the Law God looks not at what we can do but at what
we ought to do.
[2] *Institutes* II, 7, 13; *OS* III, pp. 338-39.
[3] *Institutes* II, 7, 12; *OS* III, p. 337.
[4] Commentary Matthew 5: 21; *CO* 45: 174-75.
[5] Commentary Matthew 5: 17; *CO* 45: 171.

does not leave the Law in full force, Calvin means that Christ does not undo the Law and substitute his new Law for it.[1] He does not set aside the old Law at all, but rather is its faithful expounder; it never ceases to have a salutary role in aiding the Christian to live freely in obedience to God. When the Law is contrasted with the Gospel, it contains only the outline of spiritual blessings which are shown in their fulness in Christ; to separate the Law from Christ leaves nothing but empty forms.[2] Even in describing Christian liberty, Calvin does not say the Law itself is abrogated for believers. Christian liberty means believers no longer seek justification by the Law, they freely obey the will of God since they are freed from the yoke of the Law, and they are not bound to the *adiaphora*.[3]

THE BREAKDOWN OF THE CHURCH-WORLD DICHOTOMY

The twofold sense of "Church"

The word "Church" as it is used in Scripture, says Calvin, refers to two groups of people. One is the children of God who, by the grace of adoption, are members of Jesus Christ by the sanctification of his Spirit; within the Church so defined are not only the saints who now dwell on earth but all the elect who ever were, from the beginning of the world. The other consists of those people in various parts of the world who profess to honor Jesus Christ, who are baptized, who participate in the Lord's Supper, who keep the preaching of the Word; in this Church there are many hypocrites.[4] All associated with the visible Church are not willing subjects of Christ; only the elect are freely obedient to him as their prince and leader in one body.[5]

This body of the elect within the visible Church is known only to God; it is invisible not in that it cannot be seen in the world or in the ranks of the visible Church, but only in that its corporate identity is known to God alone. In the preface to the *Institutes*, Calvin says the

---

[1] *Institutes* II, 8, 7; *OS* III, p. 349.

[2] Commentary John 1: 17; *CO* 47: 18.

[3] *Institutes* III, 19, 2-7.

[4] *Institutes* IV, 1, 7; *OS* V, p. 12.

[5] "Fontem unde ecclesia scaturit, iam inspeximus: quae nobis hoc loco credenda proponitur in hunc finem ut confidamus universum electorum numerum, per fidei vinculum in unam coire ecclesiam ac societatem, unumque Dei populum, cuius Christus Dominus noster dux sit et princeps, ac tanquam unius corporis caput: prout in ipso, ante mundi constitutionem, sunt electi, ut in Dei regnum omnes aggregarentur. Haec autem societas catholica est, id est universalis, quia non duas aut tres invenire liceat....." (*Catechism* [1538]; *CO* 5: 341.)

points of contention between Rome and the Reformers are that the
Romans always require one particular form of the visible and apparent
Church, and that they make this form the see of the Roman Church
and the estate of their prelates.

> Against this we contend that the Church can exist without being
> apparent, and that its form is not to be judged by that external pomp
> which they senselessly admire but by quite another mark: the pure
> preaching of the Word of God, and the authorized administration
> of the Sacraments. [1]

His point is not that the true Church has no appearance, but that its
form is not as the Romans conceive it to be; it consists in the pure
preaching of the Word and the administration of those Sacraments
which were instituted. Moreover, Calvin's concern for the Church is
not for the abstract theological question of what is its essence but
for how, in fact, the people of God live in the world and how they can
be recognized. One of his answers is given in the light of the persecu-
tion experienced by the evangelical party in France and elsewhere,
and it is that the people of God must not think that because they do
not have the external show of pomp and prosperity on their side the
Church of God has ceased to be constituted among them.[2]

It must not be inferred that these references to the invisible Church
of the elect carry with them a devaluation of the visible Church in
Calvin's thought. God rules by means of his visible Church, but—and
this is what is preserved by Calvin's doctrine of the elect community
whose identity is known only to God—those who are freely obedient
are not the same in number as those who are associated with the em-
pirical Church. The special reign of Christ over his willing subjects is
pre-eminently over those included in the Church Calvin calls the
"mother of all the pious," meaning the empirically observable Church
in history.

> But because right now it is my intention to speak of the visible Church,
> we learn from the one title of Mother how useful, indeed how neces-
> sary, the knowledge of her is. For there is no entry into life unless this
> one conceive us in the womb, give birth to us, nourish us at her
> breasts, and keep us under her care and governance until, putting

---

[1] "Nos contra asserimus, et Ecclesiam nulla apparente forma constare posse,
nec formam externo illo splendore, quem stulte admirantur, sed longe alia nota
contineri: nempe pura verbi Dei praedicatione, et legitima sacramentorum
administratione." (*Praefatio ad Regem Gall.*; OS III, p. 24.)
[2] *De Scandalis*; CO 8: 23-25.

off mortal flesh, we will be like the angels. For our weakness does not allow us to be released from this school until we shall have been disciples during the whole course of our life. [1]

There is no room in Calvin's thought for rejecting the means of grace because the Church is weak or because the elect, being already chosen, have no need of the ordained but imperfect visible Church. "God could no doubt in one moment perfect his saints; but he wills that they should not grow to maturity apart from the discipline of the Church."[2] Sanctification is a gradual process, accompanied by much limping, stumbling, falling, and crawling, and perfection is never attained in this life.[3]

The twofold sense of "world"

"World" for Calvin may be that which, by definition, is opposed to God's purposes: the sinful effects of man's rebellion and pride, the disorder threatening to become chaos unless continually checked by God's ordering power. Or, "world" may be the created sphere which exsts because of a gracious act of God's will and power and which is rigihtly pronounced by God as good. The Fall produced, for Calvin, an overlapping of these two.[4]

It is accurate to categorize Calvin's ethic as "other-worldly," but only if one recognizes that his concentration on the other world is for the purpose of providing an impetus for Christian life in this world.[5] There is a strong equation of "heavenly" with that state in which our affections are properly directed to God and of "worldly" with that state in which our affections are attached to idols. Man

---

[1] *Institutes* IV, 1, 4; *OS* V, p. 7.

[2] *Institutes* IV, 1, 5; *OS* V, p. 8.

[3] *Institutes* III, 6, 5; *OS* IV, p. 150.

[4] It is man's rebellion which darkens the goodness of creation. The entire creation, spiritual and material, visible and invisible, is good. The spiritual is created with a permanence the material does not have. The material is inferior in the sense that it is that plane on which appearance, disappearance, arrival, departure, deterioration take place. But the limited duration of the material is not punishment for sin; rather, it serves to relate properly the creature to the creator. But since the Fall, "world" no longer describes only the good; it becomes synonymous also with what is in opposition to God as the sphere of creation over which Satan exercises his power—not unlimited power, however, and with Christ's death and resurrection, decisively defeated power.

[5] "[For Calvin] the aspiration towards heavenly life cannot therefore imply any flight from the world but rather impels us already in this world to live another kind of life." (Heinrich Quistorp, *Calvin's Doctrine of Last Things*, trans. Harold Knight [London: Lutterworth Press, 1955], p. 43.)

cannot come to Christ without first humbling himself by putting away desire for earthly glory and worldly ambition and flattery: he can obey the heavenly teaching only when he makes the main quest of his whole life the approval of God.[1]

Our homeland is not this present life and our hearts and attentions are not to be diverted away from that other life which we approach as pilgrims in this one.[2] But this other-worldly gaze does not become in Calvin an occasion for irresponsibility by disdaining what God has here ordained for man's use. Thus, the truth that we are pilgrims here does not mean Christians should throw away their present lives which are wondrous gifts of God. ". . . This is the right way to love life: to remain in it as long as it shall please God and to be prepared to move on at his wish—or, to say it in a word, to carry our life in our hands and offer it to God as a sacrifice."[3] To tempt God means, in the context of Matthew 4:7, to neglect those means which God has put in our hands.[4] Those who take away the supports God provides for life in this world rip humanity away from man.[5]

CHRIST'S REIGN ETIAM EXTRA ECCLESIAM

If Calvin singles out the Gospel as that instrument which Christ wields to govern his chosen people, he gives special attention to the order of nature as the instrument of Christ's reign *etiam extra ecclesiam.* This order derives from the eternal justice of God no less than does that exhibited within the Church by those freely obedient to Christ.

The order of nature is God-given sustenance even for the unbeliever, and is the foundation for judicial laws peculiar to each nation. The God who so cares for and governs the world is not just God the Father or the Son or the Spirit, but the one Triune God. Christ as the Eternal Son of God is the ruler of the world beyond the Church no

---

[1] Commentary John 5:44; *CO* 47:127.

[2] Wallace calls attention to the Christocentric character of this meditation on the future life; the ascended Christ is our inspiration and the subject on whom we look. (*Calvin's Doctrine of the Christian Life, op. cit.,* pp. 87-90.)

[3] Commentary John 12:25; *CO* 47:289.

[4] Commentary Matthew 4:7; *CO* 45:135.

[5] "Sin ita est voluntas Dei, nos dum ad veram patriam aspiramus, peregrinari super terram: eius vero peregrinationis usus talibus subsidiis indiget: qui ipsa ab homine tollunt, suam illi eripiunt humanitatem." (*Institutes* IV, 20, 2; *OS* V, p. 473.)

less than the Father and the Spirit.[1] The theme of Christ's rulership over the world is surely present in Calvin's thought, but it never becomes synonymous with the primary meaning he gives to the kingdom of Christ: the spiritual reign over the Church. He never allows the specificity of the Church's task to preach the Gospel to be substituted with a general ethic which would blur the distinction between Church and world, and which would define the Church in terms of a works righteousness in social ethics rather than in terms of an open confession of Christ by his elected ones.

Our common humanity and the order of nature

Order and justice beyond the Church are not for salvation but are for the preservation and maintenance of society. Through them, God protects his creation from chaos so that it remains the milieu of redemption and sanctification. Calvin takes special notice of those provisions which enable *humanitas* in history: the liberal sciences, the family, and the state.

---

[1] Calvin distinguishes three modes of God's governance over the world: "Premierement il y a une operation universelle, par laquelle il conduict toutes creatures, selon la condition et proprieté qu'il leur a donnée à chacune en les formant," that is, the order of nature. (*Contre la secte phantastique* . . .; *CO* 7: 186.) The second is that he makes his creatures serve "sa bonté, iustice et iugement, selon qu'il veut maintenant aider ses serviteurs, maintenant punir les mechants, maintenant esprouver la patience de ses fideles ou les chastier paternellement." (*CO* 7: 187.) And "la troisieme espece de l'operation de Dieu gist et consiste en ce qu'il gouverne ses fideles, vivant et regnant en eux par son sainct esprit." (*CO* 7: 190.) It is the Triune God who rules in these three ways. Lest one think the First Person alone is intended by "God the Creator," the following shows explicit ascription of providential ordering to Christ: ". . . nostre Seigneur Jesus Christ, combien qu'il ait esté envoyé en la plenitude des temps, ne laisse pas pourtant d'estre Fils eternel de Dieu: et mesmes qu'il a esté constitué Redempteur devant la creation du monde. Car il est le premier né de toutes creatures, voire d'autant que c'est en luy et par luy que tout a esté fait, et aussi que selon le conseil admirable de Dieu il devoit tout restaurer, d'autant qu'il n'y a eu que dissipation et haut et bas après la cheute d'Adam, qui a ruiné toutes creatures avec luy. Mais tout a esté restauré par nostre Seigneur Jesus Christ. Ainsi cognoissons, comme dit l'Apostre au dernier chapitre des Ebrieux, que Jesus Christ n'est pas seulement auiourd'huy, mais qu'il a esté dès hier, c'est à dire de tout temps: que sa vertu s'est demonstrée, comme elle se demonstrera iusques à la fin. Voila donc comme il nous faut recourir du tout à ceste vertu (laquelle les Peres mesmes ont sentie et experimentée devant qu'il fust manifesté en chair) ne doutans point, combien que nous soyons absens de luy, et qu'il y ait longue distance entre le ciel et la terre: toutesfois que nous serons tousiours vivifiez de sa vie, que nous serons enrichis de ses biens, soustenus et preservez par sa vertu." (Second Sermon de Melchisedec; *CO* 23: 659-60.)

In *Institutes* II, 2, 13, Calvin says knowledge of earthly things includes the mechanical arts, the liberal disciplines, and politics; and knowledge of heavenly things includes a pure knowledge of God, the way of true justice, and the mystery of his heavenly kingdom. Of the former knowledge it must be confessed:

> Since man is by nature a social animal, by natural instinct he also has a propensity to cherish and preserve that society. Therefore, we perceive in the minds of all men universal stamps of civil probity and order. That is why no person can be found who does not understand that all associations of men ought to be governed by laws or who does not mentally apprehend the principles of those laws. [1]

Man as created is a societal creature; the family and the state are ordained by God for preserving men in society. Part of the goodness of creation is the family, including both the husband-wife and the parent-child relations. Without his wife, man is only half man: ". . . a wife is a help to the husband for a happy life: that is by the institution of God. For from the beginning God so ordained it that man without a wife was, as it were, half a man and alone felt himself lacking the necessary aid. Therefore, the wife was a sort of completion of man. Subsequently, sin attacked, so that it spoiled that institution of God."[2]

---

[1] ". . . Quoniam homo animal est natura sociale, naturali quoque instinctu, ad fovendam conservandamque eam societatem propendet: ideoque civilis cuiusdam et honestatis et ordinis universales impressiones inesse omnium hominum animis conspicimus. Hinc fit ut nemo reperiatur qui non intelligat, oportere quosvis hominum coetus legibus contineri, quique non earum legum principia mente complectatur." (*OS* III, p. 256.) Also: "[Let us observe] duplex esse in homine regimen: alterum spirituale, quo conscientia ad pietatem et ad cultum Dei instituitur: alterum politicum, quo ad humanitatis et civilitatis officia, quae inter homines servanda sunt, homo eruditur." (*Institutes* III, 19, 15; *OS* IV, p. 294.) cf. also Commentary I Corinthians 1: 20; *CO* 49: 325.

[2] Calvin reminds us of the distinction ". . . inter puram Dei ordinationem et poenas peccati . . ." (Commentary I Corinthians 7: 1; *CO* 49: 402.) As created, marriage was entirely good: ". . . uxor marito adminiculum est ad felicem vitam, id esse ex Dei institutione: ita enim initio Deus ordinavit, ut vir uxore carens, quasi dimidius esset homo, seque singulari et necessario auxilio destitui sentiret: uxor autem esset quasi viri complementum. Postea supervenit peccatum quod illam Dei institutionem corrumperet," and yet there remains something of the first benediction. (*ibid.*; *CO* 49: 401.) "*Non est bonum ut sit Adam solus.* Nunc Dei consilium exponit Moses in creanda muliere: nempe ut essent homines in terra qui mutuam inter se societatem colerent . . . Principium ergo generale est, conditum esse hominem, ut sit sociale animal . . . Caeterum quanquam hoc de Adam pronunciavit Deus, quod illi non esset utile esse soli: non tamen ad solam eius personam restringo, sed potius existimo communem esse humanae vocationis regulam: ut sibi quisque dictum accipere debeat, non esse bonam solitudinem,

Before the Fall the family stood as the society in which men's lives were ordered in relation to one another in free obedience to God; there was no need for the compulsion of judicial action and the sword. The Fall introduced lust into the husband and wife relationship, as signified by Adam and Eve's search for covering after their disobedience. Since the Fall, marriage has a bitterness along with its original sweetness.[1]

Unlike the family, the state is provided specifically because of man's fallen condition. Its primary aim is to bridle the chaotic ambitions of men and so to be a powerful means of sustaining the goodness of creation: man's societal character. It keeps the peace in which genuine humanity can thrive. Had man remained in his created integrity the state would have been unnecessary; in the office of policing, "we have a mirror of our perversity, in that it is necessary for us to be directed by force to follow equity and reason."[2] Saying that we are forced by the state to follow equity and reason is saying more than that the state keeps the world from perishing until Christ's final return. There is a positive function of the state, even as it is the mirror of our perversity: God's justice will indeed be administered, and if because of our perversity we do not and cannot follow justice and equity freely, we are forced to do so by the instrument which God has ordained for that purpose.

The order of nature and Christ's free and reluctant subjects

It is the order of nature which is at the base of the general maintenance of society because it is universally observable, binding, and above all, an expression of God's eternal and unchangeable justice.

---

nisi quem Deus velut singulari privilegio exemit." (Commentary Genesis 2: 18; *CO* 23: 46.) Monogamy, according to Calvin, is a part of the goodness of the created order. Lamech violated the right of nature by his polygamy. "Statuerat Deus ut essent duo in carnem unam, atque iste perpetuus erat naturae ordo: Lamech belluino Dei contemptu naturae iura corrumpit." (Commentary Genesis 4: 19; *CO* 23: 99.)

[1] Commentary Matthew 19: 10; *CO* 45: 532.

[2] "Si nous estions demeurez en integrité de nature, telle que Dieu l'avoit creee: l'ordre de iustice, qu'on appelle, ne seroit point tant requis: d'autant qu'un chacun porteroit la Loy en son coeur, tellement qu'il ne faudroit nulle contrainte pour nous ranger: chacun sauroit sa reigle, et d'un accord nous suyvrions ce qui seroit bon et iuste. Et pourtant la iustice est comme un remede de ceste corruption qui est aux hommes. Toutes fois et quantes qu'on parle de la police terrienne, cognoissons que là nous avons un miroir de nostre perversité: d'autant qu'il faut que par force nous soyons amenez à suyvre equité et raison." (Sermon 101 on Deuteronomy 16: 18-19; *CO* 27: 409.)

This order of nature is expressed in the moral law, the content of which forms the principal part of the Mosaic Law and the essence of which is summarized in Christ's great commandment that God should be worshipped and that men ought to love one another. This is the immutable and eternal will of God, the true and eternal rule of righteousness. Such is the moral law which is unchangeable and binding on all men; but it may be altered in its application on the ceremonial and judicial levels.[1] Equity is common to all mankind and therefore should be the goal of all laws on all subjects.

"Since the law of God which we call the moral law is nothing but the testimony of the natural law and the conscience which is inscribed by God on the hearts of all men, the whole rule of the equity of which we are speaking here is prescribed in it."[2] This statement of the basis of social justice is remarkable for the way it connects moral law, conscience, natural law, and equity.

Calvin is not consistent in the way he describes the relation between conscience and natural law. Sometimes he seems to equate natural law with conscience,[3] and sometimes he defines one as a testimony of the other's existence.[4] Calvin usually means by natural law that inner law which is engraved on all men and which has the special purpose of condemning them.[5] He occasionally ascribes to natural law a positive

---

[1] The moral law "vera est aeternaque iustitiae regula, gentium omnium ac temporum hominibus praescripta, qui ad Dei voluntatem vitam suam componere volent." (*Institutes* IV, 20, 15; *OS* V, p. 487.)

[2] "Iam quum Dei Legem, quam moralem vocamus, constet non aliud esse quam naturalis legis testimonium, et eius conscientiae quae hominum animis a Deo insculpta est, tota huius de qua nunc loquimur, aequitatis ratio in ipsa praescripta est." (*Institutes* IV, 20, 16; *OS* V, p. 488.)

[3] *Institutes* IV, 20, 16; *OS* V, p. 488; *Institutes* II, 8, 1; *OS* III, p. 344. Marc-Edouard Chenevière, while recognizing the ambiguity of Calvin's usage, too one-sidedly adopts the view that for Calvin natural law is known by the conscience. (*La Pensée Politique de Calvin* [Geneva: Labor, 1937], pp. 62-65.)

[4] Natural law is the decision of the conscience discerning sufficiently between what is just and what is unjust. (*Institutes* II, 2, 22; *OS* III, p. 265.)

[5] "Finis ergo legis naturalis est, ut reddatur homo inexcusabilis." (*Institutes* II, 2, 22; *OS* III, p. 265.)
Josef Bohatec recognizes that Calvin employs the terms *lex naturae* and *ius naturae* interchangeably, but he detects a nuance in their usage: "Die lex naturae ist vornehmlich der Inbegriff der praktischen, dem Menschengeist angeborenen rechtlichen und sittlichen Prinzipien (iustitiae ac rectitudinis conceptiones), die die Griechen als προλήψεις bezeichnet haben." (*Calvin und das Recht* [Feudingen i. Westf.: Böhlaus, 1934], p. 4.) The *ius naturae*, or *Naturrecht* is "... das durch die lex naturae gebotene Recht ..." (*ibid.*, p. 10.) For the richness and fluidity of Calvin's language related to the order-nature-law complex, see Doumergue,

function, meaning by it the same thing he means elsewhere by the
order of nature, or simply nature.[1]

It is possible to discern a pattern in Calvin's use of the terms relating to natural law if one looks at the organization of his terminology
in the contexts of his discussion of fallen man, who is without the
aid of Scripture, and forgiven man, who has the aid of Scripture and
its illumination within the redemptive community. In the first in-
stance, natural law is said to have condemnation as its sole purpose:
but in the second, confirmation of God's will as revealed in the Scriptural account of Christ's perfect obedience is its function. Thus, if
Calvin equates natural law with conscience, and conscience either in-
dicts or acquits depending on the degree of free obedience, then the
natural law has this double character also, and is not purely negative.
And if the natural law is engraved on man as created, thereby being
a part of his original righteousness, and if regeneration constitutes

---

op. cit., V, pp. 466-69. The consistency which Doumergue discovers is that:
"Cet *ordre de la nature* donne naissance au *droit de nature*. Le *droit* de nature est ce
qui est conforme à l'*ordre* de nature, et les deux mots, droit et ordre, peuvent
être pris l'un pour l'autre." (*ibid.*, p. 466.) This interpretation of Calvin is clear
because it is minimal; but it accurately reflects all one can say with certainty
about Calvin's use of the terms. Doumergue errs, however, in going on to say
that ". . . Calvin entre dans le détail et montre successivement et incessamment
que les préceptes du Décalogue s'appuient sur la loi de nature, sur la nature."
(*ibid.*, p. 467.) This last judgment misses the point that the content of the natural
law is known, for Calvin, from the Christian's prior knowledge of God's will
from the gracious revelation in the Decalogue as fulfilled by Christ.
[1] "Porro haec ipsa quae ex duabus tabulis discenda sunt, quodammodo nobis
dictat lex illa interior, quam omnium cordibus inscriptam et quasi impressam
superius dictum est." (*Institutes* II, 8, 1; *OS* III, p. 344.) The innate knowledge
of God's law is Calvin's basis for saying that parents and rulers stand as the
means for God's preserving order in society. (Commentary Exodus 20:12;
CO 24:603, 605.) cf. Commentaries Leviticus 18:6; *CO* 24:662; Romans 3:21;
CO 49:58; and Matthew 5:43; *CO* 45:187.
Dowey's elucidation of the terms is the clearest one: "The 'order of nature'
refers to the orderliness and regularity of events within creation and implies
proper interrelationships among all things, as well as the realization by every
creature of its appropriate purpose . . . The *ordo naturae* is simply *the orderliness
or constancy of God's will within nature*." (*op. cit.*, pp. 66-67.) ". . . Since the perfect
ordo naturae in human history has been disturbed, it has a continuing significance
rather as precept, or law of God, than as a description of an existing order. Hence
lex naturae and *ius naturae* are the more appropriate terms since the Fall for what
God wills (wants) within creation." (*ibid.*, p. 68.) It would be more accurate if
Dowey were to say that the *ordo naturae* remains God's will for creation even after
the Fall, and that the natural law is the innate referent to the *ordo naturae* to which
men must conform in order to obey God's unchangeable will.

some sort of restoration of that original condition, then natural law
has a positive function for the communion of the saints.[1]

There is no possibility, for Calvin, of establishing an ethic directly
from natural law. "*Si stetisset Adam...*!" Sin has not only so weakened
our wills that we have not the freedom to obey, but our knowledge of
it is such as to leave us without excuse. Apart from Scripture, the
conscience witnesses to our distance from the fulfillment of God's
will. The conscience is an inner testimony to right and wrong which
in the unbeliever condemns (that is, he has a bad conscience) and which
in the believer attests to God's merciful forgiveness in Christ and to
the sanctification within the community of the Holy Spirit (that is, the
believer has a good conscience).[2] But through Scripture and within
the community of God's redemptive action, the conscience testifies
to the completeness of God's demands for his creatures, to the forgiveness derived from Christ's merits, and to the growth in free obedience empowered by the work of the Holy Spirit. In relation to the
unfulfilled demands of justice, conscience enables man's knowledge
of himself as a creature out of order with his creator, in need of a
redeemer and in need of the power of regeneration. In relation to the
demands of justice fulfilled by Christ as known from the Scriptures,
the conscience enables man's knowledge of himself as created, redeemed, and sanctified. Apart from Scripture man's self-knowledge
is confused and deceptive. He knows only his need for felicity but he
cannot know wherein it lies apart from the knowledge of God which
is available fully only through Christ.

Thus, it is when the order of nature is known in the light of Scripture that it and the natural law may be termed confirming descrip-

---

[1] Cf. Dowey, *op. cit.*, p. 64ff., for a description of Calvin's use of "nature."
Dowey calls attention to a double use of the term: as created perfection and as
the opposite of created perfection, because of sin, which is accidental to the
created order. "As a result of this dual usage, the 'nature' of man is both his
original, created goodness, from which any lapse is unnatural; and it is also the
sinfulness or 'natural' disposition of man as against his created goodness."
(*ibid.*, p. 66.)

[2] *Institutes* III, 19, 15, and *Institutes* III, 19, 4. The spiritual, not the civil,
government trains the conscience into piety and right worship. "Conscience"
is the sense of God's justice which brings us to judgment; a good conscience
is the tranquility of heart with which, when we are persuaded of Christ's grace
we boldly present ourselves before God. (*Institutes* III, 19, 15; *OS* IV, pp. 294-95.)
Consciences do not obey the Law as if compelled by the necessity of the Law,
but being freed from the yoke of the Law they freely obey God's will. (*Institutes*
III, 19, 4; *OS* IV, p. 284.)

tions of the ethical life.[1] They then confirm what we already know from their fulfillment in Christ. However, our total knowledge of the ethical life is not restricted to what we know only from Christ's human obedience. This retains priority as the starting point and the final criterion of ethical reflection and action. But, further, it refers to that eternal justice embodied in the order of nature which is also the Law of the Eternal Son by whom and with whose Spirit all things were made. That eternal Law, known only from its fulfillment in Christ, is the same for all ages, though obedience to it must take special forms in different times and places; and the natural law as seen through the spectacles of Scripture is a confirmation of our knowledge of the ethical action willed by God for his community in a time and place other than first-century Galilee. To conform to Christ is not to mimic his Galilean actions in the thirteenth, sixteenth, or twentieth centuries. To conform to Christ is to do here and now what Christ accomplished in the flesh, that is, to obey the Father's will freely, bearing the cross and sharing the resurrection.

Conclusion

As the knowledge of God and the knowledge of man belong together in Calvin's theology, so do the knowledge and service of God and man. Since knowledge of God is Christological for Calvin, does this mean we can transfer the language of Christological dogma to the sphere of ethical discourse, thereby wrestling the complexities of

---

[1] John T. McNeill correctly shows that while Calvin clearly adopts the natural law tradition, "It is permissible to argue that natural law is, for Calvin, of secondary interest in relation to his main doctrines. This is the case only because the realm of mundane affairs is, for him, subordinate to the realm of the supernatural. Within the mundane society, natural law is not secondary but controlling—and this because it is not earthly but divine in origin, engraved by God on all men's hearts." ("Natural Law in the Teaching of the Reformers," *Journal of Religion*, XXVI [1946], p. 182.) Proper as this observation is (apart from the use of the theologically charged term "supernatural"), it would be more correct to say that natural law is of secondary importance even in Calvin's ethics but because of the priority of the Decalogue and Christ's obedience as sources for the Christian's knowledge of the intent of natural law. As Wallace has admirably put the matter, Calvin himself "does not hesitate to appeal to his hearers and readers to live according to the order of nature and the natural law, as well as according to the Gospel. In making such an appeal to the natural order he is not turning from Jesus Christ and the Scripture to some supposedly possible second and different source of guidance and inspiration. He is rather using the natural realm to illustrate and to fill out the details of the meaning of the Law of God for the Christian man." (*Calvin's Doctrine of the Christian Life*, pp. 144-45.)

ethical decision into the capsule of an *analogia unae Personae*? And can we impose the "extra Calvinisticum" as a pattern upon the material of ethics and still be dealing with Calvin's theology?

By no means—and precisely because of the "extra Calvinisticum." For it serves in part to underscore the difference between the *Una Persona* and the body of the faithful to whom the *Una Persona* is united by his Spirit.

There is, however, a parallel between what the "extra Calvinisticum" says about the relation of the Eternal Word and the flesh, and Christ's reign over the Church and his reign *etiam extra ecclesiam*. Just as the "extra Calvinisticum" sponsors the fully Trinitarian doctrine of the knowledge of God, so it sponsors a fully Trinitarian doctrine of man's knowledge of himself. This it does by accentuating the identity of the Redeemer Lord of the Church with the Eternal Word by whom and with whose Spirit the Father graciously provides for all men in the order of nature. Apart from the community of faith, man knows himself only incompletely and in bad conscience as one who is reluctantly compelled to obey the Triune God. As a member of Christ's spiritual kingdom ruled by the sceptre of the Word, man knows himself in good conscience as a freely obedient subject of the one God by whom he is justified and santified into the restoration of his created integrity.

Just as Calvin designates the Gospel as that by which Christ governs his chosen people, so he gives special attention to the order of nature as the instrument of Christ's reign *etiam extra carnem*. This order derives from the eternal justice of God no less than does that which is exhibited within the Church by those who freely obey Christ. Although Christ's human obedience remains the starting place and final criterion, our ethical knowledge is not restricted there but extends further to the eternal justice embodied in the order of nature which is also the law of the Eternal Son by whom and with whose Spirit all things were made. Obedience to that eternal law will mean different things in different times and places. The natural law as seen through the spectacles of Scripture is a confirmation of our knowledge of the action which God wills for his people even in times and places radically different from first-century Galilee; although when natural law is not illumined Scripturally it mainly, but not exclusively, functions to render men inexcusable before God.

CONCLUSION

Is the "extra Calvinisticum" inevitably bound to such slogans as "Antwerp and the ocean," "*novitas*," "*finitum non capax infiniti*," or "back to a natural theology and ethics based on the *logos ensarkos-logos asarkos* distinction"?

As it appears in Calvin's theology—*no*. Its main liability there is to reinforce Calvin's occasional minimization of the importance of Christ's bodily presence during his earthly ministry; the invisible behind the visible flesh receives disproportionate attention. Were this route systematically pursued, something Calvin fortunately does not do, the saving character of God's manifestation *in the flesh* would be seriously qualified. This in turn would go ill with Calvin's simultaneous affirmation of the goodness of our tangible world and our concrete humanity as created.

The "extra Calvinisticum," because of its widespread and ancient usage could just as well be called the "extra Catholicum"; its influence is more distinctive than its existence. In Calvin's theology, the "extra Calvinisticum" functions to support a fully Trinitarian doctrine of man's knowledge of God and of himself. It points to the identity of the Redeeming Word in the flesh with the Eternal Word by whom and with whose Spirit all things were created and are ordered. The affirmation of the "extra Calvinisticum" forces Christology back into the setting which the Church, interpreting Scripture, wisely gave it in the Creed. There it is the subject of the second article related on either side to the Church's confession of the Father and the Spirit so that the affirmation of each article presupposes the confession of the other two. The "extra Calvinisticum" lifts the knowledge of God out of the either-from-creation-or-in-Christ framework, and deposits it with the God known in nature and in Christ as witnessed to in Scripture, who is the God graciously creating, redeeming, and sanctifying man.

Man knows himself incompletely (in bad conscience) as rebellious subject of this Triune God, or he knows himself wholly (in good conscience) as the subject of God's redeeming and sanctifying action which frees him for halting but growing restoration into his created integrity.

Willing or not, man is subject to God; but there is a saving difference between being freely or reluctantly obedient. The Eternal Son never ceases to have his empire over all things. In the Incarnation he "goes out of his way," without leaving that eternal way of boundless power and majesty, to rule over the rebellious creatures attempting to disrupt the continuity of gracious order. He does not abdicate his eternal empire but extends it over sinners. He can be Lord in the human predicament he humbly assumed because he never ceases to be Lord over it according to the Father's will and with his Spirit. "... Our faith rests on him in such a way that he still presides over us; he is our brother in such a way that he is at the same time Lord; as man he was so formed by God that as eternal God he still quickens and restores all things." (Commentary Hebrews 3:3; *CO* 55:37).

BIBLIOGRAPHY

ABBREVIATIONS

CIB   Benoit, Jean-Daniel (ed.), *Jean Calvin: Institution de la Religion Chrestienne*. Paris: J. Vrin, 1957 ff.

CO   Baum, Wilhelm, Cunitz, Edward, and Reuss, Edward (ed.), *Ioannis Calvini Opera quae supersunt omnia*. Braunschweig (and later Berlin): C. A. Schwetschke & Sons, 1865 ff.

CR   Bretschneider, C.R. (ed.), *Corpus Reformatorum*. Hallis Saxonum: C. A. Schwetschke, 1837.

CT   *Concilium Tridentinum*. Freiburg: B. Herder, 1901 ff.

EKL   Brunotte, Heine, and Weber, Otto (ed.), *Evangelisches Kirchenlexikon*. Göttingen: Vandenhoeck & Ruprecht, 1956-61.

KCGG   Grillmeier, Aloys, and Bacht, Heinrich (ed.), *Das Konzil von Chalkedon: Geschichte und Gegenwart*. 3 vols. Würzburg: Echter Verlag, 1951-54.

LNPF   Schaff, Philip (ed.), *Select Library of the Nicene and Post-Nicene Fathers of the Christian Church*. Buffalo and New York: Christian Literature, 1886 ff.

MPG   Migne, Jacques-Paul (ed.), *Patrologiae cursus completus, series Graeca*. Paris, 1857 ff.

MPL   Migne, Jacques-Paul (ed.), *Patrologiae cursus completus, series Latina*. Paris, 1844 ff.

OS   Barth, Peter, and Niesel, Wilhelm (ed.), *Johannis Calvini Opera Selecta*. 5 vols. München: Chr. Kaiser Verlag, 1926-36.

RE   Hauck, Albert (ed.), *Realencyklopädie für protestantische Theologie und Kirche*. 3rd ed. Leipzig: J. C. Hinrichs, 1896-1913.

RGG   *Die Religion in Geschichte und Gegenwart*. 2nd ed. Tübingen: Mohr-Siebeck, 1927-32.

SC   *Sources Chrétiennes*. Collection dirigée par Henri de Lubac et Jean Daniélou. Paris, 1901 ff.

WA   *D. Martin Luthers Werke*. Weimar: Böhlaus, 1883-1957.

PRIMARY SOURCES

Calvin

Ioannis Calvini Opera quae supersunt omnia [*CO*].

Johannis Calvini Opera Selecta [*OS*].

Jean Calvin: Institution de la Religion Chrestienne [*CIB*].

McNeill, John T. (ed.), *John Calvin: Institutes of the Christian Religion*. Translated by Ford Lewis Battles. Vols. XX and XXI of *Library of Christian Classics*. Philadelphia: Westminster Press, 1960.

Les Commentaires à l'Ancien et au Nouveau Testament. Publication sous les auspices de la Société calviniste de France. Geneva: Labor et Fides, 1960 ff.

Torrance, David W., and Torrance, Thomas F. (ed.), *Commentaries*. Edinburgh: Oliver and Boyd. *The Gospel According to John*, translated by T. H. L. Parker, 1959; *I Corinthians*, translated by John W. Fraser, 1960.

Oeuvres de Jean Calvin. 3 vols. Paris: Je Sers, 1934-36.

Others

Acta Colloquii Montis Belligartensis ... *1586.* Tübingen: G. Gruppenbach, 1587.
Andreas, Jakob, *Epitome Colloquii Montis Belgartensis* ... Tübingen: G. Gruppenbach, 1588.
Athanasius, *De Incarnatione. MPG* 25.
——, *De Sententia Dionysii. MPG* 25.
——, *Orationes I et II Contra Arianos. MPG* 26.
Augustine, *Confessiones. MPL* 32.
——, *De Civitate Dei. MPL* 41.
——, *De Fide et Symbolo. MPL* 40.
——, *De Libero Arbitrio. MPL* 32.
——, *De Peccatorum Meritis et Remissione. MPL* 44.
——, *Enchiridion ad Laurentium. MPL* 40.
——, *Enarratio in Psalmos. MPL* 37.
——, *Epistola ad Dardanum. MPL* 33.
——, *Epistola ad Volusianum. MPL* 33.
——, *Sermo* 47. *MPL* 38.

Biel, Gabriel, *Sacri canonis missae expositio.* Tübingen, 1499.
——, *Sermones de festivitatibus Christi.* Hagenau, 1510.
Brenz, Johann, *De majestate Domini Nostri Jesu Christi* ... Frankfurt: Peter Brubach, 1562.

Chemnitz, Martin, *De Duabus Naturis in Christo.* Frankfurt and Wittenberg: Tobias Meuius and E. Schumacher, 1653.
Confessio de Trinitate propter calumnias P. Caroli. CO 9.
Cyril of Alexandria, *Epistola XVII. MPG* 77.
——, *Homilia Paschalis XVII. MPG* 77.

Ephraem Syrus, *Ephraem Syri Hymni et Sermones.* Mechliniae, 1886.
Eusebius of Caesarea, *Demonstratio Evangelica. MPG* 22.
Eustathius of Caesarea, *Ex oratione in Eccles. MPG* 83.

Fulgentius Ferrandus, *Epistola ad Severum. MPL* 9.
Fulgentius de Ruspe, "De Immensitate Divinitatis Filii Dei," *ad Trasimundum,* II. *MPL* 65.

Gerhard, Johann, *Locorum Theologicorum* ... *Tom. I.* 3rd ed. Jena: Steinmann, 1628.
Gregory of Nazianzus, *Ad Cledonium Presbyterum contra Apollinarium, Ep.* 1. *MPG* 37.
Gregory of Nyssa, *Oratio Catechetica. MPG* 45.

Hunn, A, *Assertio Sanae et Orthodoxae Doctrinae de Persona et Maiestate Domini* ... Frankfurt a.M., 1592.

John of Damascus, *De Fide Orthodoxa, MPG* 94.

LeFèvre d'Estaples, Jacques, *Commentarii initiatorii in quatuor evangelia.* Basel, 1523.

Lombard, Peter, *Sententiarum Libri IV. MPL* 192.

Mentzer, Balthazar, *Opera Latina.* Edited by Balthazar Mentzer, Jr. Frankfurt, 1669.

Niemeyer, Hermann A., *Collectio Confessionum in Ecclesiis Reformatis Publicatarum.* Leipzig: J. Klinkhardt, 1840.

Occam, William, *Centiloguium Theologicum*. Lyon, 1495.
Origen, *Contra Celsum*. *MPG* 11.
——, *De Principiis*. *MPG* 11.
——, *Series veteris interpretationis Commentarium Origenis in Matthaeum*. *MPG* 13.
Pelagius I, *Fides Papae Pelagii*. *MPL* 69.
Peter Chrysologus, *Sermo* 63 and *Sermo* 83. *MPL* 52.
Protocollum, hoc est, Acta Colloquii inter Palatinos et Wirtebergicos Theologos ... Heidelberg, 1566.
Quenstedt, Johann Andreas, *Theologiae Didactico-Polemicae Pars Tertia*, 4th ed. Wittenberg, 1701.
Scotus, Duns, *Opera Omnia*. Vols. XIV and XV. Paris: L. Vives, 1891 ff.
Theodore of Mopsuestia, *Ex Libris de Incarnatione Filii Dei*. *MPG* 66.
Theodoret of Cyr, *Expositio rectae fidei*. *MPG* 6.
Thomas Aquinas, *Opera Omnia*. Vols. VII and VIII. Parma ed. of 1847. New York: Musurgia Publishers, 1949.
——, *Summa Theologiae*. Ottawa: Institute of Medieval Studies, 1944.

SECONDARY SOURCES
Books

Aulén, Gustaf, *Christus Victor*. Translated by A. G. Hebert. London: S.P.C.K., 1950.
Backes, I., *Die Christologie des hl. Thomas v. Aquin und die griechischen Kirchenväter*. Paderborn: Schöningh Verlag, 1931.
Bainton, Roland, *Hunted Heretic*. Boston: Beacon Press, 1953.
Barth, Karl, *Church Dogmatics*. Vol. I, 2, translated by G. T. Thomson, H. Knight, and Vol. IV, 1, translated by G. W. Bromiley. Edinburgh: T. & T. Clark, 1956.
——, *Nein! Antwort an Emil Brunner*. (Theologische Existenz heute, Heft 14) München: Chr. Kaiser Verlag, 1934.
Barth, Peter, *Das Problem der natürlichen Theologie bei Calvin*. (Theologische Existenz heute, Heft 18) München: Chr. Kaiser Verlag, 1935.
Berger, Heinrich, *Calvins Geschichtsauffassung*. Zürich: Zwingli Verlag, 1955.
Berkouwer, G. C., *The Person of Christ*. Translated by J. Vriend. Grand Rapids: Wm. B. Eerdmans, 1954.
Biéler, André, *La pensée économique et sociale de Calvin*. Geneva: Libr. Univ., 1959.
Bohatec, Josef, *Budé und Calvin*. Graz: Böhlaus, 1950.
——, *Calvin und das Recht*. Feundingen i. Westf.: Böhlaus, 1934.
Boisset, Jean, *Sagesse et Sainteté dans la pensée de Jean Calvin*. Paris: Presses Universitaires, 1959.
Bonhoeffer, Dietrich, *Ethik*. Ed. by Eberhard Bethge. München: Chr. Kaiser Verlag, 1958.
Bonhoeffer, Thomas, *Die Gotteslehre des Thomas von Aquin als Sprachproblem*. (Beiträge zur historischen Theologie, n. 32) Tübingen: Mohr-Siebeck, 1961.
Borchert, Ernst, *Der Einfluss des Nominalismus auf die Christologie der Spätscholastik*. (Beiträge zur Geschichte der Philosophie und Theologie des Mittelalters, Band 35, Heft 4/5) Münster, 1940.
Breen, Quirinus, *John Calvin: A Study in French Humanism*. Grand Rapids: Wm. B. Eerdmans, 1931.
Brunner, Emil, *Natur und Gnade*. 4th and 5th ed. Zürich: Zwingli Verlag, n.d.
Cave, Sydney, *The Doctrine of the Person of Christ*. London: Duckworth, 1925.
Chenevière, Marc-Edouard, *La Pensée Politique de Calvin*. Geneva: Labor, 1937.

Cochrane, Charles N., *Christianity and Classical Culture*. (Galaxy Books) New York: Oxford University Press, 1957.

Daniélou, Jean, *Origen*. Translated by Walter Mitchell. New York: Sheed and Ward, 1955.

Dawe, Donald G., *The Form of A Servant*. Philadelphia: Westminster Press, 1963.

Devreesse, Robert, *Essai sur Théodore de Mopsueste*. (Studi e Testi, 141) Vatican City, 1948.

Dillenberger, John, *God Hidden and Revealed*. Philadelphia: Muhlenberg Press, 1953.

Dominicé, Max, *L'humanité de Jésus d'après Calvin*. Paris: Je Sers, 1933.

Dorner, Isaac August, *History of the Development of the Doctrine of the Person of Christ*. Translated by D. W. Simon. Edinburgh: T. & T. Clark, 1866

Doumergue, Emil, *Jean Calvin*. Vols. I-VII. Lausanne: Bridel, 1899 ff.

Dowey, Edward A. Jr., *The Knowledge of God in Calvin's Theology*. New York: Columbia University Press, 1952.

Elert, Werner, *Die Morphologie des Luthertums*. Vol. I. München: Beck, 1931.

Emmen, E., *Christologie van Calvijn*. Amsterdam: H. J. Paris, 1935.

Fricke, Otto, *Die Christologie des Johannes Brenz in Zusammenhang mit der Lehre vom Abendmahl und der Rechtfertigung*. München: Kaiser Verlag, 1927.

Frölich, Karlfried, *Gottesreich, Welt und Kirche bei Calvin*. München: Ernst Reinhardt, 1930.

Ganoczy, Alexandre, *Calvin: Théologien de l'Eglise et du Ministère*. (Unam Sanctam, 48) Paris: du Cerf, 1964.

Gloede, Gunter, *Theologia Naturalis bei Calvin*. Stuttgart: Kohlhammer, 1935.

Grass, Hans, *Die Abendmahlslehre bei Luther und Calvin*. Gütersloh: Bertelsmann, 1940.

Harkness, Georgia, *John Calvin: the Man and His Ethics*. New York: Henry Holt, 1931.

Henderson, Robert W., *The Teaching Office in the Reformed Tradition*. Philadelphia: Westminster Press, 1962.

Hendry, George S., *The Gospel of the Incarnation*. Philadelphia: Westminster Press, 1958.

Heppe, Heinrich, *Die Dogmatik der evangelisch-reformierten Kirche*. Ed. by Ernst Bizer. Neukirchen: Neukirchener Verlag, 1958.

——, *Geschichte des deutschen Protestantismus in den Jahren 1555-1581*. Marburg: Elwert, 1852.

Jansen, J. F., *Calvin's Doctrine of the Work of Christ*. London: J. Clarke, 1956.

Jedin, Hubert, *A History of the Council of Trent*. Translated by Dom Ernst Graf. London: Thos. Nelson, 1957 (Vol. I), and 1961 (Vol. II).

Kantzer, Kenneth S., *Calvin's Theory of the Knowledge of God and the Word of God*. Ph. D. thesis. Harvard University, June, 1950.

Kelly, J. N. D., *Early Christian Doctrines*. New York: Harper and Bros., 1958.

Koopmans, Jan, *Das altkirchliche Dogma in der Reformation*. Übersetzt von Heinrich Quistorp. München: Chr. Kaiser Verlag, 1955.

Krusche, Werner, *Das Wirken des Heiligen Geistes nach Calvin*. Göttingen: Vandenhoeck & Ruprecht, 1957.

Lietzmann, H., *Apollinaris von Laodicea und seine Schule*. Tübingen, 1904.

Loofs, Friedrich, *Leitfaden zum Studium der Dogmengeschichte*. 4th ed. Halle: Max Niemeyer, 1906.

Mackintosh, Hugh Ross, *The Doctrine of the Person of Christ*. New York: Charles Scribner's Sons, 1912.

McLelland, Joseph C., *The Visible Words of God*: *An Exposition of the Sacramental Theology of Peter Martyr Vermigli* ... Edinburgh: Oliver and Boyd, 1957.

McNeill, John T., *The History and Character of Calvinism*. New York: Oxford University Press, 1954.

Mersch, Emile, *La Théologie du Corps Mystique*. Vol. I. Paris: Museum Lessianum, 1944.

Niesel, Wilhelm, *Calvin Bibliographie 1901-1959*. München: Chr. Kaiser Verlag, 1961.

——, *Calvins Lehre vom Abendmahl*. München: Chr. Kaiser Verlag, 1930.

——, *The Theology of Calvin*. Translated by H. Knight. Philadelphia: Westminster Press, 1956.

Oberman, Heiko A., *The Harvest of Medieval Theology*: *Gabriel Biel and Late Medieval Nominalism*. Cambridge: Harvard University Press, 1963.

Parker, T. H. L., *Calvin's Doctrine of the Knowledge of God*. 2nd ed. Grand Rapids: Wm. B. Eerdmans, 1959.

——, (ed.), *Essays in Christology for Karl Barth*. London: Lutterworth, 1956.

——, *The Oracles of God*. London: Lutterworth, 1947.

Planck, Gottlieb Jakob, *Geschichte der protestantischen Theologie*. Vol. VI. Leipzig: S. L. Crusius, 1799.

Quasten, Johannes, *Patrology*. Vol. III. Utrecht-Antwerp: Spectrum, 1960.

Quistorp, Heinrich, *Calvin's Doctrine of Last Things*. Translated by H. Knight. London: Lutterworth, 1955.

Ritschl, Otto, *Dogmengeschichte des Protestantismus*. Vol. IV. Göttingen: Vandenhoeck & Ruprecht, 1927.

Robinson, J. A. T., *The Body*: *A Study in Pauline Theology*. (Studies in Biblical Theology, no. 5) Naperville, Illinois: A. R. Allenson, 1957.

Schaff, Philip, *The Creeds of Christendom*. 3 vols. 6th edition. New York: Harper and Bros., [1931].

——, *History of the Christian Church*. Vol. VII. New York: Charles Scribner's Sons, 1892.

Schmid, Johann Heinrich, *Die Dogmatik der evangelisch-lutherischen Kirche*. 3rd edition. Frankfurt a.M. and Erlangen: Heyder & Zimmer, 1853.

Schweizer, Alexander, *Die Glaubenslehre der evangelisch-reformierten Kirche*. Vol. II. Zürich: Orell, Füssli & Comp., 1847.

Seeberg, Reinhold, *Die Theologie des Johannes Duns Scotus*. Leipzig: Dieterich, 1900.

Smits, Luchesius, *S. Augustin dans l'oeuvre de Jean Calvin*. Vols. I-II. Assen: Van Gorcum, 1957-8.

Thomasius, G., *Christi Person und Werk*. Vol. II. Erlangen: T. Bläsing, 1857.

Torrance, Thomas F., *Calvin's Doctrine of Man*. London: Lutterworth, 1952.

van Bavel, T. J., *Recherches sur la Christologie de Saint Augustin* (Paradosis, X) Fribourg, 1954.

van Buren, Paul, *Christ in Our Place*: *The Substitutionary Character of Calvin's Doctrine of Reconciliation*. Edinburgh: Oliver and Boyd, 1957.

Vogelsang, Erich., *Der Angefochtene Christus bei Luther*. Berlin and Leipzig: de Gruyter, 1932.

Wallace, Ronald S., *Calvin's Doctrine of the Christian Life*. Edinburgh: Oliver and Boyd, 1959.

——, *Calvin's Doctrine of the Word and Sacrament*. Edinburgh: Oliver and Boyd, 1953.

Watson, Philip, *Let God be God*. London: Epworth Press, 1958.

Wendel, Francois, *Calvin*: *sources et évolution de sa pensée religieuse*. Paris: Presses Universitaires de France, 1950.

Werner, Karl, *Die Scholastik der Späteren Mittelalters.* Vol. I. Published 1881, reprinted New York: Burt Franklin, n.d.
Williams, George H., *The Radical Reformation.* Philadelphia: Westminster Press, 1963.
Xiberta, Bartholomaeus M., *Enchiridion de Verbo Incarnato.* Matriti, 1957.

Articles in Reference Works

Backes, I., "Die Christologische Problematik der Hochscholastik und ihre Beziehung zu Chalkedon," *KCGG*, II.
Bauke, Hermann, "Christologie II, Dogmengeschichtlich," *RGG*, I.
Cadier, Jean, "Saint Augustin et Calvin," *Augustinus Magister*, II. Paris: Congrès International Augustinien, 1954.
Grillmeier, Aloys, "Die theologische und sprachliche Vorbereitung der christologischen Formel von Chalkedon," *KCGG*, I.
Kreck, Walter, "Extra Calvinisticum," *EKL*, I.
Lau, F., "Christologie," *EKL*, I.
Lehmann, Paul, "The Christology of Reinhold Niebuhr," *Reinhold Niebuhr: His Religious, Social, and Political Thought.* Ed. by Charles W. Kegley and Robert W. Bretall. New York: Macmillan, 1956.
Loofs, Friedrich, "Christologie," *RE*, IV.
——, "Kenosis," *RE*, X.
Piolanti, A., "Il mistero del 'Christo totale' in S. Agostino," *Augustinus Magister*, III. Paris: Congrès International Augustinien, 1954.
Ternus, Joseph, "Chalkedon und die Entwicklung der protestantischen Theologie," *KCGG*, III.
Witte, Johannes, "Die Christologie Calvins," *KCGG*, III.

Secondary Sources: Articles in Periodicals

Chavannes, Henry, "La présence réelle chez St. Thomas et chez Calvin," *Verbum Caro*, XIII (1959).
Elert, Werner, "Über die Herkunft des Satzes *Finitum infiniti non capax*," *Zeitschrift für Systematische Theologie*, XVI (1939).
Galtier, Paul, "Théodore de Mopsueste: sa vrai pensée sur l'Incarnation," *Recherches de Science Religieuse*, XLV (1957).
Goudel, A., "La Théologie de l''Assumptus Homo'," *Revue des Sciences Religieuses*, XVII (1937).
Jacobs, Paul. "Pneumatische Realpräsenz bei Calvin," *Revue d'Histoire et de Philosophie Religieuse*, XLIV (1964).
Joussard, G., " 'Impassibilité' du Logos et 'impassibilité' de l'ame humaine chez saint Cyrille d'Alexandrie," *Recherches de Science Religieuse*, XLV (1957).
Kratz, Wolfgang, "Christus — Gott und Mensch: Einige Fragen an Calvins Christologie," *Evangelische Theologie*, XIX (1959).
Lebon, J., "Une ancienne opinion sur la condition du corps du Christ dans la mort," *Revue d'Histoire Ecclesiastique*, XXIII (1927).
Maury, Pierre, "La Théologie naturelle chez Calvin," *Bulletin de la Société de l'Histoire du Protestantisme Francais*, LXXXIV (1935).
McNeill, John T., "Natural Law in the Teaching of the Reformers," *Journal of Religion*, XXVI (1946).
Oberman, Heiko A., "Quo Vadis, Petre? The History of Tradition from Irenaeus to *Humani Generis*," The Dudleian Lecture 1962, *Harvard Divinity Bulletin*, XXVI (1962).
Pollard, T. E., "The Impassibility of God," *Scottish Journal of Theology*, VIII (1955).
Reid, J. K. S., "The Office of Christ in Predestination," *Scottish Journal of Theology*, I (1948).

INDEX

Alciati, A., 75
Alexandrian, 50, 58
Ambrose, 43
Andreas, J., 12, 15f.
Angels, 47f., 64f., 70f., 73, 76, 135
Antioch, 4, 49f., 56, 66, 74
Apollinaris, 58
Arius, 64, 67
Athanasius, 35, 56ff., 60
Aubéry, C., 16
Augsburg, Peace of, 11, 13
Augustine, 5, 28ff., 43ff., 60f., 67, 71, 75, 95
Aulén, G., 75

Backes, I., 39
Barth, P., 102
Barth, K., xi, 1ff., 5, 8, 21, 26, 36, 101ff.
Baucke, H., 2, 4f., 8, 21, 74
Being (Essence), 3, 22, 27, 33, 37, 40, 56, 61, 70, 79, 122f.; ontology, 37, 66ff., 113; substance, 29, 48, 52, 54, 65; power, 55f., 69, 84
Benoit, J.-D., 8, 26
Berkouwer, G. C., 4
Bèze, T. de, 16ff., 20f.
Biel, G., 42ff., 60
Blandrata, G., 64
Bohatec, J., 148
Bonhoeffer, T., 39
Borchert, E., 42
Bouquin, P., 12
Brenz, J., 9, 12, 20
Brunner, E., 101ff., 121
Bucer, M., 12, 122
Bullinger, H., 12

Cadier, J., 45
Calvinist (Reformed), 1, 5, 9, 11ff., 16, 18, 23ff., 60, 78, 112
Caroli, P., 122
Cave, S., 1
Chalcedon, 5, 39, 49, 56, 66, 134
Chemnitz, M., 9ff., 16, 20
Chenevière, E., 148
Christ, 1ff.; language about, 32, 61, 100, 119, 133ff., 151; relation of person and work, 27, 51, 56, 61f.,
73, 84f., 88, 99
Unity of Person: incarnation, 22ff., 27, 37f., 40, 47ff., 52, 55, 59, 63ff., 74ff., 91, 100, 134, 154; assumption of flesh, 18, 38ff., 42, 55, 62, 68, 72, 81, 83, 98, 154; communicatio idiomatum, 1, 9ff., 20, 24, 28ff., 42, 65ff., 95, 112; God manifest in the flesh, 32, 47, 62ff., 78f., 83, 93, 97f., 109f., 117, 124f., 130; hypostatic union, 17f., 24, 38, 40, 42, 47f., 50f., 55, 59f., 62f., 73, 79, 82, 93, 100, 135, 152; kenosis, 20, 24, 39, 78ff., 86, 97
Divinity: image of God, 47, 66, 73, 80, 114, 120, 126; boundless power, 20, 32, 38, 41, 57, 61f., 73f., 81, 88ff., 94, 112f., 116, 154; descent from heaven, 27, 29f., 38, 43, 47f.; Son of God, 22f., 27, 32, 39, 47f., 52, 59ff., 62, 67, 74, 109, 117, 151; head of the angels, 64, 70ff., 76ff.; majesty, 15, 24f., 52, 63, 73ff., 80, 86, 134, 154; ubiquity, 15, 16ff., 20, 22ff., 29ff., 41ff., 78, 93, 95f.
Humanity: 15, 17f., 20, 22, 27ff., 37, 40, 43, 47f., 54, 58f., 60, 66f., 72, 76, 78ff., 91ff., 97ff.; body, 17f., 20, 27f., 32, 36ff., 57, 89, 73, 92, 100, 153; flesh, 24, 27, 31, 64f., 98; soul, 40, 46, 53, 58f.
Work: ascension, 15, 28f., 32, 42ff., 73, 89ff., 134; cross, 27ff., 40, 43ff., 50f., 71, 78f., 90ff., 132ff., 138, 150f.; descent into hell, 28, 34f., 40, 42, 46, 58; healing, 88f.; humility, 47, 67, 69, 72f., 81, 83, 86, 89, 111, 154; judge, 29, 40, 53, 78, 136; ruler, 28f., 40f., 46, 53, 56, 59, 73, 76, 87, 94, 135ff., 142, 144ff., 152, 154; mediator, 30f., 47, 63f., 67ff., 85, 87, 90, 99f., 110, 131; miracles, 87f., 113; obedience, 72, 80, 84ff., 90, 97, 100, 111; prophet, 86ff., 108, 114, 118; resurrection, 28f., 36, 58, 75, 91f., 134, 151; eucharistic presence, 14, 27f., 30, 32, 41, 91, 93, 95f., 141

Christopher, Duke of Würtemberg, 12
Church, 6, 7, 32, 35f., 49, 121, 126, 128, 130ff., 135, 137, 141ff., 145, 149f., 152; catholic, 5, 60, 99, 139f.; Christ head of, 61, 70f., 91, 118, 132, 136ff.; word and sacrament, 14, 27f., 30, 32, 41, 89, 91ff., 106, 118, 136f., 141; visible and invisible, 141f.
Cochrane, C. N., 49
Concord, Formula of, 9, 16
Constant, P., 35
Contarini, G., 139
Creation, 3f., 6f., 18, 28, 41f., 51, 54, 58f., 71, 76, 83, 120, 124, 126, 128, 143, 153; order of, 51, 54, 57f., 70ff., 99, 144ff., 152; nature, 101f., 135, 144ff., 148ff.
Crocius, J., 22
Crocius, L., 22
Cyril of Alexandria, 55, 58ff.

Daniélou, J., 53f.
Dawe, D., 4
Devreese, R., 56
Didymus the Blind, 58
Diepen, H., 59
Dominicé, M., 71, 79, 91
Dorner, I., 4, 11, 14, 48f.
Doumergue, E., 122, 148f.
Dowey, E., 3, 103f., 110, 121, 123ff., 149
Duns Scotus, 40f.

Election, 7, 40, 71, 115ff., 135f., 141, 145
Elert, W., 2, 4, 5, 74
Ephesus, 5
Ephraem Syrus, 49
l'Etoile, P. de, 75
Eusebius of Caesarea, 49
Eustathius of Antioch, 49
Eutyches, 63f.

Faith, 1, 48, 61, 90, 105, 107f., 115, 118, 132, 138ff., 154
Farel, G., 12, 122
Father, 42, 46, 52ff., 57, 61, 70f., 83f., 86, 88, 98, 154
Faye, A. de la, 16
Finitum non capax infiniti, 2ff., 7, 18, 74f., 100, 153
Florovsky, G., xi

Frederick, Elector of Palatinate, 11ff., 32
Frederick, Count of Würtemberg, 16
Fricke, O., 10f.
Fröhlich, K., 135
Fulgentius Ferrandus, 35
Fulgentius of Ruspe, 43, 49

Galtier, P., 55
Ganoczy, A., 5, 99
Gerhard, J., 20
Gilbert, M., 37, 39
Gloede, G., 102
God (Cf. „Trinity"), 1ff., 27, 50ff. 73ff., 105, 114f., 126, 129
Gospel (Cf. "Church: word and sacraments"), 4, 118, 136f., 140ff., 152
Goudel, A., 40
Grace (Cf. "Spirit: gifts"; "Justification-Sanctification"), 15, 33, 103, 136, 138
Gregory of Nazianzus, 34
Gregory of Nyssa, 49
Grillmeier, A., 56

Harkness, G., 137
Heaven, 10, 27, 32, 47, 75, 94f.
Heidelberg Catechism, 11, 15
Henderson, R., 119
Heppe, H., 11
Heshusius, T., 32
Hilary of Poitiers, 35
History, 7, 49, 124, 149
Hubner, P., 16
Hunn, A., 18f.
Hypostasis (Cf. "Christ: hypostatic union"; "Trinity"), 22, 34f., 40, 43, 62, 79, 122

Idols, 56, 105, 110, 143
Institutes of the Christian Religion, 2, 26ff., 45, 86, 103, 121ff., 131
Irenaeus, 3, 129

Jacobs, P., 5
Jansen, J., 86
John of Damascus, 34, 39
Joussard, G., 59
Justification-Sanctification (Forgiveness, Reconciliation, Regeneration), relation of justification and sanctification, 137ff.; justification, 70f., 76,

86, 88, 132, 136ff.; works, 139f.; double justice, 139f.; sanctification, 57, 132f., 137ff., 141, 143, 145, 153; obedience, 134ff., 150, 154; freedom, 132, 140f.; regeneration, 47, 56, 138, 150; conformity to Christ, 132, 134, 151; union with Christ, 33, 47, 55, 89, 92, 134; vision of God, 98; ascension with Christ, 28, 47, 73, 92, 114

Kantzer, K., 103
Kelly, J., 54, 56
Kierkegaard, S., 89
Kingdom of God (Cf. "Christ: ruler"; "Creation: order"), 28, 61, 78, 98, 115, 126, 135f., 154
Knowledge: of God, 1, 6, 56, 60, 101ff., 107f., 129, 131, 124, 153; of Christ, 61ff., 105ff., 109ff., 130; of Holy Spirit, 123, 131; and obedience, 132ff.; of man, 133, 152ff.; trinitarian character of, 104f., 120ff., 152ff.
Kratz, W., 5, 8, 113
Kreck, W., 8, 26
Krusche, W., 3, 8, 26, 82, 84

Lau, F., 74
Lausanne, Synod of, 122
Law, 3, 75, 106, 140f., 144, 148
Lebon, J., 35
Le Fèvre, J., 43f.
Lehmann, P., xi
Liberal Arts, 32, 108, 130, 145ff.
Loofs, F., 1, 4f., 8, 21, 26, 74
Luther, M., 12, 24, 111f.
Lutheran, 1f., 8ff., 23f., 65, 111

Mackintosh, H., 5, 8, 26
McLelland, J., 8
McNeill, J., 151
Man, xi, 1, 5, 18, 35, 40, 65, 73, 99, 115, 126, 128, 144, 146ff.; image of God, 73, 101; conscience, 128, 146, 148, 150; and order of nature, 145ff.; happiness, 105f., 136, 150; senses, 46, 115, 127; body and soul, 28ff., 46, 65, 99; weakness, 68, 94, 98; sin, 69, 73, 76, 85, 90, 107, 129, 147, 150; inexcusability, 129, 133, 152; ascension of, 28, 47, 73, 92, 114
Manichaean, 27
Marcion, 27ff., 63

Maulbronn, Colloquy of, 11, 15f., 23
Maury, P., 102f.
Melancthon, P., 9f., 12, 14, 78
Mentzer, B., 21ff.
Mersch, E., 36
Montbéliard, Colloquy of, 16ff.
Musculus, Abraham, and W., 16
Musculus, Andreas, 9, 16
Myconius, O., 122
Mystery, 27, 29f., 46, 49, 56, 116f.

Nestorius, 4, 19, 56, 58, 63f., 74
Niebuhr, R. R., xi
Niesel, W., 1f., 8, 62, 101

Oberman, H., xi, 42, 119
Occam, G., 42
Oecolampadius, 12
Oliveanus, K., 12, 15f.
Origen, 51ff., 60
Osiander, A., 17, 69, 72f.
Osiander, L., 17

Parker, T., 103, 113f.
Pelagius I, 49
Peter Chrysologus, 49
Peter Lombard, 28, 31, 40, 44, 60, 71, 95
Pezel, C., 19, 21
Philosophy, 1, 3f., 7, 32, 54, 56, 74, 94, 100, 106
Piety, 4, 52, 58, 107f., 120, 129f., 132, 142, 150
Piolanti, A., 35f.
Planck, G., 12
Providence (Cf. "World: rule of"; "History")

Quenstedt, J., 22
Quistorp, H., 143

Ratisbon, Colloquy of, 14, 139
Redemption (Cf. "Christ"; "Justification-Sanctification"; "Creation: order"), 3, 6f., 51, 63, 67, 73, 78, 80, 83, 120f., 124, 128, 145, 150, 153
Revelation, xi, 2f., 6, 20, 24, 56ff., 60ff., 67, 78, 101, 104, 112ff., 115ff., 120, 124, 126f., 129; and concealment, 20, 24, 56, 78, 112ff.; and election, 115ff.
Ritschl, O., 11, 111
Robinson, J. A. T., 36

Sadoleto, J., 122
Schaff, P., 12, 15, 122
Schmid, J., 10
Schnepff, E., 12f.
Schnepff, T., 12
Scriptures, 1, 6, 32, 54, 60, 65, 68f., 99, 102f., 110, 115, 118f., 120, 122, 124, 128, 130f., 135, 149ff.
Schweizer, A., 2, 101
Schwenkfeld, C., 12
Seeberg, R., 40
Selnekker, N., 16
Seripando, G., 139
Servetus, M., 65
Smits, L., 45
Sohn, G., 21
Spirit, 3, 6f., 10, 38, 42, 51, 84, 87, 92, 99, 108, 113f., 119f., 127, 131f., 134, 139, 150, 152f.; gifts of, 3, 6f., 10, 84, 138ff.; knowledge of, 123, 131; and Word, 68, 87f., 108, 116ff., 136; and Christ, 15, 82ff., 125
Stancaro, F., 9, 69f.
Staphylus, F., 9
Strigel, V., 13

Ternus, J., 1, 8
Tertullian, 75
Theodore of Mopsuestia, 54ff., 60
Theodoret of Cyr, 49
Theology (Cf. "Church: message"; "Knowledge"; "Revelation"), xi, 1f., 5, 24, 110ff.; doctrine, 27, 87, 108f., 118, 120
Thomas Aquinas, 35ff., 44, 60
Thomasius, G., 9, 21
Thornton, L., 36
Thumm, T., 21
Totus-Totum Distinction, 30ff., 36f., 44, 46, 95
Tradition, 1, 5, 8, 26, 29ff., 37, 39, 43ff., 49, 60, 64, 67, 75, 119, 122
Tremellius, E., 12
Trent, Council of, 139
Trinity (Cf. "God"; "Knowledge"; "Revelation"), xi, 1, 3, 6, 27, 36, 42,

51, 83, 98f., 103, 120ff., 133, 144ff., 152ff.; and man's self-knowledge, 133, 152ff.; and structure of Institutes, 121ff.

Ursinus, Z., 12, 20

van Bavel, J., 44f.
van Buren, P., 3, 101
Vermigli, Peter Martyr, 12
Viret, P., 122
Virgin Mary, 24, 27f., 42f., 46, 57, 59
Visibility-Invisibility, 10, 28, 46f., 53, 105, 114, 126

Vogelsang, E., 111
Wallace, R., 95ff., 110, 139, 144, 151
Watson, P., 112
Wendel, F., 1, 2, 8, 26
Wendelin, M., 23
Werner, K., 40
Westphal, J., 12
Witte, J., 2, 5, 8, 26, 62, 65f.
Word (Cf. "Christ"; "Church; message"; "Scriptures"; "Spirit"), meanings of, 117ff.; person of, xi, 2ff., 17f., 22, 38f., 46, 52ff., 109, 124f.; boundless, 27, 30, 32, 48, 51ff., 57, 59; containing all things, 56f.; clue to history, 49; logos ensarkos-asarkos, 1, 5, 7ff., 11, 14, 18f., 21ff., 50f., 60, 101, 109, 135ff., 153; logos-Mensch, 56; immutability, 48, 57, 59; and Spirit, 116ff.; self-authenticating, 119
Worms, Conference of, 12
World (Cf. "Creation"), 20f., 24f., 27, 32, 43, 46, 50f., 56ff., 78, 88, 91, 143f., 154; meanings of, 143f.; other-worldly ethics, 143f.; rule of, 20f., 24f., 32, 40f., 43, 46, 50f., 56ff., 78, 88, 91, 145, 154

Zanchius, G., 20f.
Zürich, Consensus of, 13f.
Zwingli, U., 4, 11ff., 19, 21ff.